BUILDING BRIDGES

BUILDING BRIDGES

by

DAVID A. RAUSCH

MOODY PRESS

CHICAGO

© 1988 by
THE MOODY BIBLE INSTITUTE

All Scripture quotations in this book are from the *New International Version*.

ISBN: 0-8024-1076-6

1 2 3 4 5 6 7 8 Printing/BC/Year 93 92 91 90 89 88

Printed in the United States of America

TO MY SISTERS AND BROTHERS

Brynith Anne O'Hara
William E. Rausch
Paul D. Rausch
Constance Rausch Amarel
Sandra Rausch Scott

and to my "elder" brother in Ashland,
Merle "Pat" Patrick,
86 years young

CONTENTS

Acknowledgments

I am indebted to Dr. Joseph R. Shultz, president of Ashland College and Seminary, and to Dr. Lucille G. Ford, vice president of Academic Affairs, for their support and constant encouragement. Darwyn J. Batway, director of the Ashland College Library, and his competent staff were always helpful. A number of individuals from diverse walks of life have read portions of this manuscript for clarity. I would especially like to thank Gordon H. Fliegel, Jake Jacobs, Katheryne M. Larimore, Pat Patrick, Patti Brown, Carl Hermann Voss, Irvin J. Borowsky, and Lynne Stevenson Rausch. My graduate assistant, Janice M. Boville, came through when I needed it the most; and Gerald A. Davis and Alvin Kastan constantly filtered materials to me. Textbook editor Garry Knussman gave special attention to this manuscript, for which I am extremely grateful.

Last, but certainly not least, was the help afforded by Rabbi Michael Stevens, who read each part of this manuscript and offered helpful suggestions. The final decisions, of course, were my own and any errors should not reflect upon his expertise. I have appreciated his friendship, however, for nearly two decades.

Unnamed in this manuscript, but certainly to be acknowledged, are the hundreds of Jewish friends who have been willing to build bridges with me, and the scores of Christian friends involved in Christian-Jewish relationships that have helped along the way, including the American Institute for the Study of Religious Cooperation. It has been an interesting and profitable journey.

Introduction

Jesus was a Jew. Those who first followed Him were Jews. He selected only Jews as His disciples. His chosen earthly environment was within first-century Judaism, and because of this the roots of the Christian faith are firmly planted in Jewish soil. Jerusalem was the center of Christianity in the early decades of the church. Even the apostle Paul was taught by the great rabbi Gamaliel, and Paul appears to have remained an observant Jew his whole life. A vibrant Jewish Christianity, considered by the Romans a sect of Judaism, developed in Judea during the apostolic period.

Little wonder, then, that modern Christians are endeavoring to know more about Jewish tradition in an attempt to understand better the foundations of their own faith. In the past few decades, conscientious Christians have realized the importance of understanding other cultures and the danger of looking at life through the narrow lens of Western secular culture. The mature Christian is impressed with a new sense of responsibility to gain accurate knowledge and exhibit unconditional love toward all human beings.

In addition, a sobering and embarrassing awareness of Christian complicity in the history of anti-Semitism and in the extermination of six million Jewish men, women, and children during the Holocaust has led some Christians to rededicate their lives to the principles of their Lord— to love people as Jesus Himself did. This new impetus to model Christ by thwarting bigotry, recognizing structures of evil, and pursuing the justice of God has given Christians the opportunity to develop friendships within the Jewish community. Jews are beginning to view some Christians as "caring" human beings.

And Christians indeed are caring. In response to my book *A Legacy of Hatred: Why Christians Must Not Forget the Holocaust* (Moody Press, 1984), I have received hundreds of letters from sensitized Christians asking questions about Jewish people, about anti-Semites in their areas, and about Christian options in dealing with structures of evil. Many of these Christians have bluntly inquired concerning the Jewish community: "Where do we go from here? What can we do?"

The goal of this book is to acquaint such a reader with the fascinating and complex world of Judaism and to offer helpful suggestions in nurturing relationships with Jewish people. Because I am a Christian who has experienced this fellowship, I know the spiritual value and profound depth that accompanies such sharing. Because I spend much of my time explaining Christians to Jews and Jews to Christians, I am aware of the questions and fears in both communities. And, because I too started "at the bottom," I believe the possibility of learning, sharing, and caring is open to all.

Nevertheless, not all will want to understand or care. I have seen college professors and students welcome dialogue with Jews or become sensitized to Jewish concerns, but I have also witnessed Jewish students being tormented and ostracized in similar institutions. I have watched seminary students and ministers from a broad spectrum of denominations learning more about their Jewish roots and passing on this sensitivity to their congregations, but I have also encountered the few students and ministers who refrain from preaching from "Jewish Scriptures" (Old Testament) and a few more who ridicule their fellow laborers for their interest in "all this Judaica business." I have watched Christian men and women thrilled in their newfound friendships with Jewish families, but I have also met professing Christians who pass out anti-Semitic literature, totally immersed in their hatred for Jews and Judaism. This book is for those with the desire to learn more about and develop friendships within the Jewish community.

COMMON MISCONCEPTIONS

Common misconceptions about Jewish people must be dispelled before attempting such an understanding. No people in history seem to have been stereotyped more than the Jews. Christians do not like to be stereotyped, caricatured, or categorized to the point of losing their individual identity. Jewish people feel much the same.

"ALL JEWS ARE RICH"

Contrary to common opinion, all Jews are not rich. On the scale of wealth and possessions, there are many poor or middle class Jews in the United States and even more throughout the world. In the United States, the Jewish population of six million may include upward of five hundred thousand poor.

One hesitates to quote such figures, because the Jewish community (or any community) must not be penalized for being a successful community. Indeed, the *average* income of Jews may be higher than that of most other religious groups. This is a testimony to their initiative and to their religious heritage of caring for their own poor (something the early Christian church was instructed to do).

I have found that even those who appear to live a rich, easy life work very hard in their professions and have sacrificed countless hours in education and career. Often, an understanding of an individual's background sheds much light on the reasons for his success. For example, I once overheard a Christian comment on the "rich Jew" who lived near the country club in a midwestern city. During the Christmas holidays a large Star of David lit up his roof, attesting to his religious background. Little did the Christian realize that that particular home belonged to a Jewish auto parts dealer who owned a small store downtown and who worked in coveralls from 7:00 A.M. to 6:00 P.M. six days a week to operate that store. In fact, he had purchased and built his home before the country club existed, and, as has occurred in many parts of the nation, Jews were excluded from joining that club until a couple of decades ago.

"JEWS CONTROL THE WORLD"

Anti-Semites in the nineteenth and twentieth centuries have used extensively the argument that Jews control the world. Russians massacred thousands of Jews at the turn of this century under the guise of limiting "Jewish control of the world," and Adolf Hitler attempted to justify the Holocaust with the same argument. These Jewish "controllers" of the world could not, however, stop Hitler's mania, even as they have been unable to eradicate centuries of anti-Semitism.

The truth is that Jews cannot even control the New York City press, let alone the world. Despite common assumption, few newspapers are

owned or directed by Jews, and even fewer Jews are directors or trust-
ees of banks. This holds true even in New York City, which has a large
percentage of Jews in its population. Ironically, until the last two decades, Jews were actively discriminated against in the top management
of such institutions. In the latter 1970s, studies finally disclosed that the
religious persuasion of a large portion of the board of directors of the
Fortune 500 companies was *not* Jewish, but rather Episcopalian. That the
stereotype of the "Jewish banker" or "Jewish controller of the press"
persists in spite of such information attests to the diabolical deception of
anti-Semitism.

"JEWS ARE PROFESSIONAL TYPES WHO ARE TIGHT WITH THEIR MONEY"

It is true that there are many professionals among the Jewish people. This is because of Judaism's emphasis on learning for learning's sake
and obtaining an education (no matter what the cost). Judaism also
places an emphasis on the duty of entering the professions "if God has
given one the mind" to do so. These are the traditional helping professions—doctors, nurses, lawyers, teachers. Nevertheless, one must remember that many of the grandfathers and great-grandfathers of these
young Jewish professionals pushed peddlers' carts throughout the cities
or skimped and scraped in small businesses to send their children
through college and graduate school. Historically, a Jew was just as apt to
be in the junkyard business as to be in the medical profession. Judaism
has never been a stranger to hard work and menial tasks.

Judaism teaches that charity is a concept of justice that is to be actively pursued. A man or woman is not especially virtuous if charitable; if
one does *not* give to those less fortunate, one is *unjust*.[1] No group that I
know helps out others more than the Jewish people, and the caricature
that labels Jews as tight with money and selfish is criminal. As we shall
see, Judaism teaches that money, time, even one's very being is ultimately God's. Jews believe that the world's social conditions fall short of
God's will for humankind, and when it comes to philanthropy, historically or currently, the Jewish community is second to none. From helping
the boat people of Cambodia to the starving masses of Africa, from providing homes for orphans to local charity campaigns, the Jewish people

---

1. The Hebrew word for "charity" (*tzedakah*) literally means "righteousness." One is to
   give to charity to help those in need, not because of a reward, but rather because it is
   the *right thing to do*. Jews are commanded to work in partnership with God to make the
   world a better place.

are often in the vanguard of leadership and the backbone of support. In light of such a noble and generous spirit, it is with great sorrow that I have had to explain to a Jewish immigrant what an American Christian neighbor meant when he said that he was going to "Jew down" a salesperson.

JEWISH FEATURES

The accurate portrayal of Jewish people is that of a warm and loving community who, in spite of persecution through the centuries, does not repay evil for evil and attempts the magnanimous effort to welcome and be hospitable to the stranger—giving the benefit of the doubt to all who seem to be friendly and balanced.

I was amazed at the small Conservative Jewish congregation that was one evening confronted by a man who introduced himself as "Jesus Christ—you can call me Jesus." Rather than being laughed at or ushered out of the service, he was introduced from one member to the other as "Jesus," cordially welcomed in the service itself, and treated to the hospitality of refreshments and fellowship at the Oneg Shabbat following the service. For all of his mental problems, that man left the synagogue feeling loved and accepted—a reception he rarely experienced elsewhere.

Unfortunately, to those who stereotype and caricature, certain physical characteristics have been employed historically to depict Jews, to emphasize "Jewish features." Hitler's Third Reich made much of this "science" of physiognomy—the art of judging character by physical features. Actually, as some Nazis soon learned and as one must emphasize today, Jewish people come in all shapes, sizes, and degrees of beauty. Often their features defy the physical stereotypes, just as Gentile features often resemble caricatured Jewish ones. For instance, in Berlin's West End on July 15, 1935, two hundred Nazis attacked Jews in restaurants and theaters, shouting, "The best Jew is a dead Jew." A tall, blond Nazi leader mercilessly beat a short, dark-complexioned man he thought was a Jew. The brutalized man, however, proved to be a Bavarian SA leader—a commander of Hitler's infamous Brown Shirts!

THE TASK BEFORE US

History teaches us that relying on stereotypes can have awesome consequences. The Bible teaches us that libel is sin. To approach the study before us, negative preconceptions should be abandoned. The millstones of prejudice hung on our necks in childhood must be thrown off. Certainly, intensive contact with the Jewish community is the best way to handle false preconceptions and erroneous information. Although we encourage such contact, we hope this text will convey useful information about the historic beliefs and modern composition of the Jewish community.

Part 1, "Judaism," examines the multifaceted aspects of the Jewish religion in an attempt to acquaint the reader with the beliefs and lifestyle of contemporary Judaism. Part 2, "The People," gives insight into the history and psyche of the Jewish people. From American Jewry to the Israelis, the Jewish community's diversity, as well as its common heritage, is underscored, including highlights of Jewish social and cultural heritage.

Part 3, "Groups and Relationships," elaborates on the history and traditions of the Jewish community in the United States. With separate chapters on Orthodox, Reform, and Conservative, as well as other groups, this section discusses similarities and differences, interaction and attitudes, patterns of worship and organizational structure. Building upon the previous essential foundation, the last chapter of this section deals specifically with fostering Christian-Jewish relationships. A Christian of necessity must be aware of what it means to love one's Jewish neighbor and what is involved in friendship and interaction.

In May of 1987, a Christian school presented Celeste Raspanti's play *I Never Saw Another Butterfly*. It is about the fifteen thousand children who passed through the Terezin concentration camp. Only one hundred of those precious children survived. The play was an act of love by the Christian students and their teachers who had been sensitized to the horrors of the Holocaust.

The play was held in the sanctuary of Grace Brethren Church, which operated the school. A large authentic Nazi banner hung forebodingly as the single backdrop at the front of the sanctuary, and above it was suspended as a permanent fixture the cross. To Christians, this sight may have evoked sentiments of victory that the cross of Christ conquers the evils of Nazism. To Jewish people, however, the cross has been as much a symbol of persecution and terror as the Nazi banner. Both symbols would provoke feelings of uneasiness at the least and, for many, send a cold shudder of dread through to the bones. It is a sad commentary that so-called Christians have willfully persecuted Jewish people throughout the centuries out of hatred, ignorance, and superstitious fear while proudly displaying the cross during their missions of cruelty and violence. Adolf Hitler himself claimed to stand for "positive Christianity."

As you embark on this journey of understanding and sensitivity, perhaps you, your family, your friends, and your church will be a part of a movement to try to help reinterpret the symbol of the cross to our Jewish neighbors. Perhaps in your study of the Jewish people, you will come to know better the Jewish Jesus and His ways.

Part 1

JUDAISM

1
Basic Concepts

Judaism has traditionally taught that a "Jew" is one who is born of Jewish parents or is a convert to Judaism. Being a Jew not only entitles one to be part of the "holy nation" and "kingdom of priests" described in Exodus 19:6, but also carries with it the obligation to obey God's commandments and to live responsibly upon the earth.

The word *Jew* comes from the Hebrew *Yehudi,* a word originally referring to members of the tribe of Judah [*Yehudah*]. By the time of King David, 2 Samuel 5:5 tells us that David "reigned over Judah [*Yehudah*] seven years and six months, and in Jerusalem [*Yerushalayim*] he reigned over all Israel [*Yisra'el*] and Judah [*Yehudah*] thirty-three years." Thus, the term had come to refer to those who dwelt in the area of the Kingdom of Judah, the Southern Kingdom. When the Northern Kingdom, Israel, fell to the Assyrians in 722 B.C., *Yehudi* was used by surrounding nations as the designation for those in the land, and thus the word *Jew* came to signify much more than a specific tribe. It was a broadened word that connoted a religious and national entity. For example, in the book of Esther, Mordecai is referred to as a "Jew," a *Yehudi,* even though he was from the tribe of Benjamin (Esther 2:5).

Although the term *Jew* was in common usage by those Gentiles and Jews who lived outside the Holy Land, the Hebrew-speaking Jews who remained inhabitants of the land referred to themselves as "Israelites." This is apparent in the gospel of Mark, where Pilate asked if Jesus was "the King of the Jews" (15:2), whereas a few of the resident chief priests mocked Him as "this King of Israel" (15:32). Through the Greek *Iou-*

daios and the Latin *Judaeus,* the word *Jew* passed into the early English language around A.D. 1000.

The word *Judaism* was derived from the Greek *'Ioudaismos* and came to signify among the Greek-speaking Jews of the Roman Empire their religion, philosophy, and way of life. The term was used to distinguish Jewish culture from the Greek or Hellenistic culture that permeated the ancient Western world. The apostle Paul used the word twice in his letter to the Galatians (1:13-14) to describe his firm adherence to the Jewish way of life and traditions of his ancestors before his conversion experience. The term has no other parallels either in the Hebrew or Greek Scriptures or in rabbinic literature (although it is popularly used today). *Torah* is the term generally used in ancient Hebrew sources for the whole gamut of Jewish teaching.

Although Judaism and Jewish people have historically emphasized particular aspects of their belief, they have always put more stress on the actual living of one's faith rather than on a particular creed or doctrinal formula. The cornerstone of Judaism is *deed*, not *dogma*. When one fully comprehends this, the Jewish Jesus' emphasis on practice rather than mere verbalization comes to life.

GOD

In every Jewish worship service today, the *Shema* is recited. It literally means "Hear!" (or "Understand!") and is the first word of Deuteronomy 6:4, which the congregation sings in unison: *"Shema Yisrael Adonai Eloheinu Adonai Echad"* ("Hear, O Israel: The Lord our God, the Lord is one"). Judaism has traditionally held to the unity and eternal spirit of the one true God. God created everything and actively governs the universe. Monotheism is never questioned, and, historically, God's existence can never be proved. It is taken for granted. "The fool says in his heart, 'There is no God' " (Psalm 14:1).

Whereas the essence of God is hidden and unfathomable, the attributes of God (such as justice, mercy, and wisdom) are visibly active in the universe. God has established order, meaning, and purpose in the world, and has created men and women in His own image. He is a caring God, who fellowships with His creatures and lovingly sustains them. In Judaism, God as Creator is a continuing reality, not merely the initiator of a single act.

For the Jew, the weekly Sabbath observance symbolizes the truth of God's personal activity in the affairs of humankind. On the seventh day of the week God culminated His work of creation and declared the day blessed and holy (Genesis 2:1-3). The Sabbath also celebrates God as the Redeemer of His people in world history. The day commemorates the Exodus from Egypt, in which God liberated the Hebrew slaves, presented the Torah, and led His people into the Promised Land.

GRACE AND FAITH

In Judaism, the relationship between God and man is one of grace and faith. Grace is the divine side of the connection, whereas faith that leads to devotion is the human side. *Hesed* is the Hebrew word used for the undeserved love that God has for His creation. Psalm 118:1 calls on the believer to "give thanks to the Lord, for he is good; his *hesed* endures forever." As Jacob prepared to meet Esau he prayed: "O God of my father Abraham, God of my father Isaac, O Lord, who said to me, 'Go back to your country and your relatives, and I will make you prosper,' I am unworthy of all the *hesed* and faithfulness you have shown your servant" (Genesis 32:9-10).

Moses and the Israelites upon crossing the Red Sea sang to the Lord, "In your unfailing *hesed* you will lead the people you have redeemed" (Exodus 15:13). In asking God for wisdom, Solomon acknowledged at the outset that God had "shown great *hesed*" to his father David (1 Kings 3:6); and as he dedicated the Temple, Solomon prayed, "O Lord, God of Israel, there is no God like you in heaven above or on earth below—you who keep your covenant of *hesed*..." (1 Kings 8:22-23).

Often translated as mercy, love, kindness, as well as grace, the Hebrew word *hesed* connotes God's beneficence in the creation of the world, in His relationship to His creatures, and in His covenant with the Jewish people. It portrays a gracious, forgiving, and just God who is exceptionally kind and compassionately patient. As the psalmist declared: "When I said, 'My foot is slipping,' your *hesed*, O Lord, supported me" (Psalm 94:18). Undeserved by humankind, God's *hesed* has been, and continues to be His favor and blessing freely bestowed.

In Judaism, men and women are to respond to God's grace and unmerited love through faithful devotion to God. Underlying all of the commandments is Deuteronomy 6:5, the continuation of the Shema: "Love the Lord your God with all your heart and with all your soul and with all your strength." Jesus understood this divine concept well. When questioned by a first-century expert in Jewish law, "Of all the commandments, which is the most important?" Jesus declared: "Hear, O Israel, the Lord our God, the Lord is one. Love the Lord your God with all your heart and with all your soul and with all your mind and with all your strength" (Mark 12:28-30).

The Jewish concept of faith is one of being faithful or holding firm in the faith. Faith is an ongoing process and must mirror God's faithfulness. It links the soul of the human being to God, creating an awareness of and an attachment to the divine that produces deeds of kindness. In this way, the "faithful ones" *(emunim)* mirror the grace of God in acts of human grace.

God provides the model of both faithfulness and grace. For example, in Deuteronomy 7 one of the key Hebrew words for faith, *emunah,* is linked to *ḥesed.* In this chapter, the Israelites are told that God did not choose them because of their numbers or strength. Rather, He chose them because He loved them and because of His covenant with their forefathers. "Know therefore that the Lord your God is God"; verse 9 continues, "he is the faithful God, keeping his covenant of *ḥesed* to a thousand generations of those who love him and keep his commands."

Christian tradition has often drawn a picture of Judaism as "law" and Christianity as "grace." Such a dichotomy is not accurate and has led to much misunderstanding. Both Christian theologians and Jewish theologians have historically held to a wide range of views on such topics as law and grace. And, as shall be seen, Judaism gives a differing perspective and emphasis on the place of personal salvation. Nevertheless, Judaism has never taught that the observance of the law or man's works *alone* elevate him to God. Indeed, even today, one of the preliminary supplications to be recited by the traditional Jew before the opening of his daily worship, begins:

> Master of all worlds,
> Not on account of our acts of righteousness
> Do we lay our supplications before You,
> But on account of Your great compassion.
> What are we?
> What is our life,
> What our piety,

What our righteousness,
What our helpfulness,
What our power,
What our strength.[1]

The Jewish worship service is replete with similar statements appealing to God's compassion, mercy, kindness, and love; all the while relating the faithful worshiper's failures and shortcomings. In Judaism, God is certainly the originator of grace, and yet God does respond with more *hesed* to the *emunim*, the faithful ones. Grace produces faith, and such faithfulness engenders more unmerited love.

In such a context, James's declaration, "Faith by itself, if it is not accompanied by action, is dead" (James 2:17), and his whole discussion of faith and deeds takes on new meaning. In fact, Jesus' teaching in this regard in the Sermon on the Mount is grounded firmly in Jewish thought. He insists: "Not everyone who says to me, 'Lord, Lord,' will enter the kingdom of heaven, but only he who does the will of my Father who is in heaven" (Matthew 7:21).

TORAH

One learns the will of the Father through *Torah*. Christians have often mistranslated this word as "law," but it actually is related to the root "to teach" or "teachings." In the most narrow sense, it specifically refers to the first five books of the Bible (Genesis-Deuteronomy), the foundation stones of Jewish tradition. As Moses blessed the Israelites before his death, he referred to the Torah that he gave them (Deuteronomy 33:4). In like manner, the Lord commanded Joshua upon entering the Land: "Be strong and very courageous. Be careful to obey all the *Torah* my servant Moses gave you" (Joshua 1:7). When Cyrus decreed that the Jews could return from exile and rebuild the Temple, they began to rebuild

1. There are a number of English translations of prayers and worship services, both old and new, that may be referred to throughout this book. Note, especially, *Sabbath and Festival Prayer Book, with a New Translation, Supplementary Readings and Notes* (The Rabbinical Assembly of America and the United Synagogue of America, 1946); *Gates of Prayer: The New Union Prayerbook: Weekdays, Sabbaths, and Festivals, Services and Prayers for Synagogue and Home* (New York: Central Conference of American Rabbis, 1975); Bernard Martin, *Prayer in Judaism* (New York: Basic Books, 1968). Helpful for the weekly Torah and Haftorah readings would be J. H. Hertz, ed., *The Pentateuch and Haftorahs: Hebrew Text, English Translation and Commentary*, 2d ed. (London: Soncino, 1968).

the altar "in accordance with what is written in the *Torah* of Moses the man of God" (Ezra 3:2). Ezra himself is described as "a teacher well versed in the *Torah* of Moses" (Ezra 7:6).

And yet, the Jewish concept of tradition is that truth is given once and for all. Torah is revelation—the revelation of God. As revelation, the word *Torah* describes the Hebrew Bible as a whole. Its teaching rests on God's authority, not only the written words but also the interpretation of those words. In this broader sense, far from being a narrow law code, Torah is a "way of life"—God's way of life.

Traditionally, the Hebrew Bible is the base of the Jewish tradition that God revealed. Through Torah one comes truly to know God. It is inerrant, God's Word to His children. Even the original words of the Bible (including every letter) were revealed by God. From this basic concept all Jewish discussion and interpretation builds. Throughout Jewish history, the commentaries and codes, the philosophy and the mystical analysis, all attempts at interpretation and discussion in Jewish religious literature form the larger body of Torah or instruction. Because God originally revealed the interpretation of His Scriptures, most discussion is attempting only to rediscover His original meaning. Nothing is new; God revealed it all at Sinai. Because God's truth is given once and for all, commentary rather than systematic theology is the form in which the Jewish philosophical and theological literature takes shape.

This is where the Jewish concept of Oral Tradition originates. In Judaism, Torah demands interpretation. The word *Torah* also implies the concept of guidance. In an effort to explain the message of the written Torah, a vast body of Jewish literature arose even before the birth of Jesus, conveying an oral inheritance that had been passed down through centuries of teaching through memorization. Such deliberations by rabbinic sages continued to expand until the Oral Tradition was eventually written down to form the Talmud (see chap. 4).

In Judaism there is no New Testament or Old Testament. The Hebrew Scriptures *are* the Bible, often referred to by the acronym *Tanach* (from TaNak, pronounced tah-nahk). This refers to the three sections of the Hebrew Scriptures: the Pentateuch *(Torah:* Genesis-Deuteronomy); the Prophets *(Nevi'im:* Joshua, Judges, 1 & 2 Samuel, 1 & 2 Kings, Isaiah, Jeremiah, Ezekiel, and the latter prophets, Hosea-Malachi); and the Writings *(Ketuvim,* in this order: Psalms, Proverbs, Job, Song of Songs, Ruth, Lamentations, Ecclesiastes, Esther, Daniel, Ezra, Nehemiah, 1 & 2 Chronicles). Thus, the Hebrew *Tanach* that Christians refer to as the "Old Testament" ends with 2 Chronicles.

Originally the books of the Bible were in an order different from the Christian Old Testament. In fact, any Jewish Bible written in Hebrew today maintains the above-listed order. In addition, before the Bomberg edition of these Hebrew Scriptures in 1521, there were only twenty-four book divisions (rather than the thirty-nine with which the Christian is familiar). This is because in ancient times the twelve latter prophets were written on a single scroll and counted as one, Ezra and Nehemiah were combined, and Samuel, Kings, and Chronicles were undivided.

WORSHIP

Judaism is a liturgical religion. It has a prayer book and a fixed liturgy for worship. Although spontaneous prayer and private expressions toward God are never discouraged, the prayer book (known as the *Siddur,* "order") is used in both the synagogue and the home. This Jewish liturgical tradition had an important influence on the early liturgical tradition of the Christian church. In both traditions, prayer continues to be a central element.

PRAYER

Judaism maintains that "the man who objects that he cannot pray on schedule often does not pray at all." Thus, *keva* (fixed times and fixed liturgy) has been an operating principle since ancient times. David, as all other male Jews, prayed a minimum of three times a day. Fixed times of prayer are viewed as part of God's order and are an important aid when one is in no mood to pray. Fixed liturgy provides inspiration as a person reads the words on the page. The illumination that may result can lead to a beautiful spontaneous expression toward God.

Inwardness and spontaneity, *kavanah,* are the proper intention of Jewish prayer. Prayer is seen as an encounter with the divine and must be expressed in the language of the heart. Private prayer has always been highly regarded among the Jewish people. In fact, prayer has been defined as the "service of the heart," and as such is an integral part of Jewish worship. It confirms and renews the Jew's covenant with God, and it is said that even an iron wall cannot separate God and Jew in prayer.

Throughout Jewish history, the principles of *keva* and *kavanah* have operated to produce the *Siddur* (prayer book) of today. One generation's spontaneous expressions were compiled to become another generation's fixed liturgical heritage. For example, there are different prayers of praise and thanksgiving to be said whenever one smells the first blossoms of spring, upon hearing thunder, upon smelling aromatic spices, upon eliminating bodily wastes to maintain health, or upon hearing a learned man share his knowledge, to name only a few instances. Even so, Judaism teaches that prayer must not become a matter of mundane routine but in every instance should mean that the worshiper is putting his or her soul in his hands and offering it to God. Judaism takes for granted that God and human beings are involved in continual dialogue, God speaking through the Bible and human beings directing words of praise, thanksgiving, supplication, petition, confession, and intercession to Him. Because there is an eternal God who cares about men and women and communes with them, prayers are to be found in every part of the Bible. Ironically, as a contemplation of the innermost being, the heart of humankind, Judaism teaches that words alone are insufficient in prayer. Attitude, once again, is the key.

To be effective, prayer must begin with the understanding that God's will comes before man's, and prayer should not be abused. A case in point from the Talmud would be of a man who, upon hearing a fire alarm in the city, prays that the fire not be in his home. Such a prayer is actually asking that this misfortune befall someone else, which is immoral. It is also asking God to move the fire from where it is already burning or praying that facts are not facts. Prayer must strive for the highest and noblest (God's will), which man is not always capable of understanding. Jewish tradition, because it so highly esteems prayer, insists that it be used carefully. This may be one of the reasons the disciples were so concerned that Jesus teach them to pray.

Individual prayer is important, but in Judaism communal prayer has greater worth and effect. The local community reflects in miniature the entire covenanted congregation standing before God. Each Jewish person derives strength and purpose from uniting with his people under God in prayer. That is why when Jesus replied to His disciples' request for instruction in prayer, He began the communal prayer, *"Our* Father." Even today, prayers are recited toward Jerusalem, and the Hebrew language as the holy tongue of the Torah is held in special reverence.

In traditional Judaism, prayers are offered evening and morning *every* day; and evening, morning, and afternoon during the Sabbath.[2] The two pillars of these prayers are the *Shema* and the *Amidah*. These are also the same pillars of the public worship service.

PUBLIC WORSHIP

The synagogue is firmly grounded on an equalitarian spiritual structure. That is, it upholds the principle of "the priesthood of all believers." Even the humblest man is permitted to lead the public worship service if he is familiar with its content and order. Wealth and social status should have no bearing on those who lead the service. A *minyan* of ten is the quorum needed to conduct all prayer services.

The basic framework of the Jewish Prayer Book (Siddur) dates back to at least the period of the Second Temple and, next to the Hebrew Bible and Talmud, is the most revered book of Judaism. It has never been considered "completed" or "canonized," and the principles of keva and kavanah work freely in its translation and composition.

Preliminary psalms of praise are read to prepare the worshiper's heart for the public service. In fact, the book of Psalms is the basic source of the Jewish Prayer Book. Examples of such psalms used in preparation would be Psalm 95 ("Come, let us sing for joy to the Lord; let us shout aloud to the Rock of our salvation"), Psalm 19 ("The heavens declare the glory of God, the skies proclaim the work of His hands"), and Psalm 34 ("I will extol the Lord at all times; His praise will always be on my lips").

Following such preparation, the ancient "Call to Worship" is delivered by the leader, "Bless the Lord who is to be praised"; the congregation responding, "Praised be the Lord who is blessed for all eternity."

The Shema (Deuteronomy 6:4) follows soon after, "Hear, O Israel: the Lord our God, the Lord is One." As a pillar of Jewish worship, the Shema and its accompanying readings are a central part of every service. Deuteronomy 6:5-9 is read as a reminder of the responsibility that ac-

---

2. Technically, every morning, afternoon, and evening of every day. The traditional *Siddur* includes the weekday afternoon service, most often recited right before sundown and therefore virtually back-to-back with the evening service. The *Aleinu*, a prayer proclaiming God as King over a united humanity, has been recited as the closing prayer of the three daily services for many centuries. Anticipating the day when all will acknowledge the one true God, the *Aleinu* reminds: "So it is written in your Torah, 'The Lord shall reign forever and ever,' " and, "And it has been said: 'The Lord shall reign over all the earth; on that day the Lord shall be One and His name shall be One.' "

companies their decision to accept God's election of them to be His servants as a light to the nations (the yoke of God's rulership):

> Love the Lord your God with all your heart and with all your soul and with all your strength. These commandments that I give you today are to be upon your hearts. Impress them on your children. Talk about them when you sit at home and when you walk along the road, when you lie down and when you get up. Tie them as symbols on your hands and bind them on your foreheads. Write them on the doorframes of your houses and on your gates.

Then Deuteronomy 11:13-21 is added as the terms of the agreement for accepting His challenge (the yoke of the commandments of God). They will be well cared for: "So if you faithfully obey the commands I am giving you today—to love the Lord your God and to serve Him with all your heart and with all your soul—then I will send rain on your land." The Lord promises them plenty to eat and a long life.

Finally, Numbers 15:37-41 is recited:

> The Lord said to Moses, "Speak to the Israelites and say to them: 'Throughout the generations to come you are to make tassels on the corners of your garments, with a blue cord on each tassel. You will have these tassels to look at and so you will remember all the commands of the Lord, that you may obey them and not prostitute yourselves by going after the lusts of your own hearts and eyes. Then you will remember to obey all my commands and will be consecrated to your God. I am the Lord your God, who brought you out of Egypt to be your God. I am the Lord your God.' "

Because of the last verse, this is often referred to as "The Exodus from Egypt."

As will be discussed in part 3, the amount of Hebrew versus English in an American Jewish congregational service will depend on its particular prayer book and its affiliation with the Orthodox, Reform, or Conservative movement. Most Christians visit a Conservative or Reform congregation on a Friday evening their first time. The Sabbath is welcomed in during such a service, often with the singing of *L'cha Dodi* (the congregation standing and facing Jerusalem during a verse in this song), "Come, my beloved, with chorus of praise, Welcome Bride Sabbath, the Queen of the days." The English language is used at least part of the time. Some prayer books even have the Hebrew phonetically re-spelled with English characters so that those who lack expertise in Hebrew can participate.

In such services, readings may follow the Shema, such as the responsive reading that begins:

> True and certain it is that there is one God,
> And there is none like unto Him.
> > It is He who redeemed us from the might of tyrants,
> > And executed judgment upon all our oppressors.
> Great are the things that God hath done:
> His wonders are without number.

Other selections and songs may follow, imploring the keeping of the Sabbath as an everlasting covenant or recognizing a certain festival through prayer.

The second pillar of Jewish prayer and the Jewish worship service is now observed: the *Amidah. Amidah* means "standing" and consists of a set of petitions silently prayed while standing before God. It is considered *the* prayer of the service and is of ancient origin.

The Amidah's first concern is contemplation of God:

> Praised art Thou, O Lord our God and God of our fathers,
> God of Abraham, God of Isaac, and God of Jacob. . . . Faithful
> art Thou to grant eternal life to the departed.

In contemplating God, the petitioner acknowledges God as the God of history, the daily helper of the faithful, and the author of life. God's holiness is also recounted: "Holy art Thou and holy is Thy name and unto Thee holy beings render praise daily."

The Amidah then proceeds to needs—spiritual needs, physical needs, Israel's needs, and the world's needs. During weekdays personal needs are listed, but the main emphasis on the Sabbath and during festivals is on thanksgiving. The worshiper recounts God's setting aside the seventh day and asks God to "sanctify us through Thy commandments and grant our portion in Thy Torah. Give us abundantly of Thy goodness and make us rejoice in Thy salvation. Purify our hearts to serve Thee in Truth."

Finally, the Amidah thanks God for His precious gifts, such as the opportunity to worship and God's gift of peace. Passages from Scripture inundate the Amidah, and even during the ancient period it became customary for the petitioner to add personal prayers at the end of the Amidah. "O Lord, guard my tongue from evil" is based on a meditation from a fourth-century sage that now is included in the Amidah after a prayer for peace. It is one of my favorite prayers.

> O Lord,
> Guard my tongue from evil and my lips from speaking guile,
> And to those who slander me, let me give no heed.
> May my soul be humble and forgiving unto all.
> Open Thou my heart, O Lord, unto Thy sacred Law,
> That Thy statutes I may know and all Thy truths pursue.
> Bring to naught designs of those who seek to do me ill;
> Speedily defeat their aims and thwart their purposes
> For Thine own sake, for Thine own power,
> For Thy holiness and Law.
> That Thy loved ones be delivered,
> Answer us, O Lord, and save with Thy redeeming power.

> May the words of my mouth
> And the meditation of my heart
> Be acceptable before You,
> Lord, my rock and my redeemer.
> May He who makes peace
> In His high heavens
> Make peace
> For us and for all Israel,
> And say: Amen.

This prayer recognizes that an evil tongue is the most insidious enemy of peace and calls upon the believer to bear oppression without hatred. As the Talmud asserts: "Whosoever does not persecute them that persecute him, whosoever takes an offense in silence, whosoever does good because of evil, whosoever is cheerful under sufferings—is a lover of God" (*Shabbat* 88b).

THE CANDLES, THE KIDDUSH, AND THE KADDISH

In Conservative and Reform synagogues on Friday evenings, the home ceremony of welcoming in the Sabbath by the blessing over the Shabbat candles and the Kiddush over the wine has been incorporated into the public worship service. The candles are lighted at the beginning of the service, while the Kiddush over the wine is recited after the *Amidah*.

At sunset in Jewish homes throughout the world, the Sabbath (Shabbat or Shabbos) is welcomed in by a candlelighting ceremony before the Sabbath blessings over the meal. In Jewish tradition, the table is an altar. In fact, the home is called *mikdash me'at*, "a small sanctuary." This is the tradition that Jesus followed and the tradition that is so evident in the early church. Early Christians gathered frequently as a community around the table.

The woman of the household covers her head, lights at least two candles, and wafts the aura of serenity toward her, ceremonially laying aside all of the cares of the week. She covers her eyes with both hands and recites the blessing: *Baruch ata Adonai Eloheinu melech ha'olam asher kiddeshanu b'mitzvotav v'tzivanu l'hadlik neir shel Shabbat* ("Blessed are You, Lord our God, Ruler of the universe, Who has sanctified us with His commandments and commanded us to kindle the light of the Sabbath").

Traditional Jewish women for several centuries have added another brief prayer, a prayer for messianic times, the *Yehi Ratzon:*

> May it be Your will, Lord, our God and God of our fathers, that the Temple be speedily rebuilt in our days, and grant our portion in Your Torah. And there we will serve You with awe as in days of old and as in ancient years. And may the offerings of Judah and Jerusalem be as pleasing to You as ever and as in ancient times.

Kiddush is the formal sanctification of the day and is recited over a full cup of wine. The Sabbath is such a special time that there are no words in Hebrew for the days of the Jewish week. Instead, each day is known by the number of days until Shabbat. Sunday, for instance, is known as *yom rishon beshabbat*, "the first day toward Shabbat."

Kiddush acknowledges the setting apart of this day as the culmination of the week, a time of joy and devotion. Festive songs are sung and the importance of every family member is acknowledged by a special blessing or Scripture reading. The man of the household recites the Kiddush, the blessing over the wine ("Blessed art Thou, O Lord our God, King of the universe, Who creates the fruit of the vine"). All present respond with "Amen," and are given a sip. After ritual washing, two loaves of hallah (bread) are blessed in the "Ha-Motzi" prayer ("Blessed art

Thou, O Lord our God, King of the universe, Who brings forth bread from the earth"). One hallah is then broken and portions are given to each person at the table. Jesus followed this same Jewish custom of breaking bread.

In the Friday evening service of Conservative and Reform congregations, a similar lighting of the candles and Kiddush takes place. After the Kiddush, the ark holding the Torah scrolls is opened with accompanying blessings. The *Aleinu*, which proclaims the kingship of God and expresses the fervent hope for the coming of the kingdom of God, is recited, anticipating the day when all humankind will be united under God in a completed, perfected world.

A Mourner's Kaddish follows. This is in remembrance of loved ones who have died, and close relatives stand in remembrance on the anniversary of the death of their loved one. It is significant that the Mourner's Kaddish does not mention death or sorrow at all but is rather a beautiful prayer of praise to God speaking of life and peace:

> Magnified and sanctified
> Be God's great name
> In the world He has created
> According to His will.
> May He establish His kingdom
> During your lifetime and days
> And during the lifetime
> Of the whole house of Israel
> Speedily and soon:
> And say: Amen.
>
> May His great name be blessed
> Forever and to all eternity.
>
> Blessed and praised,
> Glorified and exalted,
> Extolled and honored,
> Magnified and lauded
> Be the name of the Holy One, blessed be He,
> Though He is high above
> All the blessings and hymns,
> Praises and consolations
> That are spoken in the world;
> And say: Amen.

May there be great peace from heaven
And life for us and all Israel;
And say: Amen.

May He who makes peace in His high places
Make peace for us and all Israel;
And say: Amen.

Death, like birth, is viewed as a part of life, and Christian psychologists are only beginning to understand the "grieving process" already existent in Jewish practice—a process today recognized as being extremely important to the emotional health of every human being (see chap. 3).

The rabbi or a guest lecturer speaks in the Conservative or Reform synagogue after this Friday evening worship service. At this service the ark holding the Torah scrolls is opened in reverence, but Saturday morning the Torah is actually taken out, read, explained, and discussed.[3] Following an ancient Palestinian custom, one-third of Pentateuch weekly sections are read aloud, in an effort to cover the books of Genesis through Deuteronomy in one year; to read every word in three years. Each section has accompanying readings from other books of the Hebrew Bible. For example, the first reading of the year is *bereshith* ("beginnings") and covers Genesis 1:1–6:8. One-third of this will be read aloud in Hebrew each year on a three-year cycle. The *haftorah* ("conclusion") lesson from the Prophets for Bereshith is Isaiah 42:5–43:10. The entire haftorah portion is read on Sabbath morning immediately following the reading of the Torah. Because so much of this morning service is in Hebrew and because of its length of worship, the English/Hebrew worship service on Friday evenings has become the most popular service in Conservative and Reform congregations. In spite of this fact, this late Friday evening service (around 8:00 P.M.) is not to take the place of the other required services. It is the service that most Christians will attend first, however, and therefore it has been explained in detail.

After the sermon, the Friday evening worship service is concluded with a song glorifying God and a benediction by the rabbi. One such song is *Adon Olam* ("Lord of the World"):

> Lord of the world, the King supreme,
> Ere aught was formed, He reigned alone,

3. Many Reform congregations do not have regular Shabbat morning services and have begun reading the Torah on Friday evening (see chap. 8).

When by His will all things were wrought,
Then was His sovereign name made known.

And when in time all things shall cease,
He still shall reign in majesty.
He was, He is, He shall remain
All-glorious eternally.

Incomparable, unique is He,
No other can His Oneness share.
Without beginning, without end,
Dominion's might is His to bear.

He is my living God who saves,
My Rock when grief on trials befall,
My Banner and my Refuge strong,
My bounteous Portion when I call.

My soul I give unto His care,
Asleep, awake, for He is near,
And with my soul, my body, too;
God is with me, I have no fear.

An *Oneg Shabbat,* a time of Sabbath fellowship with refreshment and good conversation, follows this service.

DAILY ATTITUDES

Judaism teaches that God has shown men and women the way of truth. Torah goes far beyond individual laws and statutes to include religious concepts, ethical teachings, and historical lessons. One's daily pattern of behavior is to glorify God and to love one's neighbor as oneself.

That is why Jesus added without interruption to the "most important" commandment, "The second is this: 'Love your neighbor as yourself.' There is no commandment greater than these" (Mark 12:31). The command to love one's neighbor as oneself is found in Leviticus 19:18 and was fundamental to Judaism. In fact, when an expert in the Torah asked Jesus, "Teacher, what must I do to inherit eternal life?" Jesus asked him what was written in the Torah. The expert answered with the two commandments. Jesus replied, "You have answered correctly" (Luke 10:25-28). The parable of the Good Samaritan, which followed (an object lesson on the definition of "neighbor," "love," and "mercy"), served to underscore the importance of this command of God. A verse in Micah sums up this Jewish doctrine nicely: "He has showed you, O man, what is good. And what does the Lord require of you? To act justly and to love mercy and to walk humbly with your God" (Micah 6:8).

The sanctity of every human life is central to the account of the Good Samaritan, because the sanctity of life is a very important concept in Judaism. It is to mold daily living patterns. Humankind was created in the image of God, and, because of this, life itself is sacred. "Whoever saves one life, it is as if he or she had saved the entire universe" is a maxim in Jewish tradition that reflects the importance of the individual person, irrespective of age, social standing, or physical and mental development.

Because God has revealed His way, He has granted men and women the privilege either to follow or to reject that way. In the case of rejection, God provides the remedy of repentance and applies His forgiveness through grace. Men and women actually share the responsibility with God for rectifying a wrong. Redemption (or deliverance) is both personal and national, entailing obedience to God's teachings and commandments, i.e., following in His way. And yet, a Jew does not *earn* redemption, but is constantly in process, preparing by building his faith in God and faithfully discovering opportunities to serve the Lord. *Mitzvot* ("good deeds" or "commandments," both ritual and ethical) are a means to further faith, *not* a substitute for faith. God's grace and the believer's turning toward His way are the ingredients of salvation.

Thus, in Judaism, mitzvot are not what one does *above and beyond* (as in the common Christian conception of "charity"). Rather, good deeds are the *expected* thing to do—the way of the faithful's life. In Judaism, the admonition is *zedek zedek tirdof* ("Justice, Justice pursue"). Through such a way of life and drawing close to God's gracious deliverance, a Jewish person becomes a *ben Olam Haba,* a son of the world to come. The quantity of legal adherences is no substitute for the quality of one's way of life.

That is why the Orthodox Jew wears a *kippah* (head covering) at all times and why some other Jews wear it at prayer or in the synagogue. To the ancients the uncovered head symbolized freedom and human strength. By covering the head, a Jewish person acknowledges in one more way that he or she is subject to God. The Yiddish word for this "skull cap" is *yarmulke.* An abbreviation of *Yare Me-Elohim, yarmulke* symbolizes this whole aspect of walking in God's way. It is simply translated, "Stand in awe of God." Some Jewish women, for example, keep a kosher and prayerful home as an act of worship and reverence to God. "Obedience is better than sacrifice" is a standard for the Jewish faith.

Broadly conceived, Torah presents the Jew with the opportunity for individual salvation as well as national redemption. Non-Jews are also provided the opportunity for salvation by following God's way as He instructed in the seven commandments given to Noah (Genesis 9). In Judaism, the "righteous" from all nations who follow God's way inherit the "world to come." God's grace is available to all humankind.

Abraham Joshua Heschel (1907-1972) once said, "A Jew must strive to be Torah incarnate." Once a Christian understands the basic concepts of Judaism, Jesus' words in the Sermon on the Mount (Matthew 5-7) become even more powerful and less culturally bound.

2

Yearly Cycle

In Leviticus 23 the Lord says to Moses, "Speak to the Israelites and say to them: 'These are my appointed feasts, the appointed feasts of the Lord, which you are to proclaim as sacred assemblies'" (vv. 1-2). As the Sabbath was appointed "a day of sacred assembly" (23:3) to order each week, so too the Jewish festivals to this day are "seasons of the Lord" to order the year.

Although some originated in the Pentateuch and others were added later on, the annual cycle of fasts, festivals, and holy days provides a yearly rhythm for the Jewish community. Through the yearly cycle a sense of history and a sense of the passing of earth's time are communicated, the Jewish peoplehood is grounded, family ties are strengthened, and Jewish tradition and identity are passed along to younger generations.

For the individual, the yearly cycle internalizes the Jewish experience and dictates an understanding of life itself. Through this cycle, a Jew reflects on past and present dependence upon God as well as on hopes and aspirations for the future. The continual experience of the Jewish peoplehood and the adventure of life itself thus turn mere commemorations into vehicles for witness and mission. The festivals denote obligation to God as well as to one's people.

THE JEWISH CALENDAR

The Jewish calendar is based on a lunar-solar calendar, which uses the moon for its basic monthly calculations and uses the sun to adjust to the seasons. Such an adjustment is needed because the moon completes its cycle of phases approximately every 29 1/2 days. Thus, 12 Jewish months add up to only 354 days per year (as compared to the 365 1/4 days of the solar year). If left to such calculations, a spring festival (such as Passover) would soon be celebrated in the fall, and a fall festival (such as Sukkot) would soon move to spring.

To keep these holidays in the proper season, a nineteen-year cycle of seven "leap years" is used. An extra month is added after the twelfth month Adar on the third, sixth, eighth, eleventh, fourteenth, seventeenth, and nineteenth years of the cycle. Thus, Adar I and Adar II appear during these leap years of the Jewish calendar. To even out the twenty-nine and one half-day period among the months, some Jewish months have twenty-nine days and others have thirty days.

In the Bible, each month is numbered rather than named, for example, "the first month, the second month." Names for these months today were fixed by the important Jewish community of scholars that flourished in Babylon after the Exile (note chap. 4). Thus, they are Babylonian rather than Hebrew names. In order they are: (1) Nisan, (2) Iyyar, (3) Sivan, (4) Tammuz, (5) Av, (6) Elul, (7) Tishri, (8) Heshvan, (9) Kislev, (10) Tevet, (11) Shevat, and (12) Adar.[1] With the exception of Heshvan, every month has some special observance.

It is important to note that Nisan is the first month of the year, and yet Rosh Hashanah (the New Year) occurs in Tishri, the seventh month. That is because Rosh Hashanah marks the creation of the world. In Jewish thought this is a different celebration from the first month of the year. As we shall see, every new month is celebrated in Judaism.

As calendars throughout history have changed, including both the Jewish and Christian calendars, so too the counting of years has changed. Although Jesus was born between 6-4 B.C., our calendar today, through miscalculation, dates the year A.D. 1 from His perceived birthdate. In the ancient period, the Jewish year was fixed from the Exodus from Egypt. After the destruction of the Temple in A.D. 70, various other focal points were used to date the Jewish year. The system that gained the most popularity and is used today in the Jewish community is the number of years from the traditional perceived date of Creation (fixed by counting the personal life-spans or generations in the book of Genesis). Thus, the evening of September 11, 1988, marks the beginning of the Jewish New

---

1. In current convention, the biblical numbering is not usually used. Jews often call Tishri the first month, Adar the sixth. The use of Adar II keeps Passover from starting *before* the first day of spring.

Year of 5749; the evening of September 29, 1989, the year 5750; and the evening of September 19, 1990, the year 5751. Most calendars in English mark the day after as the Jewish holiday, but one must remember that biblical days (and therefore Jewish days) are calculated evening to morning. Be careful of this or you will miscalculate the inception of the festival by one day every time you use a regular calendar.

The Jewish community uses the world calendar as well, but replaces the letters B.C. with B.C.E. (Before the Common Era) and A.D. with C.E. (Common Era). Many scholars now commonly use the B.C.E. and C.E. designations to denote the dual era of Judaism and Christianity or to show deference to other religious traditions.

THE NEW MOON

The new moon marks the beginning of the Jewish month. In ancient times it was announced by the Sanhedrin and signaled by the blowing of trumpets and special offerings. To Israel, it testified that even though life fluctuates between comfort and persecution, God was firmly in control of the future and the faithful rhythms of the universe.

Rosh Hodesh celebrates the new moon and the new month. Much of the Blessing of the New Moon ceremony speaks of the hope of redemption. In traditional Jewish circles, the hope is in the Messiah, and the prayer is for the restoration of the Davidic kingdom. Psalm 89:37 is cited to prove that David's line and throne "will be established forever like the moon, the faithful witness in the sky."

In early centuries the proclamation of the new moon was heralded with rejoicing and dancing. In Numbers 10:10 the Lord said to Moses: "Also at your times of rejoicing—your appointed feasts and New Moon festivals—you are to sound the trumpets over your burnt offerings and fellowship offerings, and they will be a memorial for you before your God. I am the Lord your God." To this day, a custom persists that part of the blessing is given while rising on the tips of one's toes.

Judaism has never abandoned visual observation for cold calculation when it comes to time. Each night the moon is different, and traditionally the Blessing of the New Moon is delayed until the third day because one should be able to see a significant portion of the new moon's light before blessing it. If possible, the ceremony should be said in a standing position in the open air with the moon visible.

Shalom Aleichem ("Peace be to you") is customarily said to those around, and they respond, *Aleichem Shalom* ("to you be peace").

Through the years, portions of psalms (such as Psalm 148:1-6 and Psalm 8:4-5) and other readings have been added to the basic text found in the Talmud. The reading of *ha-Maariv Aravim* is used in some Rosh Hodesh ceremonies and is indicative of the spirit of the blessing:

> You abound in blessings, Lord our God, Source of all Creations:
> shading evenings with intent, brightening morning by design,
> causing time to pass and seasons to alternate,
> setting stars in their courses in rhythmic sway.
> You are the Source of day and night
> rolling light before darkness and dark before light,
> passing on day and bringing on night,
> yet always distinguishing day from night.
> Lord-of-Heavenly-Hosts is His Name!
> O God of Life, living eternally,
> sway us too through time without end.
> You abound in blessings, Lord,
> shading skies as evenings descend.

In some ways, many of us have lost an appreciation for this rhythm of God's universe through our twentieth-century technological separation from creation and its order. Such appreciation has been, however, the heartbeat of the Jewish experience.

Rosh Hashanah

The Jewish New Year, Rosh Hashanah, begins in the fall on the first day of Tishri, the seventh month, initiating a period of ten days that is referred to as the Days of Awe, Days of Repentance, or High Holy Days. It culminates with Yom Kippur, the Day of Atonement.

The preceding month, the biblical sixth month of Elul, is viewed as a time of preparation and introspection for this important period of renewal and repentance. Spiritually, emotionally, and intellectually, one is to review the past year. The graves of relatives and teachers are visited to remember their contributions and encouragements. Traditionally, the Shofar (a wind instrument made from a ram's horn) is sounded in the synagogue most of the month.

Beginning the Saturday night before Rosh Hashanah, Selihot (penitential prayers) are recited for at least four days. These are prayers for forgiveness and mercy. If Rosh Hashanah begins on a Monday or Tuesday, these prayers are said a week before. During this period, one meditates on the attributes of a merciful God and one's duty to forgive others as God forgives us.

The Bible records that the Lord said to Moses, "On the first day of the seventh month you are to have a day of rest, a sacred assembly commemorated with trumpet blasts" (Leviticus 23:24; cf. Numbers 29:1-6). This Feast of Trumpets goes unnamed, but may have been considered the beginning of the agricultural or economic year, since crops were harvested and sold around this time (the month Tishri comes from the root "to begin"). It was also on the first day of the seventh month that Ezra read the Torah aloud from daybreak until noon to the assembled Israelites (Nehemiah 8:1-3). The reference to Rosh Hashanah ("head of the year," cf. Ezekiel 40:1) came to designate this important period and corresponding festival. Originally celebrated for one day, the two-day festival arose out of a concern to safeguard against error as to when the new moon actually appeared.

Special synagogue services with High Holy Day prayer books are held during the two days of Rosh Hashanah, with intensive prayer being a central component. God's sovereignty as judge over mankind and ruler of the universe is affirmed. In fact, a tradition has developed that it is during Rosh Hashanah that God opens the books of the deeds of men and women and on Yom Kippur closes them once again. An essential ritual is the sounding of the curved shofar, symbolic of man's bowing in submission to God's will. Numbers 29:1 declares: "It is a day for you to sound the trumpets," and the shofar is sounded after the reading of the Torah, during the repetition of the Amidah and sometimes at the end of the service. More than one hundred notes may be sounded.

During Rosh Hashanah, it is the custom to send friends and relatives special wishes for a good and happy New Year. In Israel, gifts are given. For your Jewish friend to receive a Rosh Hashanah greeting card from you would be an unexpected delight.

This is not only a time for introspection, reconciliation, and confronting the past, but is also a time of joy and sweetness. Fine meals are prepared and festivity abounds. Rosh Hashanah is viewed as the anniversary of creation, and God is thanked for giving life, sustenance, and for allowing each person to reach this day once again. God is recognized not only as Judge but also as the Compassionate One. New clothes are worn, and white is the color of the day. White yarmulkes are provided in the synagogue and in the homes. "May you be inscribed and sealed in the Book of Life" is a customary greeting.

At the first evening meal, a piece of apple is dipped in honey after the Kiddush and Ha-Motzi (the blessing over the bread) have been said. "Blessed are You, Lord our God, King of the Universe, who creates the fruit of the tree" is recited before eating the apple. "May it be Your will, God and God of our fathers, to renew for us a good and sweet year" is said after eating the apple dipped in honey. On the second evening, it is customary to eat a new fruit not yet eaten that season. In addition, the hallah (bread) prepared for these meals is circular in shape, symbolizing both a crown (the kingship of God) and the continuous cycle of life.

YOM KIPPUR

The days of repentance between the beginning of Rosh Hashanah and ending in Yom Kippur are called "the ten days of turning." It is customary to ask forgiveness of those we have hurt or slighted and to forgive those who approach us. Judaism teaches that unresolved guilt and animosity shackle the spirit. Some rabbis speak of the "four Rs" of repentance—*recognizing* what one has done wrong, *regretting* that act, *resolving* not to repeat it again, and *restraining* oneself when faced with the same situation and temptation.

The Torah reading for the Sabbath during this period deals with the last days of Moses (Deuteronomy 31-34). This Sabbath is called *Shabbat Shuvah* ("Sabbath of Returning") because the Haftorah readings begin with a portion from Hosea 14:1-9, "Return, O Israel, to the Lord your God." This is followed by Micah 7:18-20:

> Who is a God like you,
>   who pardons sin and forgives the
>   transgression
>   of the remnant of his inheritance?
> You do not stay angry forever
>   but delight to show mercy.
> You will again have compassion on us;
>   you will tread our sins underfoot
>   and hurl all our iniquities into the
>   depths of the sea.
> You will be true to Jacob,
>   and show mercy to Abraham,
> as you pledged on oath to our fathers
>   in days long ago.

This passage is also read during the Day of Atonement afternoon service along with the book of Jonah. The Haftorah reading ends with Joel 2:15-27.

The Day of Atonement, Yom Kippur, the tenth day of Tishri, is the climax of the ten-day period and is the most important day in the liturgical year. "This is to be a lasting ordinance for you: On the tenth day of the seventh month you must deny yourselves and not do any work," the Lord commanded the Israelites in Leviticus 16:29-31, "because on this day atonement will be made for you, to cleanse you. Then, before the Lord, you will be clean from all your sins. It is a sabbath of rest, and you must deny yourselves; it is a lasting ordinance."

As the most solemn and holiest day of the Jewish year, fasting is required from before sundown of this "Sabbath of Sabbaths" to nightfall (when three stars are visible) the following day, approximately twenty-five hours. In the ancient Jewish community, it was customary to spend the whole day praying in the Temple. In the modern community, much time is spent praying in the synagogue. It is the only day of the year with five Amidah prayer periods, giving rise to the speculation that the Muslim custom of prayer five times a day toward Mecca was based on this ancient rite.

Clothing for men and women on Yom Kippur is white or beige, and more traditional men wear a *kittel,* a white robe. White clothing or a white robe is traditionally worn as a symbol of the white burial shroud *(tachrichim)* in which people are to be wrapped at death. White also serves as a consoling reminder of Isaiah 1:18: "Though your sins are like scarlet, they shall be as white as snow; though they are red as crimson, they shall be like wool." Gold is usually not worn, because it brings back memories of the apostasy with the golden calf in the wilderness. Leather products, including leather shoes, are avoided for precisely the same reason. Special white coverings, including curtains for the ark, are characteristic of the synagogue decor, and many traditional men have a special white-on-white Yom Kippur tallit.

A spirit of holiness and love, remorse and reflection, permeates the atmosphere. As a woman lights the candles to usher in the period, a sense of awe pervades. Profound and touching liturgy encompasses the services:

> May our words and deeds of penance rise at dusk,
> our pardon come to greet us with the dawn,
> and let atonement cleanse us all at dusk.

> May our prayers of confession rise at dusk,
> our anguish at our imperfection meet the dawn,
> and let reconciliation make us whole at dusk.

The center of the Yom Kippur worshiper's experience is perhaps captured in the words:

> As clay in the hand of the potter, to be thickened or thinned
> as he wishes, are we in Your hand. Preserve us with Your love.

The conclusion of Yom Kippur is marked by a single long blast of the shofar. Hugging, kissing, and well-wishing abound in a climate of emotional release from the ten-day period. The fast is now broken; the New Year has "officially" arrived.

SUKKOT

Preparations for Sukkot, the Feast of Booths, or Tabernacles, begin after sunset of the twenty-five-hour Day of Atonement. Among some traditional Jews, construction plans are made immediately on the *sukkah*.

A sukkah is a booth built by the family to commemorate the temporary shelters used by the Israelites in their wanderings after leaving Egypt. As a harvest festival, it also commemorates Jewish farmers who built temporary shelters at the edge of their fields. The sukkah has at least three sides and must have an open roof covered by leaves and branches. Meals are eaten inside it; some Jews even sleep inside it during the eight-day festival to observe the commandment to *live* in booths for seven days.

Leviticus 23:39-43 instructs in part: "So beginning with the fifteenth day of the seventh month, after you have gathered the crops of the land, celebrate the festival to the Lord for seven days; the first day is a day of rest, and the eighth day also is a day of rest.... Live in booths for seven days: All native-born Israelites are to live in booths so your descendants will know that I had the Israelites live in booths when I brought them out of Egypt. I am the Lord your God."

This Feast of Tabernacles is one of the most joyous of Jewish holidays. It has messianic overtones in that Zechariah 14:16 states that even Gentiles will celebrate Sukkot. "Then the survivors from all the nations that have attacked Jerusalem will go up year after year to worship the King, the Lord Almighty, and to celebrate the Feast of Tabernacles."

Verses 17-19 refer to "the punishment of all the nations that do not go up to celebrate the Feast of Tabernacles."

For the Jewish community, Sukkot symbolizes the transitory nature of life itself and the sacrifice required for those who follow God. Leviticus 23:40 instructs the Israelites to take "choice fruit from the trees, and palm fronds, leafy branches and poplars, and rejoice before the Lord your God for seven days." To this day, these four species (the *etrog,* or yellow citron fruit; the *lulav,* or date palm branches; *hadas,* or myrtle leaves; and *aravah,* or willow branches) are held together, and each day of Sukkot they are waved in all directions (first east, then south, west, north, up and down). The latter three are tied together and waved by the right hand while the *etrog* in the left hand is held against the *lulav.*

In the synagogue services during the first two days of Sukkot, a scroll of the Torah is taken from the ark where it is kept, and the assembled fruit and branches are carried by each participant in procession around the synagogue. Children often lead the procession, some waving flags inscribed with Bible verses. A portion of the singing and chanting proclaims:

> For the sake of Thy truth, Thy covenant, Thy greatness and glory: for the sake of Thy Torah, Thy majesty, Thy fidelity and Thy fame; for the sake of Thy mercy, Thy goodness, Thy unity, Thine honor, and Thy wisdom; for the sake of Thy sovereignty, Thine eternity, Thy mystic bond with us, Thy strength and Thy splendor: for the sake of Thy righteousness, Thy holiness, Thine abundant mercies, and Thy divine presence, do Thou save us; for the sake of Thy praise, do Thou save us, we beseech Thee. O Eternal, do Thou save us.

On *Hoshana Rabba,* the seventh day of Sukkot, seven circuits are made around the synagogue, in similar fashion to the seven circuits made around the Temple in Jerusalem in ancient days. Psalms are recited; Torah is studied diligently. In the midst of joy and hope, willow leaves are beaten off their stems in an act of supplication signifying the "beating off" of sin and despair. As in ancient days, prayers for rain occur, having spiritual as well as physical connotations. The water from God is needed for life. The prayers for rain continue on the eighth and concluding day of Sukkot, *Shemini Atzeret* (cf. Lev. 23:36).

It was during the festival of Sukkot, on "the last and greatest day of the Feast" (John 7:37), that Jesus made allusion to "streams of living water" and the Spirit of God. Understanding the festival and the prayers for rain not only puts Jesus in His Jewish social setting, but brings forth the message of the Jewish Jesus with greater clarity and impact. In addition, our American Pilgrim forefathers seem to have modeled their first Thanksgiving after the Sukkot festival.

SIMCHAT TORAH

Simchat Torah ("Rejoicing of the Torah") coincides with *Shemini Atzeret* in Israel, but is celebrated the next day (23d day of Tishri) in the Jewish community outside of Israel.[2] This festival celebrates the end of the yearly reading of the fifty-four sections into which the Pentateuch is divided and the beginning of the new annual cycle. By reading the last verses of Deuteronomy and the first verses of Genesis, one's love for the Torah as well as the never-ending pursuit of the knowledge of God's Holy Word is underscored. Synagogues are filled with whole families on Simchat Torah eve, as the Torah scrolls are carried around the synagogue in seven circuits. This is the only time the Torah scroll is read in the synagogue at night, and the closing chapter of Deuteronomy is read aloud.

Young and old sing and dance, the youngest children waving Simchat Torah flags inscribed with Scripture verses. Even in the Soviet Union, the Jewish community turns out in defiance of Russian oppression and celebrates the Torah and Judaism. *"Am Yisroel Chai"* ("The Jewish People Lives") reverberates throughout the halls and around the world.

Prior to the reading of the Torah, verses are chanted and rechanted. Some sing:

> You have been taught, and you know:
> The Lord is God; there is none else.
>
> He alone performeth wondrous things,
> For His lovingkindness endureth forever.
>
> There is none like unto Thee among the mighty, O Lord,
> And there are no works like unto Thine.

---

2. Reform Judaism follows the biblical and Israeli calendar, that is, seven days of Sukkot, with *Shemini Atzeret* and *Simchat Torah* observed together on the eighth day.

May the glory of the Lord endure forever;
May He rejoice in His works!

May the name of the Lord be blessed
From this time forth and forever.

May the Lord our God be with us as He was with our fathers;
May He not leave us nor forsake us.

Save us, O God of our salvation,
Gather us, and deliver us from among the nations
That we may give thanks unto Thy holy name,
And find honor in praising Thee.

The Lord is King, the Lord was King,
The Lord shall be King for ever and ever.

May the Lord give strength unto His people,
May the Lord bless His people with peace.

We pray that our words may find favor
Before the Lord of all mankind.

As the ark is opened and the Torah scrolls are seen, the congregation breaks into song about Moses and his words; David and his faith. "For out of Zion shall go forth the Torah," the congregation sings, "and the word of the Lord from Jerusalem." As the singing and chanting increases, the scrolls are taken from the ark and carried around the synagogue. Joyful hymns accompany the return of the scrolls to the ark—an exuberant testimony to the primacy of the Word of God.

On the Simchat Torah morning, another procession takes place. The Torah reading begins with the last chapter of Deuteronomy and ends with the first section of Genesis. It is a powerful object lesson. "For no one has ever shown the mighty power or performed the awesome deeds that Moses did in the sight of Israel" (Deuteronomy 34:12). "In the beginning God created the heavens and the earth" (Genesis 1:1).

HANUKKAH

Hanukkah literally means "dedication." It is an eight-day festival of freedom and light beginning on the 25th of Kislev and lasting through the 2d of Tevet. Hanukkah was instituted after the *Tanach* (Old Testament) was written, but it is referred to in the intertestamental and rabbinical writings. John 10:22 refers to "the Feast of Dedication at Jerusalem" in the winter.

First and Second Maccabees record that the "Maccabees" revolted against the Hellenistic Syrians of the Seleucid Empire (see chap. 4) to free the Jewish people in 165 B.C. The Seleucid king, Antiochus IV "Epiphanes" (ruled 175-164 B.C.) upon returning from a military expedition to Egypt had stormed the city of Jerusalem. He killed thousands of Jews and sold others into slavery. Second Maccabees 5:12-14 describes the gruesome scene: "And he [Antiochus] commanded his soldiers to cut down relentlessly every one they met and to slay those who went into the houses. Then there was killing of young and old, destruction of boys, women, and children, and slaughter of virgins and infants. Within the total of three days eighty thousand were destroyed, forty thousand in hand-to-hand fighting; and as many were sold into slavery as were slain."

Antiochus IV determined to turn the Jewish people from Judaism to Greek culture. He polluted the Temple with sacrifices of swine's flesh and proclaimed it a temple of Olympian Zeus. Orgies abounded, and the Jewish people were compelled "to forsake the laws of their fathers and cease to live by the laws of God" (2 Maccabees 6:1). Jews were forbidden to read their Scriptures and to practice the act of circumcision.

A guerilla army of fighters was organized in the hills of Judah by Mattathias of the priestly Hasmonean family and his five sons. Actually, his son Judah took the command. Judah received the nickname Maccabee ("the hammer"), and his band of guerillas became known by this name. He has been called Judah Maccabee ever since.

Upon miraculously defeating the large army (reportedly 60,000 infantry and 5,000 cavalry) of Antiochus's general, Lysias, Judah declared: "Behold, our enemies are crushed: let us go up to cleanse the sanctuary and dedicate it" (1 Maccabees 4:36). A new altar was built according to the Torah, and "Judah and his brothers and all the assembly of Israel determined that every year at that season the days of the dedication of the altar should be observed with gladness and joy for eight days, beginning with the twenty-fifth day of the month of Kislev" (1 Maccabees 4:59).

The central motif of Hanukkah is light. Josephus speaks of the Maccabean revolt and notes: "From that time onward unto this day we celebrate the festival, calling it 'Lights' " *(Antiquities* 12:325). Rabbinic tradition states that when the Temple was purified, only one flask of pure consecrated olive oil sealed by the high priest (one day's supply) was found to keep the eternal light burning before the holy ark. This was a 6-feet-high, 107-pound, golden, seven-branch candelabrum that stood in the inner sanctuary (today, an "eternal light" burns before the holy ark in every synagogue to symbolize it). Miraculously, the oil lasted eight days 'and eight nights. Hence, the key observance of this festival is to "kindle lights" in a special Hanukkah menorah (candelabrum) each night.

This menorah, which can be found in varying artistic designs, contains holding cups for oil or candles. Eight of these holders represent the eight-day length of the miracle. The ninth is the *shamash* ("servant") used to light the others. The *shamash* is never extinguished, but allowed to burn with the other flames. One candle is lit the first night, two on the second, and so forth, until all eight candles (plus the *shamash)* burn brightly on the last evening. To proclaim both the miracle of light and the freedom expressed in the holiday, the Hanukkah menorah is set up in front of a window for the benefit of passersby. In early centuries it hung at the entrance of a Jewish home. During times of persecution and danger, rabbinic tradition allowed it to be moved inside for safety's sake.

At least one Sabbath occurs during the festival. The special Haftorah for *Shabbat Chanukah* contains verses from chapters 2-4 of the book of Zechariah. The prophet Zechariah was one of the exiles who returned from Babylon under Cyrus's decree of restoration in 537 B.C. He began his prophecies nearly two decades later, when the hostility of neighbors and disastrous harvests had discouraged the people so much that they had ceased rebuilding the Temple. Zechariah roused the people from their despondency, assuring them that even in the darkest hour God was with them. This haftorah reading begins with chapter 2, verses 10-13 (2:14-17 in the Hebrew Bible, which, as in many cases throughout this text is numbered slightly different):

> "Shout and be glad, O Daughter of Zion. For I am coming, and I will live among you," declares the Lord. "Many nations will be joined with the Lord in that day and will become my people. I will live among you and you will know that the Lord Almighty has sent me to you. The Lord will inherit Judah as his portion in the holy land and will again choose Jerusalem. Be still before the Lord, all mankind, because he has roused himself from his holy dwelling."

The message is appropriate, for although in American society Jewish children receive gifts every night of the eight nights of Hanukkah, and although a very joyous celebration takes place, the overall message is one of God's faithfulness in the midst of the quest for freedom; of the struggle for the worship of the only true God in the midst of the worldly lures of assimilation and sensuous pleasures. It is the challenge of a handful of Jewish citizens that were prepared to die so that the light of revealed truth and righteousness would not be extinguished in a heathen world. It signifies to the Jewish people the disastrous consequences of total assimilation—enslavement to the dictates of the prevalent worldview and its culture. On the other hand, American Jews also view it as a commemoration of that precious principle of religious freedom—a heritage to which our nation subscribes, for which our ancestors settled here, of which we must never lose sight.

PURIM

Purim, the Feast of Lots, is considered the happiest festival of the Jewish annual cycle. It is celebrated in the spring on the fourteenth day of the twelfth month of Adar (in leap years in the second month of Adar). It commemorates the story of young Queen Esther of Persia and the deliverance of the exiled Jewish people from the plot of the king's wicked prime minister, Haman (who in Esther 3:7 had the lot, or *pur,* cast to ascertain the date of the destruction of the Jewish community).

Mordecai was a relative of Esther's, who had adopted and raised her, and had forbidden her to reveal her nationality (Esther 2:10) when the king was choosing a new queen. Esther 3:5 records that Mordecai would not kneel before or honor prime minister Haman as custom decreed. When he learned that the Jewish community was to be punished for his actions, Mordecai "tore his clothes, put on sackcloth and ashes, and went out into the city, wailing loudly and bitterly" (Esther 4:1). He convinced Esther, whose Hebrew name was Hadassah, to risk her life and go before the king to plead for her people. In the end, Haman was hung on the very same gallows that he had prepared for Mordecai (Esther 7:10). Haman suffered the fate he had planned for the Jewish people.

Esther 9:18-32 records the story of the inception of Purim as a Jewish holiday, mentioning Adar "as the time when the Jews got relief from their enemies, and as the month when their sorrow was turned into joy and their mourning into a day of celebration" (9:22). In both the Purim eve and subsequent morning synagogue service, the *Megillah,* the scroll of the book of Esther, is read in its entirety, and a spirit of rejoicing, frivolity, and sundry antics abounds. Every time Haman's name is mentioned during the reading of Esther, children and adults alike shout, stomp, jeer, and twirl *greggers* (clackety noisemakers often distributed before the service) to symbolically blot out Haman's name. This is quite a contrast to the traditional day of fasting, *Taanit Esther,* that precedes Purim, recalling the three days of fasting Esther required of the Jewish people (Esther 4:16) before she went unsummoned to the king.

Purim is also a time of gift-giving and charity. It is little wonder that the largest Jewish women's organization in the world, which promotes medical relief and welfare enterprises, is called Hadassah. The lesson that Hadassah (Esther) learned, as well as illustrated through her life's example, reminds the Jewish community yearly of its duty to heritage and peoplehood. Mordecai's answer to the young queen's explanation that certain death by law would face her for such boldness, has had universal implications for Jews of all persuasions and theologies:

> Do not think that because you are in the king's house you alone of all the Jews will escape. For if you remain silent at this time, relief and deliverance for the Jews will arise from another place, but you and your father's family will perish. And who knows but that you have come to royal position for such a time as this? (Esther 4:13-14)

The young queen responded with courage, judiciously requesting the community to fast, and resolving: "I will go to the king, even though it is against the law. And if I perish, I perish" (verse 16).

PESACH

Pesach (pronounced, pay-sock) is the Hebrew term for Passover, the historic commemoration of Jewish emancipation. It is also called the Feast of Unleavened Bread. This spring festival is designed as a learning exercise, a yearly reminder of God's deliverance of His people from Egyptian bondage.

In Exodus 12:17-18, God commands the Israelites: "Celebrate the Feast of Unleavened Bread, because it was on this very day that I brought your divisions out of Egypt. Celebrate this day as a lasting ordinance for the generations to come. In the first month you are to eat bread made without yeast, from the evening of the fourteenth day until the evening of the twenty-first day."

So central is the Passover motif in Judaism that tradition teaches that every Jewish person is to regard his life and deeds as though he personally had been delivered from bondage and gone out of Egypt with Moses. Exodus 13:9 instructs that observing Passover and the eating of unleavened bread "will be for you like a sign on your hand and a reminder on your forehead that the law of the Lord is to be on your lips." Deuteronomy 16:3 insists that Passover must be observed "so that all the days of your life you may remember the time of your departure from Egypt." To this day, the Exodus is a part of daily prayers, synagogue worship, and grace after meals.

The Passover reminds the faithful that God hears the cries of those who are oppressed, personally cares for each of His children, remembers His covenant, and provides redemption. More than mere "escape," it is a cooperative act between God and man, between grace and faith. Little wonder, then, that God preferred to describe Himself that way as He gave the Ten Commandments. "I am the Lord your God, who brought you out of Egypt, out of the land of slavery" (Exodus 20:2).

In ancient times, the paschal lamb was offered as a sacrifice on the eve of the feast, roasted whole, and eaten in a family setting (cf. Deuteronomy 16:1-8). By the time of Jesus, millions gathered in Jerusalem to participate in the festival. The Last Supper (Matthew 26:17-30; Mark 14:12-26; Luke 22:7-38) appears to have been the *seder* meal of Passover; Matthew and Mark prefaced their accounts with the words, "On the first day of the Feast of Unleavened Bread." It was the custom of the early Christian community to recall the resurrection on Passover.

After the destruction of the Temple, the offering of the paschal lamb ceased (although there is some evidence that for a time it continued in some Jewish circles). The Samaritans still sacrifice the paschal lamb on Mt. Gerizim to this day. The *seder* meal, however, continues throughout Jewish history.

PREPARING FOR PASSOVER

The Pesach home ceremony developed in the ancient Jewish community as a response to God's command to tell the children, "I do this because of what the Lord did for me when I came out of Egypt" (Exodus 13:8). The entire *seder* ("order") and the specific food items are designed for this end.

Although it is an honor for one to be invited to the Passover seder, and the ceremonial meal is spiritually uplifting and rewarding, it is doubtful that many Christians have the slightest idea of the amount of preparation involved. The elaborate meal is only one small undertaking compared to the long list of obligations preceding it. Preparations must begin right after Purim in order to have everything completed in time for Pesach.

The basic observance of Pesach comes from the commandment in Exodus 12:15: "For seven days you are to eat bread made without yeast," and Exodus 12:19: "For seven days no yeast is to be found in your houses." The word "yeast" here refers to the Hebrew word *chametz,* which is the leavening product caused by fermentation that results from water touching a grain such as wheat, oats, barley, rye, and spelt (a wheat containing two light red kernels). Ashkenazic Jews (those of eastern European origin) expand this list to include rice, corn, beans, peas, and lentils. Because chametz is a symbol of corruption and impurity, the orthodox treat it like a dreaded cancer.

In order to rid the house of chametz, there are the obvious items to throw out, such as flours, breads, cookies, crackers, noodles, spaghetti, cereals, packages of baking yeast, baking powder, baking soda, and (for the Ashkenazic) the above mentioned additional grains and vegetables, as they are also capable of fermenting. There are, however, the not so obvious items, such as vitamins in a grain base, cough syrups in grain alcohol base, vanilla, some flavoring extracts, and pet foods for parakeets, gerbils, hamsters, and the like. A leading pet food maker carries a line of "kosher for Passover" pet foods for the strict observers. Constructing this "fence around the law" ensures that one will not even get *near* breaking the Lord's commandment.

The search for chametz is an exhausting and time consuming observance of Passover. It involves cleaning the entire house from attic to basement, in corners, under and behind furniture, under sofa cushions, cleaning out drawers and closets (including turning pockets and pant cuffs inside out—a real adventure for the mother of small boys!), suitcases, school bags, overturning mattresses, and vacuuming the floor, seats, cushions, and glove compartment of the car. Each book is taken from the bookcase, turned over, shaken, and dusted before returning it to a clean shelf. In the process of all this searching and cleaning, there is the temptation to go all the way and wash curtains, shampoo carpets, wax floors, and wash windows.

The drawers and cupboards of the kitchen must be cleaned, vacuumed, scrubbed, and new lining paper put down. Pots and pans must be *kāshēred* (made right, proper) for Passover by thoroughly scouring all surfaces and dipping them in boiling water. This practice dates back to ancient times when bacteria could hide in the cracks and pores of wooden and earthen vessels. (The Egyptians discovered that the old, porous jars with a lot of cracks made the best beer due to the fermentation action of the bacteria hiding there.) If a woman can afford it, she can save herself a lot of trouble with a separate set of Passover cooking and baking utensils.

The kitchen sink must be scoured and boiling water poured over all surfaces before replacing the sponge with a new one. The stove and oven must be thoroughly scrubbed in all parts and the heat turned up until the metal glows (or a blowtorch can be applied to grates and oven surfaces). The refrigerators (some traditional households have one for dairy products and another for meat from their interpretation of Exodus 23:19; 34:26; and Deuteronomy 14:21) must be washed out, paying careful attention to the folds in the rubber gasket linings where crumbs can accumulate. Toasters are totally removed from the house.

Once all this chametz is "rounded up," the problem arises as to what is to be done with it. Ideally, the supply has been allowed to run very low, but burning all the rest can be a very costly proposition. Therefore, the rabbis have devised a method of "disowning" chametz. This can be done either by selling it (figuratively speaking) to a Gentile and buying it back after Pesach, or boxing, sealing, and removing all usable chametz to a far corner of the basement where it will be out of sight and thus symbolically disowned. Pets on a grain diet must also be given to a Gentile for the duration of the holidays or be put on a Passover diet. A final ceremony, *B'dikat Chametz,* takes place the night preceding the first seder. Every family member searches for crumbs of bread purposely left in conspicuous places and burns them in a fire. The search at night is done with a candle, a feather, and a wooden spoon. The burning is done in the morning. Children are taught in this way the importance of following the commands of the Lord, of taking the Bible seriously.

The seder menu must be thoughtfully planned and labels carefully read when shopping. Products bearing the words "kosher for Passover" and signed by a rabbi ensure that the item is suitable for the holidays. For instance, *matzah* (unleavened bread) that is kosher for Passover has been carefully watched and supervised by a rabbi during its production from the harvesting of the grain in the field to the baking in the factory. The time it takes for flour and water to ferment is, traditionally, the time it takes to walk a Roman mile (or approximately eighteen minutes). Therefore, Passover matzah must be baked well within eighteen minutes after water touches the flour and the dough is mixed.

Meats must be purchased from a kosher butcher. This ensures that the animal was mercifully and painlessly killed by a kindhearted and devoutly religious *shochet* (slaughterer). The blade of his long knife is sharpened keener than a razor's edge and with one deft stroke, without applying any pressure, he severs both the carotid artery and jugular vein in the neck of the animal. The animal swiftly loses consciousness as the blood supply to the brain is diminished. The blood is then drained from the body.

A Jewish cook will further purge the meat of capillary blood by soaking and salting it for a total of an hour and a half. It is ironic that anti-Semites have accused the Jewish people throughout history of using the blood of Christian women and children to make matzah (the "blood libel" against Jews) when, in fact, a Jewish cook will not even use an egg in a recipe without first breaking it in a clear glass bowl to check for a blood spot. As incredible and disgusting as it seems, there are anti-Semites today who still propagate this "blood libel" against the Jewish people.

In addition to the foregoing physical preparation for Pesach, spiritual preparation is also necessary. Five special Sabbaths precede Passover. Additional portions of Torah are read in remembrance of the Temple, moral purification, the paschal sacrifice, and future redemption of humankind from all physical and spiritual oppression. This latter Sabbath is known as the Great Sabbath, *Shabbat Hagadol,* where the haftorah reading is from Malachi 3:4–4:6 (3:4-24 in the Hebrew text). This passage ends with a section on the "day of the Lord," commanding the people to remember "the law *[Torah]* of my servant Moses, the decrees [statutes] and laws [judgments] I gave him at Horeb for all Israel" (4:4). As an expression of gratitude to God for sparing the Jewish firstborn in the final plague, firstborn males traditionally fast on the day before the Passover celebration.

THE SEDER MEAL

The first two evenings of Pesach are set aside for the Passover *seder* (order or arrangement) conducted in the home. The text used for the festive Passover meal is called the *Haggadah* (from the Hebrew *haggeyd,* "to tell"), a guidebook that explains how to conduct the seder and what the symbols of Passover mean. It also contains songs, stories, narrative, and prayers. More extensive books on the Passover seder are listed in the Suggested Reading at the back of this book, but a brief synopsis of the stages of the seder is as follows:

THE ORDER OF THE SEDER

1. *Blessing over the wine:* The cups of wine are filled, and the *kiddush* is sung. It is a common custom to stand for *kiddush* and to sit for drinking (varies).

2. *Washing the hands:* Ritual washing is required before any food is dipped in liquid. This is accomplished by filling a cup with water and pouring it over each hand two or three times, alternating hands.

3. *Eating the karpas:* Dipping the vegetable in saltwater is the first dipping ritual. The saltwater symbolizes the sweat and tears of a people in bondage.

4. *Dividing the matzah:* The seder leader takes out the middle of the three *matzot,* breaking it into two uneven pieces. The largest of the portions is wrapped in a napkin, becoming the *afikoman.* The children watch attentively (this act traditionally keeps their attention throughout the seder) and attempt to "steal" the *afikoman* (variations on this tradition). Later, the seder leader "ransoms" the *afikoman.*

5. *Telling the Passover story:* The seder plate is lifted momentarily, the *matzot* are uncovered, the wine cups are refilled. This signifies the beginning of the Haggadah. The youngest child proceeds to recite the four questions (see below). Sometimes the story of Pesach is read aloud together, but more often the participants take turns.

6. *Washing the hands:* A blessing accompanies the washing because bread will be eaten.

7. *Blessings over the matzah:* All *matzot* are lifted, and a *matzah* blessing is given. The bottom *matzah* is then put down. Each participant receives part of the whole top *matzah* (symbol of freedom) and part of the broken middle one (symbol of slavery). As usual, all are eaten while reclining to the left.

8. *Eating the bitter herb:* The *maror* (bitter herb, usually horseradish) is blessed, dipped in the *charoset* (a delicious chopped apple and nut concoction, symbolizing mortar and clay). This is the second act of dipping after the blessing over the *maror*.

9. *The sandwich (Hillel):* A sandwich is made out of the bottom matzah, with *maror* in between. This is in remembrance of the great sage Hillel's interpretation. He did not separate the *maror* and the matzah in the traditional way.

10. *The festival meal:* Traditional items include: celery and olives, *gifilte* fish with beet horseradish, beef brisket, potato *kugel,* fresh asparagus, assorted nuts, lettuce salad, strawberries, matzot, roast turkey or chicken, beet and egg salad, applesauce, chopped eggs and onions, chicken soup with matzah balls, pot roast with vegetables, honeyed carrots, cole slaw, melon or fruit bowl, Passover cake or Passover macaroons.

11. *Eating the afikoman:* The *afikoman* is "ransomed." It is the last item to be eaten, signifying the paschal lamb, which was the last item to be eaten in the ancient period of the Temple. Everyone gets a piece.

12. *Grace After Meals:* The third cup of wine is filled, and the Grace After Meals is recited. Based on passages such as Deuteronomy 8:10 ("When you have eaten and are satisfied, praise

the Lord your God"), Grace After Meals was a tradition at the time of Jesus and was no doubt one of the central features of His home meal. After Grace, the blessing over the third cup of wine is delivered, and the wine is drunk. The cups are immediately filled again, as well as a large goblet for Elijah. A door is opened for Elijah. *(If you do not drink wine, grape juice is a legal substitute—your hostess, however, should be forewarned.)*

13. *Hallel:*   Songs and melodies of praise are sung.

14. *Nirtzah:*   In conclusion, the call for "acceptance" (see below). All participants hope that Passover will be celebrated "Next year in Jerusalem!" More singing occurs throughout the evening.

Passover Haggadahs may be purchased at most Jewish bookstores, ranging from inexpensive paperback editions of sixty pages to elaborate hardback copies. The order remains the same, some portions dating from long before the time of Jesus. Beautiful passages abound. For example, one of the oldest portions is recited as the *matzah* is raised on the ceremonial plate. The head of the home reads aloud:

> This is the poor bread which our fathers ate in the land of Egypt. Let anyone who is hungry, come in and eat; let anyone who is needy, come in and make Passover. This year we are here; next year we shall be in the land of Israel. This year we are slaves; next year we shall be free men and women.

As a teaching excercise, the youngest in attendance (who is able) asks four questions preceded by the well-known introduction, "Why is this night different from all other nights?":

1. On all other nights, we eat either leavened or unleavened bread. Why on this night do we eat only unleavened bread?
2. On all other nights we eat all kinds of herbs. Why on this night do we eat only bitter herbs?

3. On all other nights we do not dip the vegetables even once. Why on this night do we dip them twice?
4. On all other nights we eat either in a sitting or a reclining position. Why on this night do we all recline?

The story of the Exodus is then read aloud from the Haggadah. Each participant old enough to read usually takes turns around the table.

It is significant that as each plague is recounted in unison, a drop of wine (the symbol of joy) is dipped from the glass. This signifies that their joy cannot be full because of the suffering the Egyptians had to endure (cruel as they were to the Israelites). Remorse is felt that redemption came through the suffering of others. This compassion toward an enemy is entirely in accordance with Judaism. Proverbs 24:17 warns: "Do not gloat when your enemy falls; when he stumbles, do not let your heart rejoice." Proverbs 25:21 instructs: "If your enemy is hungry, give him food to eat; if he is thirsty, give him water to drink" (cf. Exodus 23:4-5; Proverbs 20:22).

The seder meal is eaten while resting on cushions. This posture symbolizes the reclining position of free men and women. Kings and noblemen used to eat this way. It is customary for guests and family members to wear brightly colored clothes of fine cloth or silk, whereas the head of the household may wear a plain white garment (especially in traditional circles). This is to keep the leader of the seder from pride —the plain white garment clothes the dead for burial (see chap. 3).

Singing abounds at the close of the seder. *Nirtzah,* the "acceptance," rings out:

> Ended the act of Pesach night,
> Each law and custom kept aright:
> As we've lived to do it without a stain,
> God grant we do it time and again.
> Pure One, Dweller in height august,
> Raise up the folk of countless dust!
> Soon lead the stem-shoots of thy ward,
> Redeemed and singing, Zionward.
>
> NEXT YEAR IN JERUSALEM!

SHAVUOT

On the second night of Passover, a counting ritual called the Counting of the Omer *(sefirah)* begins. After the special blessing is recited, the forty-nine days from this night until *Shavuot* are counted, making mention of the number of each day and each week, for example, "Today is the first day of Omer," "Today is the second day of Omer," "Today is the ninth day, which is one week and two days in the Omer." Thus, the biblical injunction concerning the firstfruits in Leviticus 23:9-14 is acknowledged as "a lasting ordinance for the generations to come, wherever you live" (verse 14).

Omer means "sheaf" (of grain), and Leviticus 23:15-16 goes on to instruct:

> From the day after the Sabbath, the day you brought the sheaf of the wave offering, count off seven full weeks. Count off fifty days up to the day after the seventh Sabbath, and then present an offering of new grain to the Lord.

The fiftieth day is a holiday, *Shavuot,* the Festival of Weeks, "a sacred assembly" in which one does "no regular work" (Leviticus 23:21). In the Bible, in Israel, and in Reform Judaism, *Shavuot* is a one-day holiday, whereas in Conservative Judaism and Orthodox synagogues outside Israel, it is celebrated for two days.

On Shavuot, the synagogues are decorated with plants and flowers to commemorate the bringing of the firstfruits of the harvest to the Temple in ancient times. It has also come to symbolize the giving of the Torah to Moses and the Jewish people at Mount Sinai. Dairy products are eaten at home signifying the "milk" of the Word of God. In Conservative and Reform synagogues, confirmation ceremonies (see chap. 8) are held during this holiday. Traditionally, one should stay up the entire night of Shavuot, studying and discussing a small section from each portion of the Torah.

The last of the agricultural holidays of the Jewish sacred year, Shavuot (in addition to Sukkot and Pesach), was a time when Jesus' family would travel to the Temple in Jerusalem to bring an offering in accordance with the Torah. From the Greek word for "fifty," this Festival of Weeks was also known as *Pentecost.* That is why the Jewish disciples of Jesus in Acts 2 "were all together in one place" and "there were staying in Jerusalem God-fearing Jews from every nation under heaven" (vv.1 and 5). They were all assembled for Shavuot or Pentecost.

In the synagogue, it is customary to read the book of Ruth as part of the regular holiday service. Much of this book takes place in a harvest setting, and Ruth's great-grandson King David traditionally was thought to have been born and died on Shavout. The story of the faith and devotion of this Moabite woman who converted to Judaism is indicative of the love God has for all people, whether Jew or Gentile, and the honor He bestows on those who love Him and Torah. Ruth 1:16 records her decision: "Where you go I will go, and where you stay I will stay. Your people will be my people and your God my God." The account is also an illustration of how God can cause good to come out of trial and tragedy.

The Torah reading on the first day of Shavuot is Exodus 19:1–20:26 —the "great theophany" (appearance of God) at Sinai. The haftorah for this day is Ezekiel's remarkable vision of God in Ezekiel 1-2. This personal encounter with God marked the commencement of Ezekiel's prophetic ministry.

A portion from Habakkuk is read on the second day of the Festival of Weeks, beginning with Habakkuk 2:20:

> But the Lord is in his holy temple;
> let all the earth be silent before him.

TISHA BE-AV AND CONTEMPORARY COMMEMORATIONS

A number of other commemorations have come into prominence in the yearly cycle of Jewish life after the destruction of the Second Temple. These fasts and commemorations are deeply wedded to the history of the Jewish people.

TISHA BE-AV

Tisha Be-Av, the ninth day of Av, is the saddest day on the Jewish calendar. Traditionally, it is a fast day for mourning the destruction of the First and Second Temples in Jerusalem. Viewed historically as a time of calamity, it has become the "Friday the 13th" of Jewish life.

Not only were the First and Second Temples destroyed during this period (by the Babylonians and Romans respectively), but the children of Israel were forbidden to enter the Promised Land on that date, condemned to wander forty years in the wilderness. In A.D. 135, the last bastion of the Second Jewish Revolt against the Romans (Betar) was captured on Tisha Be-Av, and the following year Emperor Hadrian built a pagan temple and a pagan city on the original Temple site. Hadrian renamed Jerusalem *Aelia Capitolina;* called Judea "Palestine"; and, on the ninth of Av, forbade Jews access to or even a look from afar upon their sacred city.

In more modern times, the "Christian" Crusades destroyed entire Jewish communities on the ninth of Av. On this date in 1290, Jews were expelled from England, and, again on the ninth of Av during the Spanish Inquisition in 1492, Jews were expelled from Spain. Four hundred fifty years later, in 1942, Polish Jews in the Warsaw Ghetto were deported by the Nazis on Tisha Be-Av to the Treblinka extermination camp. There more than 800,000 Jewish men, women, and children were slaughtered.

For Orthodox Jews, a mourning period of three weeks preceding the ninth of Av is important for intensifying the gravity of the period. Jewish weddings and other celebrations are not held during this period. Rejoicing is prohibited. Therefore, purchasing new clothes, eating meat, building a new house, or constructing additions on a home are prohibited—for these things may bring joy. *Tallit* and *tefillin* are not worn at morning prayer (not until afternoon prayer).

On the night of Tisha Be-Av and on the fast day itself, leather shoes are not worn, and customs much like those mourning the death of a close relative are observed (see next chap.). Food and drink are forbidden; cosmetic washing and perfuming are shunned; hair is not cut. In the synagogue, the book of Lamentations is read, and the study of Torah (which brings joy) is reserved for another day. The lights of the synagogue are dimmed, and the congregation sits on the floor or on low stools or benches. The curtain of the ark that holds the Torah scrolls is removed. Sometimes a black curtain is put in its place. Special songs of mourning are chanted, and melancholy tunes abound.

The haftorah portion for the morning service of the ninth of Av is Jeremiah 8:13–9:24. Invasion, siege, famines, defeat, devastation, death, and exile are all mentioned; intense sorrow and lament are recorded throughout. Jeremiah 8:22 questions: "Is there no balm in Gilead? Is there no physician there? Why then is there no healing for the wound of my people?"

Jeremiah 9:13 continues: "The Lord said, 'It is because they have forsaken my law [Torah], which I set before them; they have not obeyed me or followed my law [Torah].' " A lesson, however, comes at the end of the passage—a lesson for all humankind:

> This is what the Lord says:
> "Let not the wise man boast of his wisdom
> or the strong man boast of his strength
> or the rich man boast of his riches,
> but let him who boasts boast about this:
> that he understands and knows me,
> that I am the Lord, who exercises kindness,
> justice and righteousness on earth,
> for in these I delight," declares the Lord.
>
> (Jeremiah 9:23-24)

Appropriately, the yearly cycle continues with the Sabbath of Consolation, the weekly Sabbath that follows Tisha Be-Av. Isaiah 40:1-26 is read: "Comfort, comfort my people, says your God. Speak tenderly to Jerusalem, and proclaim to her that her hard service has been completed, that her sin has been paid for, that she has received from the Lord's hand double for all her sins" (vv. 1-2).

In some traditional Jewish circles it is believed that the Messiah will appear on Tisha Be-Av. Then, sorrow and lamentation will be turned to joy—Tisha Be-Av will become a holiday.

YOM HA-SHOAH

In 1951 the Israeli Knesset set aside the 27th day of Nisan as a "perpetual remembrance" of the six million Jewish men, women, and children exterminated by the Nazi regime and its collaborators. The date fell between the Warsaw Ghetto uprising (which began on the first day of Passover) and Israel Independence Day (on the 5th day of Iyyar; see below). The date became a part of the religious calendar of the Jewish people. It is a time to reflect on the responsibility and the persecution that has historically accompanied being Jewish.

Maimonides (1135-1204), famed Jewish philosopher, once stated: "If a Jew is murdered for no other reason except that he is a Jew, and, had he not been a Jew, he would have remained alive, then it may truly be said that he sacrificed his life for the holiness of God." The magnitude of the Holocaust and the irrationality of man's inhumanity toward Jewish people staggers the mind, making this medieval Jewish sage's words a fitting apology from out of the past.

In October 1980 the United States Holocaust Memorial Council established by the unanimous vote of Congress a national commitment to remembrance. Memorial ceremonies had been held in Washington, D.C., the year before. Across the United States (and in many parts of the world), more and more local communities are joining Israel in initiating commemorative programs. Increasingly, this is becoming an interreligious observance, as the Christian community begins to realize that anti-Semitism, stereotypes, caricatures, persecution, and extermination are universal problems. The Holocaust is not merely a Nazi problem, or a German problem, or an Eastern European problem—it is a human problem—our problem!

Without an understanding of the Holocaust, we fail to understand man's inhumanity to man, even in a civilized society. With an understanding of the Holocaust, we begin to comprehend the consequences of even latent racial and religious prejudice. Without an understanding of the Holocaust, we would not question what our reactions might be while watching others being persecuted. With an understanding of the Holocaust, we begin to see that racism in general, and anti-Semitism in particular, devour a society, causing it soon to turn on its own people like a hideous cancer.

Although the Holocaust may be approached as a case study for all racial and religious prejudice, the Jewish dimension of the Holocaust is unique. Even though millions of others died during World War II, the Nazis were determined to kill *all* Jews. They searched out every hovel to do so. Conversion was no longer a refuge for the Jewish person, because Hebrew Christians were sought out as well. "Good" Christians turned their backs on the Jewish community, and Holocaust study continually raises the disturbing question: "Are Christians really different from the rest of society? Are they really different from the world?"

That is why it is very important to stand with the local Jewish community at *Yom Ha-Shoah,* making a statement by your presence. Usually an evening memorial service at the synagogue is open to the public, and is a meaningful tribute to the victims of the Holocaust. Increasingly, Christian clergymen and their congregations are taking part in the program. Synagogue programs for the event can include films, testimonies by survivors, Holocaust literature, songs, poems, and prayers. It is a sobering necessity for all ages to "remember." For the Jewish community, the Holocaust is an atrocity in Jewish history that has burned itself on the Jewish psyche and soul. We cannot possibly hope to comprehend what we personally have never experienced, but we must nevertheless come alongside members of the Jewish community and stand with them. A Christian cannot begin to appreciate or empathize with his or her Jewish neighbor today without an understanding of the Holocaust.

YOM HA-ATZMAUT

Eight days after *Yom Ha-Shoah, Yom Ha-Atzmaut* (the Israeli "Fourth of July") is observed on the fifth day of Iyyar. In Israel, this independence day is preceded by a Remembrance Day *(yom ha-zikkaron)* of religious, civil, and military ceremonies for those soldiers who died fighting in Israel's War of Independence or who have died in active duty since that time. Psalm 9 and Psalm 144 are two special readings for the occasion. In the morning of Iyyar 4, the nation observes a two minute period of silence in tribute and remembrance. In the evening that marks the beginning of the fifth day, Israel Independence Day, Jerusalem rejoices with fireworks and festivity. Boys and girls carry multicolored flashlights. Family celebrations abound, with food and music. After two thousand years without a country, the Jewish people have a homeland of their own, the land that they had prayed to see again—"Next year in Jerusalem!"

In the United States, *Yom Ha-Atzmaut* is a time for education as well as reflection on the importance of the State of Israel. Religious services include prayers for Israel and thankfulness to God for a homeland. Although Jewish people consider their country of residence their home and Jewish tradition teaches that one must be a good citizen of the country in which one lives, the importance of the state of Israel to the survival of the Jewish people is incalculable. During the Holocaust, for example, there was no place for most Jewish people to go—no country that would take them. The state of Israel promises citizenship to Jewish people from any nation and pledges to be a haven in time of trouble.

To the contemporary Jewish community, this has come about in their own generation—in their own century. Although they realize that no nation or state is perfect, the Jewish community's love affair with the Holy Land goes back four thousand years. Much of the spirit of that "miracle" of God is found in the opening verses of Psalm 9 on Remembrance Day: "I will praise you, O Lord, with all my heart; I will tell of all your wonders. I will be glad and rejoice in you: I will sing praise to your name, O Most High."

So flows the yearly rhythm for the Jewish community. By understanding that rhythm, one understands both the Jewish people and the Christian's biblical heritage more completely. Jesus and the Jewish disciples shared in this rhythm and were an integral part of their generation's festivals and commemorations. They were part of this heritage because the holy days, fasts, and festivals were an expression of religious commitment. The purpose of the annual cycle was to remember and illustrate God's presence and activity in history. The yearly festivals underscore a personal God who cares for His creation and is active in the lives of men, women, and children every day of the year.

Tishri 1 (September 12, 1988) through Elul 29 (September 29, 1989)

Jewish holiday begins at sunset the previous evening

1989

	SEP	OCT	NOV	DEC	JAN	FEB	MAR	APR	MAY	JUN	JUL	AUG	SEP
1													Elul 1
2									Yom Ha-Shoah			Av 1	
3													
4		Simchat Torah		Hanukkah (8 days)						Sivan 1	Tammuz 1		
5													
6						Adar I 1		Nisan 1	Iyyar 1				
7					Shevat 1								
8							Adar II 1						
9				Tevet 1						Shavuot			
10			Kislev 1						Yom Ha-Atzmaut			Tisha Be-Av (9th of Av)	
11	5749*												
12	Tishri 1 Rosh Hashanah	Heshvan 1											
13													
14													

17
18
19
20 Yom Kippur
21
22
23
24
25
26 Sukkot (8 days)
27
28
29
30
31

Pesach (8 days)

Purim

Tishri 1
Rosh Hashanah
5750 New Year

*5749 is a leap year in the Jewish calendar; thus Adar II is added after Adar I

3
Life Cycle

As the Sabbath contributes to a weekly order and the festivals mark a yearly order, so too birth, circumcision, bar/bat mitzvah, marriage, and death are milestones in the life of a Jew.

BIRTH AND CIRCUMCISION

In Judaism, birth is a miracle of God, a blessing imparted to a fortunate couple. The first commandment given to man by God was to "be fruitful and increase in number" (Genesis 1:28), and a high value is placed upon children. Indeed, life is to be cherished and nurtured. The sanctity of human life is the apex of God's creation and a number one priority.

In biblical times, a couple without children were considered dead—they had failed their mission in this world. The act of childbearing and the rearing of children glorified the name of God on earth. Every infant was thought to have a calling before it came into the world, and parents viewed their children as a kingdom of priests. The duty of childrearing was perceived as a holy calling, a mission that honored God and spread His message throughout the earth. Thus, the family has traditionally been God's way of spreading Torah, His way of life, through each Jewish generation and out to the world at large. The command to "be fruitful and multiply" applies to the spiritual as well as the physical.

It is little wonder, then, that the birth of a child in the Jewish community is an event filled with great joy and a keen sense of responsibility. As in all facets of Jewish life, the covenant with God is the prime concern when a new member is born into the community, and the *b'rit mi-lah,* the "covenant of circumcision" ceremony on the eighth day of the male child's life, usually marks and spiritually confirms this special relationship. Jewish circumcision began with Abraham when God commanded in Genesis 17:9-13:

> Then God said to Abraham, "As for you, you must keep my covenant, you and your descendants after you for the generations to come. This is my covenant with you and your descendants after you, the covenant you are to keep: Every male among you shall be circumcised. You are to undergo circumcision, and it will be the sign of the covenant between me and you. For the generations to come every male among you who is eight days old must be circumcised, including those born in your household or bought with money from a foreigner—those who are not your offspring. Whether born in your household or bought with your money, they must be circumcised. My covenant in your flesh is to be an everlasting covenant.

The word "covenant" is repeated thirteen times in the seventeenth chapter of Genesis.

Although for years the hygienic value of circumcision has been upheld by the medical profession (only to be questioned by some in recent days), the Jewish response to God's "everlasting covenant" is never explained through medical or rational analysis. Rabbis have never turned to statistics of lower cervical or penile cancer among married couples where the husband is circumcised. In stark contrast, the traditional response has been, "God commanded us to do this as an appropriate response to His covenant, and this symbolizes our partnership with God."

Contrary to popular belief throughout history, circumcision does not "make" one Jewish. Birth or conversion are the only means of entering and belonging to this peoplehood. The *b'rit milah* ceremony through a physical act, however, serves as an outward sign of the covenant with God, a covenant through which all life is given meaning and a keen sense of responsibility is nurtured. So crucial is this concept of human value that in recent years it has become popular to hold a religious ceremony welcoming the female child as well into the covenanted community.

The *b'rit milah* ceremony has varied from generation to generation and from culture to culture. It is a time of great festivity that is usually held in the home. In earlier periods, the ceremony was held in the synagogue, and a man bringing his son to be circumcised was likened to a high priest bringing a meal offering or libation to the Temple altar.

According to Jewish law, it is the father's obligation to circumcise his son. Due, however, to the inability of most fathers to perform this duty, only a *mohel* (a pious, trained, religious specialist) can stand in for him. An uncertified doctor or surgeon is not qualified to carry out this important rite, which is conducted in the presence of at least ten men (the traditional quorum or *minyan* needed for a religious service). Two chairs are placed in front of the mohel, one reserved for the grandfather or uncle who holds the child during the ceremony (becoming the child's godfather). The other chair is left empty as the symbolic seat for the traditional guardian of Israel's covenant with God, Elijah the prophet.

All rise as the child is brought in, and the people remain standing throughout the ceremony. The mohel recites, "Blessed are You, Lord our God, Ruler of the universe, who commanded us regarding circumcision." He then circumcises the child with deft swiftness and efficiency, a master at his craft. A mohel must be a devout man, an observant Jew, who has received careful training. He is to consider performing such a religious act as a special privilege.

The child's father follows with the blessing: "Blessed are You, Lord our God, Ruler of the universe, who has sanctified us with His commandments and commanded us to bring him into the Covenant of our father, Abraham." Every person present responds with a hearty, "Amen!"

Those congregated, family and friends, then recite a Hebrew blessing which interpreted says: "Just as this child enters today into the Covenant of Abraham, so may he enter upon the study of Torah, a gratifying marriage and a life of good deeds." In the final prayer, the mohel announces the baby's name: "Let his name be called in Israel _____, the son of _____."

The ceremony is followed by a festive meal, often including speeches from the proud grandparents, parents, and the rabbi. Sometimes the father will explain the significance of the name during his speech. The female child is named formally in the synagogue, and the father is called up to read Torah. In fact, in some naming ceremonies, passages from the Bible are interspersed throughout.

In Judaism, beginnings are important. The *b'rit milah* is a momentous occasion for the community as well as a personal milestone for parents and child. Since Judaism is a way of life, both religious rituals and the ethical covenantal values that surround them are crucial. Responsibility before God, both collective and individual, is deeply felt. Through the covenant, human shortcomings and failures are realized, but so also are the patience, grace, and faithfulness of God.

BAR MITZVAH AND BAT MITZVAH

The Jewish child traditionally is to be given increasing spiritual responsibility as he or she grows toward adolescence. At five years of age, for example, the male child is to receive considerable instruction in the Scriptures; at ten the intense study of oral tradition. The Bar Mitzvah or Bat Mitzvah ceremony becomes the milestone in a young person's life when he or she formally assumes personal moral and religious responsibility and accountability.

At the age of thirteen, a Jewish boy becomes a *bar mitzvah,* literally "son of the commandments" or "commanded son." He formally assumes before his community and his God the privileges and obligations of being Jewish. Judaism recognizes that girls mature faster than boys, so at the age of twelve during the *bat mitzvah* ("daughter of the commandments") ceremony, a girl assumes her responsibility as a Jewish woman. In ancient times the vows of a Jewish child became the responsibility of girls and boys at the age of twelve years and one day, and thirteen years and one day respectively. Fast days were also to be observed at these ages. What is commonly referred to in the history of religions as *rites of passage* ceremonies developed around these important occasions in the medieval period.

Today, the Bar Mitzvah or Bat Mitzvah ceremony is one of the most popular events in the Jewish world. Although traditions vary from Orthodox to Reform Judaism, this time is viewed as a turning point—a period when young people are obligated to control their own desires, accept accountability for mature religious actions, and assume adult community responsibilities.

At one point in the service the father (sometimes unable to keep a straight face) says, "Blessed be He who has freed me from the responsibility for this child!"[1] This declaration usually brings a chuckle from other parents in the congregation who are identifying with his "relief." They realize that considerable financial and emotional support will be necessary for several more years. There are, nevertheless, many fathers and mothers who have tears in their eyes as they realize that their little boy

---

1. Some congregations have incorporated a parent's address to the child. In public, these are thoughtful, touching, and heartfelt.

or girl is becoming an adult. And, standing straight and tall, in the most professional voice, the Bar Mitzvah boy or Bat Mitzvah girl demonstrates to the congregation his or her proficiency in the traditions of the community and commitment to the Covenant. In the Orthodox community, Bar Mitzvah marks the period when a boy first wears *tefillin* (phylacteries). These are two sealed black boxes attached to long black leather straps. Inside each box is a tightly rolled parchment on which the scribes have finely handwritten in Hebrew the following verses: Exodus 13:1-10; Exodus 13:11-16; Deuteronomy 6:4-9; and Deuteronomy 11:13-21.

The Bar Mitzvah ceremony is conducted in the synagogue on the Sabbath following the Jewish boy's thirteenth birthday. He is called up for his first Torah reading, reciting the blessings that his forefathers recited for centuries before him. Generally, he has worked with the rabbi and his father to such an extent that he will be able to read the entire Torah portion for that Sabbath and the haftorah section as well. A spiritual electricity seems to fill the air as this child-man kisses the Torah scroll and proclaims: "Bless the Lord Who is blessed. Blessed be the Lord Who is blessed forever and ever. Blessed are You, Lord our God, Ruler of the universe, Who has chosen us from among all peoples by giving us Your Torah. Blessed are You, Lord, Giver of the Torah."

At the conclusion of the ceremony, the congregation often sings a song of *mazel-tov* (congratulations), and a reception is held after the service in the social hall. As one watches a youth dedicate himself to God, the words in the book of Hosea that are recited as the tefillin straps are wrapped around the head and left arm can be recalled: "I will betroth you to me forever: I will betroth you in righteousness and justice, in love and compassion. I will betroth you in faithfulness, and you will acknowledge the Lord" (from Hosea 2:19-20, numbered 2:21-22 in the Hebrew Bible).

The covenantal relationship begun at eight days of age in the *b'rit milah* has blossomed into a religiously mature commitment of dedication in the bar mitzvah.

MARRIAGE

In Judaism the family is the basic unit of society, and marriage is the ideal human state established by God at the time of creation. In Jewish teaching, the person who does not marry is thought to be incomplete, and marriage is to be preferred to the celibate state. It is through marriage that one obtains the ultimate in human companionship, and only as a result of this union is procreation to occur.

The biblical concept of marriage was essentially one man and one woman, a metaphor the prophets used to illustrate God's relationship to Israel. Divorce in Judaism, although always permitted, is considered a tragedy and is understood as the avenue of last resort. "Even the altar sheds tears when a man divorces his wife," ancient Jewish tradition stated. The integrity and purity of the family was to be guarded as a sacred obligation. On the Day of Atonement, an unmarried high priest was forbidden to officiate in the Temple.

According to ancient Jewish law, there were three ways to get married: with money (a ring), a legal document, and intercourse. In biblical times, anyone could perform a wedding because Jews were married by consent. There are, however, indications of wedding ceremonies with "feasts," "bridal weeks," and "wedding songs" in the Scriptures (cf. Genesis 29:22, 27; Judges 14:12; Psalm 78:63). Today, a rabbi usually presides over the ceremony.

Technically, even an arranged engagement or betrothal agreement was not to *force* a couple into marriage, since the basic principle of marriage was that of consent and free will. Such written betrothal agreements were frequently accompanied by a gift (usually a ring) from the man and a pledge of fidelity between the couple (or loyalty between families). Local custom began to dictate that breaking such an agreement was a disgraceful act and an abject humiliation for the rejected party. Soon, even Orthodox couples would not sign a formal marriage agreement until immediately preceding the ceremony in order to avoid any embarrassing breach of such agreements.

Today, even in Orthodox circles, it is not considered a disgrace to break a marriage agreement, because such an agreement does not necessarily imply a sanctioning by the community. In fact, during the arranged engagement period, an Orthodox couple gets to know one another, dining together and talking for hours, in an effort to find out if they are compatible. Judaism recognizes that a successful marriage is a difficult achievement. God is the only successful matchmaker, and yet the Talmud states that for Him the task is as difficult as splitting the Red Sea.

Wedding ceremonies are not generally permitted between Passover and Shavuot, because of the persecution of the Jewish people by Emperor Hadrian during the Bar Kokhba Revolt (A.D. 132-135). The major exception to this is the thirty-third day of the Omer, *Lag Ba-Omer,* on which persecution ceased. This is a very popular wedding day, especially among traditional Jews. Weddings are not usually scheduled as well during the three weeks preceding *Tisha Be-Av*, during the period of mourning for the destruction of the Temples, and so on. Thus, the long history of the Jewish people and their covenant relationship with God plays a crucial role in the scheduling of this most important part of the Jewish life cycle. Fortunately, for brides in the American culture, this leaves most of the month of June free for weddings.

On the Sabbath before the wedding the groom *(chatan)* is honored by being called up to participate in the reading of the Torah. This ancient tradition of honoring the groom can be seen in the Talmud's account of a gate King Solomon built in the Temple complex. Here, residents of Jerusalem would perform kindnesses to bridegrooms who came there. In the synagogue today, raisins and candy are thrown to the groom to ensure a sweet life for him and his bride.

On the wedding day itself, it is traditional for both the bride *(kallah)* and bridegroom to fast. They have been separated until the wedding ceremony, in some cases for a whole week. Weddings are usually held in late afternoon to allow the couple to fast for most of the twenty-four-hour period. The legal agreement of betrothal *(tenaim)* is usually signed by the fathers of the bride and groom right before the wedding takes place. The *ketubah*, or marriage contract, which spells out the contractual obligations of the bride and groom to each other, is then completed by putting in the couple's names, date, and place of the wedding ceremony. Two male witnesses who are not relatives sign the ketubah after the groom has stated to the rabbi that he formally accepts his obligations. The groom then takes one end of an object (such as a handkerchief) that is in the rabbi's hand. The rabbi represents the bride's interests in this preceremony ritual and later proclaims to the congregation that the groom is willing to be bound by the conditions of the ketubah.

A custom on the lighter side is the *D'var Torah*, which takes place at the groom's table. The groom chooses a Scripture text and prepares a brief discourse in honor of this occasion. But his friends keep interrupting him in jest and singing loudly so that he can never quite finish.

One of the most romantic moments of the wedding is the *bedekin*. After the groom and his attendants have finished the business of signing documents and so forth, the attendants sing and dance around the groom as they escort him to his bride. The bride is seated on a special throne surrounded by her attendants. As the eyes of the bride and groom meet, it is the first time they have seen their beloved in days. The groom then gently draws the veil over the bride's face. This act symbolizes that, unlike Jacob, he is confident that he is getting the right girl.

The Hebrew word for marriage is *kiddushin* and means "sanctification." It is from the root *kadosh*, meaning "holy." The whole wedding ceremony conveys this aspect of separation to one another and consecration to God's will. The bride and groom, dressed in white, are escorted to the *chuppah* (or canopy) where the rabbi is waiting. Each is accompanied by parents and attendants. The bridegroom is led in first by his parents, putting on a white kittel as he waits for his bride. The *kittel* is the white garment worn on Yom Kippur and symbolizes purity and forgiveness. The bride enters with her parents' arms linked through hers. In traditional circles, she walks around the groom seven times.

Unlike the American Gentile wedding ritual, the parents do not leave the couple alone, but rather stand at the side of the chuppah. Sometimes sisters and brothers will join as well, symbolizing the belief that married life encompasses the extended family. One does not marry in a vacuum. A stable marriage requires the support of all. Standing together under the chuppah (which symbolizes the couple's new home), the rabbi leads the ceremony. One must remember that wedding ceremonies differ among various Jewish groups, but the rabbi may declare: "You that come in the name of the Lord are blessed. May He who is supreme in might, blessing, and glory bless this bridegroom and bride." A cup of wine is poured, and the rabbi recites the blessing. The bride and groom then each take a sip.

Next comes the most important ritual of the entire wedding ceremony. Without it there is no legal marriage; most of the other practices surrounding it are simply deeply rooted traditions. The rabbi calls up two specially selected witnesses and, in their presence, asks the groom if this ring truly belongs to him. Historically, the ring must be one continuous band without any settings in order that there will not be any deceit about its value (such as glass in place of a precious gem). The groom slips the ring on the index finger of the bride's right hand and recites this ancient declaration: "Behold you are consecrated to me with this ring according to the Law of Moses and Israel." It is to be understood that a marriage has taken place any time, any place, with or without a rabbi, if: (1) a man gives a woman an object worth more than a dime, and (2) after she willingly accepts it, (3) he says, "Behold you are consecrated to me," in the presence of two acceptable witnesses. This act is to be viewed as serious business.

After the ketubah is read aloud in the original Aramaic language (often with a brief English translation), it is handed to the groom. He, in turn, gives it to the bride to be her possession. It is the bride's responsibility to take care of it, and the ketubah is usually framed and hung in the couple's home. If the ketubah should become lost, it must be redrawn and resigned by two witnesses. A couple may not live together without a ketubah.

The legal part of the ceremony complete, the rabbi says a few words to the couple. Seven blessings are then recited over the refilled cup of wine:

Blessed are You, O Lord our God, King of the universe,
Creator of the fruit of the vine.

Blessed are You, O Lord our God, King of the universe,
who created all things for Your glory.

Blessed are You, O Lord our God, King of the universe,
Creator of man.

Blessed are You, O Lord our God, King of the universe,
who created man and woman in Your image, fashioning woman in
the likeness of man, preparing for man a mate, that together
they might perpetuate life. Blessed are You, O Lord,
Creator of man.

May Zion rejoice as her children in joy are restored to her.
Blessed are You, O Lord, who causes Zion to rejoice at her
children's return.

Grant great joy to these beloved companions, as You did to the
first man and woman in the Garden of Eden. Blessed are You,
O Lord, who grants joy to bride and groom.

Blessed are You, O Lord our God, King of the universe,
who created joy and gladness, bride and groom, mirth, song,
delight and rejoicing, love and harmony, peace and companionship.
O Lord our God, may there be heard in the cities of Judah and in
the streets of Jerusalem voices of joy and gladness, voices of
bride and groom, the jubilant voices of those joined in marriage
under the bridal canopy, the voices of young people feasting and
singing, Blessed are You, O Lord, who causes the groom to rejoice
with his bride.

It is customary for the groom to smash a glass by stamping on it at the conclusion of the ceremony. This act has a number of interpretations, including the recollection of grief over Jewish persecution and the destruction of the Temple. Others have concluded that the smashed glass symbolizes the hope that the marriage will be irrevocable and permanent, lasting to eternity.

A festive wedding celebration ensues. The Jewish community and other guests surround the couple in love and support. Exclamations of *L'Hayyim!* (To Life!) and *Mazel Tov!* abound as the couple are escorted to the *yichud* chamber. Yichud is the occasion at the end of the ceremony when the newly married couple is given a few minutes of privacy ensured by two witnesses guarding the door. In biblical times this was the appropriate hour to consummate the marriage through intercourse and then to display the bride's blood stains as proof of her virginity. Although this ancient practice is no longer generally observed, the symbolic privacy serves to underscore the last requirement for marriage: intercourse.

Although wedding traditions and customs among the Jewish people vary from country to country, the bringing of two life cycles together to a combined living arrangement is a blessed and festive occasion. It brings the serious symbol of the Day of Atonement together with the adventure of united lives. God's presence is to spread grace and love on the home, as was felt during the ceremony.

Soul searching and introspection are wed to joy, comfort, and love to form the pillars of the Jewish home: marriage and family. At the entrance of many Jewish dwellings on the upper right doorpost is a small wooden or metal container called a *mezuzah*. It contains a rolled parchment with several passages from the Torah and the first phrases of the Shema. Through a small opening in some designs the word *Shaddai* shows through: "God the Almighty."

DEATH

As the Jewish man or woman approaches death, the prayer that is to be recited if one is conscious enough to do so reads as follows:

> My God and God of my fathers, accept my prayer;
> do not ignore my supplication. Forgive me for all
> the sins which I have committed in my lifetime.
> I am abashed, and ashamed of those wicked deeds and
> sins which I committed. Please accept my pain and

suffering as atonement and forgive my wrongdoing,
for against You alone have I sinned.

May it be Your will, O Lord my God and God of my fathers,
that I sin no more. With Your great mercy cleanse me of
my sins, but not through suffering and disease.
Send a perfect healing to me and to all who lie sick
in their beds.

Unto You, O Lord My God and God of my fathers,
I acknowledge that both my healing and death
depend upon Your will. May it be Your will to heal me.
Yet if You have decreed that I shall die of this affliction,
may my death atone for all sins and transgressions which
I have committed before You. Shelter me in the shadow
of Your wings and grant me a share in the world to come.

Father of orphans and Guardian of widows,
protect my beloved family, with whose soul
my soul is bound.

Into Your hand I commit my soul. You have redeemed me,
O Lord God of truth.

Hear O Israel, the Lord our God, the Lord is One.
The Lord, He is God. The Lord, He is God.

Jews have always considered it a particular grace of God if they die uttering the last two lines of this prayer of confession.

In traditional Judaism, death is the inevitable outcome of life, a part
of the very fabric of a created world. The soul existed before the Jewish
person was born and continues to live after his or her mission on earth
is completed. This world is a corridor leading to the world to come. At
death, the soul leaves the body with a cry that reverberates from one end
of the world to the other. And yet, death is "good" for the upright of
heart, just as God found creation to be "very good." In death, the righteous ones are finally released from the struggle with evil inclinations;
whereas the wicked perish from their polluted souls and finally stop an-
gering God. Rabbis have debated and contemplated throughout the ages
the mystery of the future life, but have insisted that one's key concern
should be our actions in this life.

In Judaism, there appears to be an acceptance that all living things—insects, flowers, animals, human beings—must one day die. To be alive means to bear within oneself the seeds of death. Avoiding death means that one has neither lived nor fulfilled his or her mission on earth. Thus, death is to be faced with spiritual strength and fortitude that only God can give.

It has been noted earlier that the Mourner's Kaddish, or sanctification of God's name, does not mention death at all but is rather a prayer of praise to God. Some have suggested the parallels found between this kaddish and the "Lord's Prayer" Jesus taught to His disciples. After the death of a parent, spouse, or close relative, the Mourner's Kaddish is to be said while standing in the synagogue service for eleven months of Sabbaths as a memorial of respect to the departed. It is only part of an elaborate grief process that helps the Jewish individual cope with the passing of a loved one.

Judaism emphasizes respect for the dying and the dead, and visiting the sick is an important mitzvah. When a person dies, the first words uttered by those who hear the news are *Baruch dayan emet* ("Blessed be the true Judge"). The idea is that God is all-wise and understands, ruling the earth in mercy and wisdom. "The Lord hath given and the Lord hath taken away: blessed be the name of the Lord." Close relatives make a slight tear in their clothing, *keriah,* near their heart as a symbol of mourning. Children tear the garment on the left, over the heart; spouses, parents, and siblings tear on the right side. They display this for one month.

Since the body is a holy vessel, created in the image of God, it is treated with utmost respect. It is not left alone from the time of death to the funeral, and psalms are often recited in the same room. Jewish communities usually have *Chevrah Kaddishas* (Sacred Burial Societies), composed of groups of volunteers who wash and dress the body of the deceased and make arrangements for the burial. The act of preburial purification is called *taharah.* A few members wash the body lovingly and carefully with warm water from head to foot. *Chevrah* comes from the root word "friend," and this act is one of the greatest *mitzvot* one can perform. Blessings are even recited before washing to connote respect and to express sorrow for any unintended disrespectful washing, and so forth.

Regardless of status, the deceased is dressed in *tachrichim,* simple white shrouds made of cotton or linen. If a brutal disfiguring accident has occurred, where blood has soaked into the clothing, the deceased is not washed but is buried in the same clothes. This is because the blood is viewed as sacred and deserving of burial as well. Only burial in a wooden casket under the earth is permitted. Burial usually occurs within twenty-four hours, unless an extension is needed to bring in family members from out of town. A funeral may not be conducted on the Sabbath.

The funeral is simple and dignified. There is no open casket and no makeup. At a Jewish funeral you will not hear anyone saying, "My, doesn't he look good?" or, "How lovely she appears today!" The deceased is not "asleep" in the casket. The mourner is to come to grips with this fact, and between death and burial should be confronting the reality that death has occurred. He has denied himself (according to Talmudic law) eating meat, drinking wine or liquor, bathing for pleasure, shaving, haircuts, marital relations, self-adornment, parties, and festive meals. Even the study of the Torah with its accompanying joy has been prohibited. Now he faces the casket, surrounded by friends. Family and friends follow the casket to the cemetery. Some dirt is thrown by the mourner onto the casket when it is lowered into the ground. After the burial, friends prepare the mourner's first meal.

Shiva, a seven-day period of intense grieving, follows the burial. It is required of those losing a parent, child, spouse, brother, or sister. Added to the prohibitions that occurred between the death and burial are the Shiva stipulations that leather shoes are not to be worn, greetings are not to be made, sitting on soft couches or beds is prohibited, no scripture (except Job and Lamentations) is to be read, and so forth. One is not to conduct normal business practices. Friends may stop by and visit, and Shiva services are held evening and morning in the home each day. Psychologists say that this is an excellent start to the grief cycle, that is, the mourner faces his grief head-on and is reinforced by his community.

Shiva gives way to *Sheloshim,* a thirty-day period in which the mourner leaves the house and begins to return to a normal schedule. The ties to society, community, and God are once again being reestablished. All prohibitions observed during Shiva are dropped, with the exception of the pursuit of entertainment, amusement, the cutting of hair, and shaving. If a parent has died, Sheloshim is observed for one year; the Mourner's Kaddish is recited at all public synagogue services for eleven months. The mourner thus affirms the justice of God and the meaningfulness of life. The tombstone, or *matzevah,* is erected or "unveiled" about one year after the death of the loved one. Friends and family assemble once again to pay honor to the dead.

Each year, on the anniversary of the death, *Yahrzeit* is observed. This is a day of solemn remembering in prayer and meditation. A twen-

ty-four-hour candle is lit and burns for a full day (evening to evening).
The dead are also remembered at various festivals during the yearly cycle of the Jewish community.

In some traditional Jewish communities, Psalm 91 is recited while
the casket is removed at the gates of the Jewish cemetery and carried to
the gravesite. Perhaps it is indicative of Judaism's attitude toward death:

> He who dwells in the shelter of the Most High
> will rest in the shadow of the Almighty.
> I will say of the Lord, "He is my refuge and my fortress,
> my God, in whom I trust."
>
> (Psalm 91:1-2)

TO LIFE!

For Jewish women and men, the proper response to life is piety
and reverence before God. Human beings have ethical choices to make,
and humankind is morally responsible before the omnipotent God. The
basic concepts, Sabbath, yearly cycle, and life cycle are geared to this
end. God judges the world.

And yet, human beings are dear to God, created in His image to be
partners in justice, love, and mercy, bringing His message and ideals to
civilization. Judaism teaches one to cherish and preserve life. In fact, the
rabbis ruled that the preservation of life supersedes the fulfillment of all
commandments (except the prohibitions against murder, unchastity, and
idolatry). For the Jewish people, this means that they are not only responsible for their lives before God, but are responsible for the well-being of all men, women, and children. In Judaism, one should be concerned as much with the preservation of others' lives as with one's own
life. Such righteousness is not without its rewards, both in this world and
in the "world to come." God will reunite body and soul in *tehiyyat ha-
metim* ("the revival of the dead") at the end of world history.

For the Christian who wants to understand the Jewish people today,
it is a mistake to envision the Jewish way of life in monolithic terms. The
Jewish people have developed in and adapted to various cultures and civilizations throughout their long history. One of the observations that
"People of the Book" make concerning Christians is that Christians have
often emphasized their particular culture's or denomination's interpretation of the "Book" to the exclusion of accurately getting to know the
"People."

Part 2

THE PEOPLE

4

Historical Experience

The history of Judaism and the Jewish people is unique. Although a minor group of individuals in comparison to the great ancient civilizations, this people has outlived them all. They have interacted with each successive Near Eastern culture and have contributed to each successive phase of Western civilization—a history spanning four millennia. They are truly a small people with a large place in the history of humankind.

The experience and creativity of the Jewish people contributed not only to the empires in which they were involved, but their interaction solidified and transformed Judaism itself. The "People of the Book" became a light to all nations, and yet Christians often forget that most of the history of this people is not recorded in *the* Book, the Bible. To understand one's Jewish neighbor—indeed one's Jewish heritage—is to have an insight into this complicated history. To understand the Jewish Jesus, one must face the historical forces that led up to the first-century environment in which He and His disciples lived.

Most important, positive Christian-Jewish relationships are fostered by the understanding that the Jewish people have had a vibrant history from the first century to the present. Contrary to some sermons one hears, Judaism did not end in the first century. The People of the Book have endured.

And they have suffered—they have suffered for their faith in God. To the polytheistic ancient civilizations, the Jewish people's belief in the one true God was blasphemous and unthinkable. Four thousand years ago, Abraham settled in the Holy Land, migrating from the seat of the first Mesopotamian civilization between the Tigris and Euphrates rivers (present day Iraq). In the midst of an idolatrous culture, he forged a covenant with the Lord. Humankind could not understand such a monotheistic religion.

Forced into slavery in Egypt, the Hebrews again suffered for their beliefs and their peoplehood. As we have seen in part 1, God's deliverance in the exodus from Egypt left a deep impression on the fledgling nation. The Jews' history became an enduring fiber basic to their beliefs, traditions, and practices. They viewed history as a partnership with God —an innovative attitude in an ancient world that believed that human history was an unchanging drama that was constantly being reenacted.

To the Egyptians, Mesopotamians, and other ancient civilizations there was no sense of the forward movement of history. It was the Hebrews by contrast who taught that men and women did not simply reenact a cyclical, divine drama patterned after nature's spring, summer, fall, and winter and orchestrated by thousands of gods and demigods. The Jews perceived history as a linear record of God's unfolding purpose for human beings. God cared and was involved in the affairs of *every* nation and people. The Hebrews interpreted history in moral terms and saw God as judging the nations of the earth. They viewed their nation's history as part of a much larger picture. Ultimately, good would triumph over evil, the lion would lie down with the lamb, there would be no more war. God's purposes were being fulfilled progressively. This Jewish perspective would eventually transform the thought processes of the entire world.

The brief splendor of the kingdoms of Judah and Israel, united under King David and amply recorded in the Scriptures, soon gave way to division, conquest, and exile. The famed Temple of Solomon was burned to the ground; thousands of Jews were taken to Babylonia by the armies of Nebuchadnezzar. Others fled to Egypt, founding strong communities there. In the Bible, one catches a glimpse of the vibrant Jewish community in Babylonia, first under the Babylonians (Chaldeans) and later under the Persians (cf. Esther, Ezra, and Nehemiah), but there is no biblical account of the Jewish community that remained there long past the time of Jesus. Indeed, between the book of Malachi and the travels of Mary and Joseph, there is unrecorded a period of four centuries of which most Christians know little, often called the intertestamental period. It is an indispensable link to understanding the formative years of Jewish tradition and the setting of early Christianity.

For example, during that period both the Pharisees and Sadducees arose, and the ancient expectations of the Messiah were discussed and disputed. During the intertestamental period the Second Temple was built, synagogues spread around the Mediterranean, Alexander the Great rose and carved out an empire, the Roman Empire evolved and expanded, and Herod the Great reigned. When one turns from Malachi 4 to Matthew 1, the historical jump is much longer than the entire history of the United States of America.

In Babylon

To the scribes of Mesopotamia, Babylon meant "gate of god," the city of the god Marduk. It was certainly a city of splendor, with vast fortifications, extensive buildings, and sprawling suburbs. The Hanging Gardens of the royal palace were considered by Greek authors as one of the seven wonders of the ancient world.

The Jewish captives began to adapt to the culture of Babylonia, adopting many customs. Some farmed, and others moved into diverse vocations in towns and cities throughout the land. The Judean exiles may have joined some of the exiles from the Assyrian conquest of Israel a century and a half earlier. This would explain Ezra's mention of the return of descendants of families who lived in northern Israel (Ezra 2). A new Jewish center was developed around Nippur, the second largest city in Babylonia, located on the Kebar River. From there, distinguished leaders from Judah, including religious leaders such as Ezekiel, led the Jewish people in their traditions. Ezekiel begins his scroll of Scripture by explaining: "In the thirtieth year, in the fourth month on the fifth day, while I was among the exiles by the Kebar River, the heavens were opened and I saw visions of God" (Ezekiel 1:1).

Babylonian sources confirm the biblical account that the repentant king of Judah, Jehoiachin, was released from the Babylonian prison by Evil-Merodach, the new king of Babylon, who "spoke kindly to him and gave him a seat of honor higher than those of other kings who were with him in Babylon" (2 Kings 25:28). By this time ("the thirty-seventh year of exile"), Jews had become merchants, contractors, bankers, and public officials as well as farmers and laborers. Elders from Judah and members of royalty would continue to lead a prosperous Jewish community in the territory of Babylonia for nearly two thousand years. The comparatively few Jews who returned to hardship in the area surrounding Jerusalem (by the decree of Cyrus the Persian and under the leadership of Ezra) were often leaving lives of considerable comfort in Babylonia. Although empires would rise and fall, the Jewish people remained a stable fixture in the ancient Near East.

THE SYNAGOGUE

The basic concepts of Jewish belief and Torah were firmly established by the time of the Babylonian Exile. And yet, as was noted in chapter 2, Babylonian names of the months of the year were adopted. Jews even adopted Babylonian names for themselves in addition to their Hebrew names. Such were the demands of commerce and culture.

Nevertheless, a deep sense of loss had engulfed the Jewish people through the destruction of their Temple and deportation to a foreign land. Religious practice had to be adapted and modified, but God and Torah were never abandoned. Jerusalem remained the center of their thoughts, and Psalm 137 reflects their pain:

> By the rivers of Babylon we sat and wept
>   when we remembered Zion....
>
> If I forget you, O Jerusalem,
>   may my right hand forget its skill.
> May my tongue cling to the roof of my mouth
>   if I do not remember you,
>   if I do not consider Jerusalem my highest joy.

To those critics who taunted the Babylonian exiles because they were far away from Jerusalem and had no Temple, God told Ezekiel: "Although I sent them far away among the nations and scattered them among the countries, yet for a little while I have been a sanctuary for them in the countries where they have gone" (Ezekiel 11:16). The Hebrew translation is, "I have been to them a *little sanctuary* in the countries where they have come," and Jewish tradition has maintained that this is a direct reference to the synagogues of these exiles.

The origins of the synagogue, the Jewish house of assembly, study, and prayer, are shrouded in mystery. Some have suggested that synagogues date back to the time of Moses, and the "meeting places" of Psalm 74:8 have been referred to as synagogues. The period of the Babylonian Exile seems to indicate synagogue worship. Ezekiel declares, "While I was sitting in my house and the elders of Judah were sitting before me, the hand of the Sovereign Lord came upon me there" (Ezekiel 8:1). Ezekiel 14:1 and 20:1 allude to the same assembly of elders.

Whatever the case, when the Temple was finally rebuilt by returning exiles, the synagogue continued as an institution wherever Jews lived—even in Judah where the Temple was being rebuilt. The Talmud ascribes to Ezra and his successors, "the men of the Great Synagogue," the formulation of the earliest liturgical prayers such as the *Amidah*. By the time of Jesus the synagogue was a well-established institution, giving every indication of centuries of growth as a center of the religious and social life of the Jewish community. Jesus used the synagogue, and in Luke 4:16-27 He follows the traditional pattern of reading Scripture.

The reading of both the Torah and the Prophets was a central element in the synagogue service. The scrolls of Scripture were kept in a receptacle called "the holy ark" (*aron ha-kodesh*) located on the wall facing the Temple Mount. In the center of the synagogue was an elevated platform, the *bema,* upon which stood a reading desk. Worshipers sat around the bema. The Scripture was read from a standing position but was explained from a sitting position. This is the pattern Jesus follows in Luke 4.

Regardless of one's interpretation of the "little sanctuary" and "assembly" of the elders, it is important to realize that when the Jewish people were taunted for their dispersion, exile, and loss of the Temple, God Himself defended them, declaring that *He* had provided for them the "sanctuary" they needed. Furthermore, He continues in Ezekiel 11:17 by proclaiming: "I will gather you from the nations and bring you back from the countries where you have been scattered, and I will give you back the land of Israel again."

When the rebuilt Temple (the Second Temple) was destroyed by the Romans in the year A.D. 70, the synagogue emerged as the central institution of Judaism. One of the gravest problems for Christian-Jewish relations in the centuries that followed was the penchant of Christians to mock the Jewish people for their loss of the Temple and their forced exile. God certainly did not look upon that mockery any less seriously than He did in Ezekiel 11:14-20.

ERETZ YISRAEL

It was Babylonian Jewry (through leaders such as Zerubbabel, Ezra, and Nehemiah) that returned to Israel, rebuilt the walls of Jerusalem, and constructed the Second Temple. This history of tens of thousands of exiles is recorded in the books of Ezra and Nehemiah and indicates the extraordinary faith of the Jewish people. Although adapting well as a minority in a foreign land, they continued to believe in a transcendent and holy God who had selected them as His holy nation. They realized they would continue to suffer until the world accepted their God, but in the meantime they determined to accept the responsibility of the "yoke" of the Lord. The Jewish people did not denounce the countries in which they were exiled, but attempted to better those kingdoms while accepting God as their ultimate leader. Their yearly cycle and life cycle traditions continued to grow. They longingly looked toward *Eretz Yisrael*—the Land continued to be their anchor.

The name *Eretz Yisrael* (the Land of Israel) is the biblical Hebrew designation that took on the connotation of the Promised Land during the Second Temple period. By the time of Jesus, it was in widespread usage. Prior to this, there was no one name in general use that denoted the Land in its entirety. The Romans recognized this important link between the Jewish people and their land, the Jewish people and their God. They determined to use the Greek term *Palestine* (derived from ancient Philistia) to replace the province of Judea and the concept of Eretz Yisrael. Emperor Hadrian after the Second Jewish Revolt (132-135 A.D.) hoped to eradicate both Jewish tradition and Jewish culture (as well as the Jewish God) by calling the area Palestine. This designation was commonly used until 1948 and the founding of the modern state of Israel. Ironically, the Jewish people in the later nineteenth and early twentieth centuries were referred to as "Palestinians."

Those who returned with Zerubbabel, Ezra, and Nehemiah celebrated Pesach, Shavuot, Sukkot, and Purim. From the Scriptures, one understands the constant spiritual warfare these Jews had to endure. Anti-Semitism was rampant, and there was a constant effort to destroy Judaism forever. Upon returning to the land, Ezra 4:4-5 records:

> Then the peoples around them set out to discourage the people of Judah and make them afraid to go on building. They hired counselors to work against them and frustrate their plans during the entire reign of Cyrus king of Persia and down to the reign of Darius king of Persia.

As one reads through the book of Ezra the deception, psychological degradation, lies, rumors, political machinations, and assimilation tactics used against the Jewish people bear a striking resemblance to modern history. The heart of man does not change. The world still attempts to destroy the very people God loves.

Nowhere is this more evident than in the Jewish people's struggle against the rising Hellenistic culture. When Alexander the Great (356-323 B.C.) in a meteoric rise conquered the Persian Empire, uniting the cultures of East and West, Eretz Yisrael was "liberated" in 332 B.C. In reality, Jerusalem and the surrounding area of Judea enjoyed the same rights they had under Persian rule. Alexander's death, however, resulted in a struggle for his throne, and the empire broke into several parts. Judea was caught between the Egyptian Ptolemies (a dynasty founded by Ptolemy Soter, one of Alexander's generals) and the Asian Seleucids (a dynasty founded by Alexander's general Seleucus Nicator). The Seleucids controlled Persia, Babylonia, and Syria, as well as Asia Minor. The ensuing struggle between the Ptolemies and Seleucids seems senseless in retrospect. Personal ambition and imperial expansion were central motives in their warfare. No matter which dynasty gained the upper hand, the crossroad of the Middle East was caught in between, and the people of Eretz Yisrael suffered. For two centuries these great empires would battle for dominance of Eretz Yisrael.

PTOLEMAIC EGYPT

After Alexander's death, an extensive Greek settlement took place throughout the Middle East, and Greek culture dominated the Western world. Jewish communities spread along the Mediterranean Sea, through Asia, and as far as China. Jewish settlers had flourished in Egypt since the Babylonian Exile, and the Ptolemies found a strong, growing Jewish community when they established their kingdom there. Synagogues abounded as relationships between the Jews and the Ptolemies were basically good. Anti-Semitism did arise from time to time, especially in grave political circumstances, but only later under the Romans did it fester unbridled.

Most of the Jewish community in Egypt were artisans, but there were some wealthy merchants. By the time of Jesus, nearly one million Jews would reside in Egypt (most in Alexandria) out of a world population of approximately eight million Jews. In fact, the earliest remains of a synagogue have been discovered at Shedia near Alexandria. A marble slab recounts that the Jewish community dedicated this synagogue to Ptolemy III Euergetes (246-221 B.C.) and his queen, Berenice.

Even in Alexandria, the new commercial and cultural center founded by Alexander, the Jewish people refused to give up their monotheistic practice for the prevailing Hellenistic culture of many gods and pagan worship. They tended, instead, to adapt and modify the Greek culture. Jewish philosophers sought to prove what the Greeks copied from the Hebrews—that all truth emanates from God. They attempted to show that the one true God was the originator of all things, that Judaism was a kind of philosophy with a spiritual God and a rational ethic. The Hebrew Bible was translated into Greek (the Septuagint), and the writings of the Greek philosophers and poets were carefully studied. Jewish poets, historians, playwrights, and philosophers coupled their perspective of Torah with Hellenistic style. They began a rich tradition of intermediary agent, transmitting the ideas of one culture to another.

Philo of Alexandria (c. 20 B.C.-A.D. 50) was the greatest among them, and his lifetime overlapped that of Jesus and Paul. Completely loyal to the Torah, Philo's ideas are biblical, but his philosophical explanations of those religious ideas are decidedly Greek (relying heavily on Plato). Thoroughly trained in the art of rhetoric, classical literature, and contemporary philosophy, it is doubtful that he had studied Hebrew. And yet he appears to have been brought up in a respected, wealthy family dedicated to the Jewish faith and synagogue practice. He traveled to Jerusalem at least once, attempting to understand Temple customs. Philo was mystical in his religious life and often allegorical in his interpretation of the Scriptures. He frequently searched for the hidden meaning, listening to what he decribed as his "God-possessed soul." Indicative of a rich Jewish philosophical heritage outside the confines of Eretz Yisrael, it is Philo who stated of human nature and divine wisdom: "When the light of God shines, the human light sets; when the divine light sets, the human dawns and rises."

Seleucid Persecution

In Eretz Yisrael, the process of hellenization was slower and less acceptable. This became quite evident when the Seleucid Empire, under Antiochus III "the Great" (222-187 B.C.), captured Judea from the Ptolemies in 198 B.C. Eretz Yisrael became part of "Greater Syria," and, although its pattern of political administration did not greatly change, the Seleucids' conflict with a growing Roman Empire enhanced anti-Jewish sentiment. Antiochus III, encouraged by the Carthaginian general Hannibal (247-183 B.C.), fought the Romans at Smyrna in 190 B.C. Completely victorious, the Romans demanded territory and exorbitant payments of gold from Antiochus III. He, in turn, robbed the temples of his kingdom to pay his debt, including the Jewish Temple in Jerusalem.

Antiochus III's successors continued the practice. Antiochus IV (ruled 175-163 B.C.), surnamed Epiphanes ("the manifest god"), perpetrated the most horrible pogroms against the Jewish people. Humiliated by the Romans, Antiochus Epiphanes intended to wipe Judaism from the face of the earth. His goal was to hellenize thoroughly the population in Judea. He decreed that the worship of Greek gods and goddesses should replace the worship of Jehovah, and that Syrian laws and customs were to be followed.

To facilitate this, Antiochus Epiphanes built Greek temples for numerous gods and goddesses, constructed race courses and public baths, introduced Greek fashions and sexual orgies, and set his hand-picked hellenized leader as high priest in Jerusalem. Thousands of Jewish men, women, and children were massacred for opposing their Greek overlords. Others were sold into slavery. Many of those were small farmers who could not keep up with the ever-increasing taxes. They lost everything.

This was the age of the Maccabees, Mattathias and his heroic Jewish family, who led a fervently religious population to oppose the Seleucids. Their victory is celebrated in the festival of Hanukkah, and the history of the heroic Jewish population who held to Torah at all cost is recorded in the books of 1 and 2 Maccabees. One particular incident of Seleucid Syrian cruelty and Jewish faith is found in the martyrdom of a mother and her seven sons. 2 Maccabees 7 begins:

> It happened also that seven brothers and their mother were arrested and were being compelled by the king under torture with whips and cords, to partake of unlawful swine's flesh. One of them, acting as their spokesman, said, "What do you intend to ask and learn from us? For we are ready to die rather than transgress the laws of our fathers." The king fell into a rage, and gave orders that pans and caldrons be heated. These were heated immediately, and he commanded that the tongue of their spokesman be cut out and that they scalp him and cut off his hands and feet, while the rest of the brothers and the mother looked on. When he was utterly helpless, the king ordered them to take him to the fire, still breathing, and to fry him in a pan. The smoke from the pan spread widely, but the brothers and their mother encouraged one another to die nobly, saying, "The Lord God is watching over us and in truth has compassion on us, as Moses declared in his song which bore

> witness against the people to their faces, when he said, 'And he will have compassion on his servants.' "
>
> After the first brother had died in this way, they brought forward the second for their sport. They tore off the skin of his head with the hair, and asked him, "Will you eat rather than have your body punished limb by limb?" He replied in the language of his fathers, and said to them, "No." (7:1-8)

Each son was tortured and killed in front of his mother. With only her youngest son left, Antiochus IV implored the mother to "advise the youth to save himself" (7:25). The mother encouraged her son instead:

> I beseech you, my child, to look at the heaven and the earth and see everything that is in them, and recognize that God did not make them out of things that existed. Thus also mankind comes into being. Do not fear this butcher, but prove worthy of your brothers. Accept death, so that in God's mercy I may get you back again with your brothers. While she was still speaking, the young man said, "What are you waiting for? I will not obey the king's command, but I obey the command of the Torah that was given to our fathers through Moses. But you, who have contrived all sorts of evil against the Hebrews, will certainly not escape the hands of God." (7:28-31)

The king fell into a rage and tortured and killed the youngest son. Then he had the mother killed.

EARLY ROMAN INTRUSION

The Romans needed a foothold in the Middle East as their Empire expanded, and they continually cultivated friendship with the Jewish community in Eretz Yisrael. In the midst of the growing unrest and civil war of Roman citizens during the late Republic (133-31 B.C.), Jewish loyalty was coveted. The Romans, however, were bound to a policy of conquest and expansion, and they had their eye on "Greater Syria." Profiting from a dispute between factions in Judea, a Roman siege of Jerusalem occurred in 63 B.C. Taking advantage of the Sabbath rest, the Roman general Pompey (106-48 B.C.) stormed the gates. The city was burned, thousands died, and Pompey entered the Holy of Holies in the Temple. The Roman Empire would have a firm grip on Eretz Yisrael for the next five centuries.

It was Julius Caesar (100-44 B.C.) who defeated Pompey. He was welcomed by the Jewish people as a deliverer, and he gave the Jews greater freedom over their affairs. Caesar allowed them to rebuild the walls of Jerusalem and gave the Jews special permission to abstain from the required pagan sacrifices and festivals that connoted loyalty to the Empire.

And yet the Romans, who were thoroughly imbued with Hellenistic culture, could never understand the ways and traditions of the Jewish people. This led to overt anti-Semitism and distrust of the Jews in many parts of the Empire. The Roman orator and statesman Marcus Tullius Cicero in 59 B.C. had described Judaism as a "barbaric superstition," and he had gloated over Pompey's capture of Jerusalem. "Even while Jerusalem was standing and the Jews were at peace with us," he noted, "the practice of their sacred rites was at variance with the glory of our empire, the dignity of our name, the customs of our ancestors." Two thousand years later, Adolf Hitler and his Nazi minions of Germany's Third Reich were mouthing the same platitudes.

PHARISEES AND SADDUCEES

Among those who united with Mattathias, his sons, and his friends to fight against Antiochus Epiphanes and the Hellenistic Syrian persecutors was a group of Hasideans ("the pious ones"). First Maccabees 2:42-43 records: "Then there united with them a company of Hasideans, mighty warriors of Israel, every one who offered himself willingly for the Torah. And all who became fugitives to escape their troubles, joined them and reinforced them."

The Pharisees were a group that appears to have risen from among these "pious ones," combating hellenization and heresy, holding firm to Torah and tradition. To the Pharisees, God's commands transcended the Temple complex, reaching to the common folk and separating the people of God from heathen nations. They believed that God cared for each individual, and although He was omnipotent and omniscient, God granted every person the free choice to follow His ways. The Pharisees stressed that there was a resurrection of the dead and that there would be rewards and punishments in an afterlife. They looked forward to a messiah, and they refused to restrict the spiritual leadership of Eretz Yisrael to a religious aristocracy. The Pharisees emphasized piety and learning, and they were a positive influence on the growth of synagogues throughout the world.

The religious aristocracy with whom the Pharisees clashed was a group called the Sadducees. Although both groups upheld the divine origin of the written Torah, the Sadducees claimed that they had descended from the high priest Zadok (cf. 2 Samuel 8:17, 15:24-37; 1 Kings 1:34-39; Ezekiel 40:46, 43:19, 44:10-16), and that they alone were qualified to interpret Scripture. Through heredity and genealogical ties, the Sadducees controlled the Temple hierarchy for centuries, becoming a wealthy and powerful class. The Sadducees denied resurrection, the immortality of the soul, rewards and punishments in an afterlife, angels, the Messiah, and the ability of the common person to interpret the Torah. In fact, the Sadducees were aloof from the common people and appear to have accommodated those Greeks and Romans who gained ascendancy over the Jewish people. Jewish tradition portrays them as worldly and heretical aristocrats, only interested in maintaining their position of privilege.

By the time of Jesus, the Sadducees had control of the Temple hierarchy in Jerusalem and were working closely with the Roman authorities. At the same time, the Pharisees greatly outnumbered the Sadducees and were the popular, growing group among the Jewish masses in Eretz Yisrael and throughout the Roman Empire. Approximately two decades after Jesus' death, the Pharisees were able finally to gain control of the Temple hierarchy, and it is Pharisaic Judaism that survived the destruction of the Temple by the Romans in A.D. 70.

It is important for Christians to realize the complex religious situation at the time of Jesus. There were many sects and movements among the Jewish people, and the majority of Jews lived outside of Eretz Yisrael, scattered in thriving communities throughout the Roman Empire. Even among the Pharisees in Judea, two schools of thought flourished at the time of Jesus' birth (6-4 B.C.)—the school of Hillel and the school of Shammai.

The exile in Babylon had not only brought the synagogue into prominence, but it had also brought about the *yeshivah,* or academy. This was a place of study where Jewish sages and their pupils learned Torah. A native of Babylonia, Hillel was a student in the yeshivah there, traveling to Jerusalem around 40 B.C. for further study under the great sages Avtalyon and Shemaiah. These men were important pharisaic teachers at the time of Herod the Great's appointment by Rome as governor of Galilee (later the Roman Senate would confer on Herod the title "King of Judea").

Avtalyon and Shemaiah worked well together and realized the gravity of interpreting Torah. Avtalyon taught that scholars must be "careful" with their words, lest their students pick up heretical teachings and suffer spiritual death. Shemaiah is noted for his attitude toward the political regime of his time. He declared: "Love work, hate lordship, and seek no intimacy with the ruling power." Tradition teaches that these great teachers descended from pagan converts to Judaism, and their student Hillel came to view God's message in Torah as universal.

Although wealthy relatives offered financial help, Hillel took no money and insisted on working a manual job while supporting his family and his studies. He appears to have chosen to remain poor his entire life, and his teachings reflect a keen social justice and love for the poor. Hillel is described as a man of deep humility, whose overriding concern was to bring men closer to the Torah. His wisdom and kind spirit were noticed early on in his studies, and he was appointed president *(nasi)* of the Sanhedrin, the supreme Jewish religious and judicial body under the Roman regime (see below). Hillel shared his leadership with Shammai, a teacher whose rigidity contrasted sharply with Hillel's merciful and mild-mannered approach.

Shammai was noted for stringent attitudes and extreme literalism. He insisted on complete separation from Gentiles. When a "heathen" came to Shammai and claimed that he wanted to convert if Shammai could teach him the entire Torah "while standing on one foot," Shammai drove him away. Hillel, however, answered the heathen kindly, stating: "What is hateful to you, do not do unto your neighbor; this is the entire Torah, all the rest is commentary—go and learn it." The heathen converted.

The first-century followers of both men seem to have in their rulings and judgments exaggerated the traits of Hillel and Shammai, and conflicts were rampant at the time of Jesus' ministry. Some scholars have suggested that Jesus' chief problems with religious leaders were with members of the school of Shammai, whereas Jesus agreed in most cases with the teachings of Hillel. Whatever the case, the Talmud itself teaches that there were unworthy and hypocritical religious leaders at the time of Jesus. In the recorded disputations, one finds most of the unflattering rhetoric that Jesus used for the hypocritical teachers of His day ("whited sepulchers," etc.) is used by competing schools of Jewish scholars against one another. Jesus was simply using the illustrations and language of His day—a language with which most of His hearers were very familiar.

In fact, the Talmud speaks of seven types of Pharisees, including those who wear their good deeds "so all the world can see and admire them" and those who say, "Wait a bit until I have done the good deed" (it *never* gets done). Only the last two types listed are the "God-fearing Pharisee" (who patterns his life after Job) and the "God-loving Pharisee" (who patterns his life after Abraham as a friend of God who really loves his heavenly father). It is a shame that with such diversity and complexity in the world of Judaism during Jesus' ministry, His negative comments to some of the hypocrites of His day have been used throughout history by Christians to stigmatize all Pharisees (and, even all Jews). The Pharisees were loved by the common people and known for their sincerity and piety. *Jesus did not hate Pharisees.* He did not attack the basic concepts of pharisaism, but (like the apostle Paul) was pharisaic in orientation. Jesus spoke against hypocrisy, wrong interpretations, and excesses. He would no doubt do the very same with "devout" Christian leaders and movements today.

The schools of Hillel and Shammai would go on to debate points of dogma and practice. Concerning the Shema, for example, the school of Shammai took the words "when you lie down and when you rise up" (Deuteronomy 6:7*b*) with extreme literalism, claiming that the Shema must be recited in a reclining position in the evening and only while standing in the morning. Hillel's school taught that the passage referred to the times of recitation rather than the posture. It was the school of Hillel within pharisaic Judaism that survived and whose interpretations endure to the present day.

The descendants of Hillel continued to hold the leadership position of *nasi* until Gamaliel VI died in A.D. 425. Gamaliel I, the grandson of Hillel, was a nasi and may well be the same Gamaliel who in Acts 5 before the "jealous" Sadducean high priest and the Sanhedrin ("the full assembly of the elders of Israel," 5:21) argued against killing Peter and the apostles. The account states:

> When they heard this, they were furious and wanted to put them to death. But a Pharisee named Gamaliel, a teacher of the law, who was honored by all the people, stood up in the Sanhedrin and ordered that the men be put outside for a little while. Then he addressed them: "Men of Israel, consider carefully what you intend to do to these men." (5:33-35)

Gamaliel concluded his speech with these words:

> Therefore, in the present case I advise you: Leave these men alone! Let them go! For if their purpose or activity is of human origin, it will fail. But if it is from God, you will not be able to stop these men; you will only find yourselves fighting against God. (Acts 5:38-39)

Acts 5:40 begins: "His speech persuaded them."

In Acts 22:3, Paul claims: "I am a Jew, born in Tarsus of Cilicia, but brought up in this city. *Under Gamaliel* I was thoroughly trained in the law of our fathers and was just as zealous for God as any of you are to-day" (emphasis added). His zealousness indicates that even within the school of Hillel there were varying personality traits and attitudes toward compliance with Torah. Understanding just how complex the religious situation was in Jesus' day gives the Christian a fuller view and a richer insight into the gospels and the book of Acts.

JUDAISM IN THE ROMAN EMPIRE

Understanding the position of the Jewish people in the Roman Empire is needed as well. Herod the Great's kingdom did not survive his death in 4 B.C. His "kingship" had been merely the creation of Roman foreign policy in the eastern Mediterranean, and at his death thousands of Jews petitioned Augustus Caesar that Herod's legal will (a will that split up his kingdom among his sons) be nullified. Herod's magnificent building programs and accompanying heavy taxation had brought about much hostility among the populace of Eretz Yisrael. Although Augustus Caesar upheld Herod's bequest to his sons, he did not name Herod's son Archelaus "King of Judea." Rather, the title of *ethnarch* was given. When sporadic rebellions continued to break out against the Roman overlords, they reorganized Judea as a province of the Roman Empire governed by a *prefect* (later these governors would be referred to as *procurators*). This occurred in A.D. 6 when Jesus was about eleven years of age. The prefect of Judea had a limited garrison of soldiers and was often dependent on the help of the Roman governor of Syria.

Under the general supervision of the prefect, Rome allowed Judea a measure of internal self-government under the Sanhedrin. There is debate among scholars as to the exact composition of this council of Jewish elders, but it appears to have been the supreme institution for the Jewish nation (and often beyond the borders of Judea) in matters of religion and worship, as well as in assisting the Romans with the collection of taxes and preserving order.

The tension between Rome and the people of Judea steadily increased between A.D. 6-66. No less than fourteen prefects were sent to Judea during that period. Most were inept administrators who made foolish judgments and were cruel. A good example of ineptitude was Pontius Pilate (governed Judea A.D. 26-36), who among other absurd actions pilfered the Temple treasury to build an aqueduct. When Jewish citizens complained, Pilate had his military units whip them unmercifully so that some citizens died from their wounds. Pilate's reign of terror ended when he attacked a defenseless group of Samaritans. He was then transferred to Vienne in southern France, where he reportedly committed suicide. This internal conflict under the prefects led to increasing calls for armed rebellion. Groups such as the Zealots gained a large following, setting the stage for both the First Jewish Revolt in A.D. 66 and the Second Jewish Revolt in A.D. 132.

In the *Diaspora* (i.e., "dispersion," all Jewish people residing outside of Eretz Yisrael) Jews formed approximately 10 percent of the Empire's population by the time of Jesus, the majority concentrated in the urban areas. Rome itself had a Jewish community at least two centuries old and numbering by the first century anywhere from ten thousand to forty thousand. Twelve synagogues and six burial galleries (catacombs) have been found dating to the first century. Most of the members of Rome's Jewish community were shopkeepers, tailors, tentmakers, and butchers, but physicians, poets, beggars, and actors were also in evidence. We have noted that Egypt had a Jewish population of approximately one million. Outside the Roman Empire, Babylonian Jewry numbered approximately one million as well.

Judaism flourished throughout the Empire as Jews were unrestricted in occupations and in living areas. Legal discrimination was minimal. The Romans excused the Jewish community from mandatory participation in the polytheistic religion of Rome and in the worship of the emperor. The Jewish devotion to the Torah and to the one true God brought, however, increasing accusations of subverting Gentile religion and Greco-Roman culture, even though many Jews spoke Greek and dressed in the fashion of their day. In Rome, Cicero had complained that too many Jews packed his courtroom. Eight thousand Roman Jews were said to have accompanied in a show of strength the Jewish delegates from Judea who, upon Herod's death, came to request the Roman Senate to abolish the monarchy.

Converts to Judaism began to appear in aristocratic circles as well as among the common people, and authors of the first century began to portray the Jewish people as an "unclean people" afflicted with the "leprosy" of Judaism. The Greek rhetorician Apion of Alexandria in the first century drew together the canards of many of the anti-Semitic writers that preceded him and of his day. He vilified the Jewish people as "haters of mankind" and claimed that once a year the Jewish community murdered a non-Jew and tasted of his entrails while secretly swearing to hate the particular nation of which he was a citizen. In Rome, Jews were expelled in A.D. 19 and again in A.D. 49. Riots broke out in Egypt against the Jews during the same period.

With the exception of the insane emperor Caligula (ruled A.D. 37-41), who ordered that he should be worshiped and his statue should be placed in the Holy of Holies in Jerusalem (an order fortunately ignored), the first-century Roman emperors upheld the freedom of religion of the Jewish people. Emperor Claudius (ruled A.D. 41-54), for example, fully confirmed the right of the Jewish community to follow the Torah in his edict to the citizens of Alexandria who had rioted against the Jews. Nevertheless, he warned Jews "not to set at nought the beliefs about the gods held by other peoples" and not to spread "a general plague throughout the world." Claudius seems to have accepted the anti-Jewish canard that the Jewish people with their monotheistic beliefs were a danger to the Gentile Greco-Roman world. When further anti-Semitic riots occurred in the Empire, Jews were massacred. It was during the reign of Claudius that Paul made his first and second missionary journeys, beginning his third missionary journey in the last year of Emperor Claudius's rule. The Jerusalem Council (Acts 15) also occurred during this time period.

With the First Jewish Revolt in Judea in A.D. 66 and the subsequent Roman destruction of the Temple in Jerusalem in A.D. 70, Jews throughout the Empire were appalled at the ruthless and evil actions of the Emperor Vespasian and his son Titus. Jews at Masada, the last bastion of Judean resistance (fell in A.D. 73), were pursued with fanatical Roman vengeance. The Romans gloried in their victory, striking coins with the inscription "Judea Is Captured" and commemorating the events with a triumphal arch (Arch of Titus) in Rome where Jewish captives were dragged with the Holy Menorah. These events brought forth a new term of forced dispersion into the Jewish vocabulary, *Galut* ("exile"), those driven into the Diaspora from unimaginable cruelty.

Incitements by local Gentile populations increased. In following years, revolts broke out among frustrated Jews in Babylonia, Egypt, Cyrenaica (Libya), and Cyprus. The Roman tax on Jews for the privilege of the Jerusalem Temple now had to be paid to support the pagan temples of Jupiter. It was during the course of examinations to decide if a man was a Jew and liable to this tax that the difference between a Jew and a Christian became known among the Romans as never before. Jews might be despised, but Christians had no special charter to practice their religion. If Christians claimed not to be Jews, according to Roman law their religion, Christianity, was illegal.

The chief chronicler of the First Jewish Revolt was Flavius Josephus (c. A.D. 38-100). Educated in the Torah and a member of an aristocratic priestly family in Jerusalem, Josephus was a moderate who hoped for a peaceful settlement with the Romans. He was appointed commander of Galilee at the outbreak of the Revolt. Battling against Vespasian and the Roman legions, Josephus met with defeat and fled with forty men to a cave. Each man resolved to die rather than be taken by the brutal and vengeful Romans. Casting lots to kill one another, only Josephus and another man remained. Josephus convinced the last man to surrender with him to the Romans. Ingratiating himself with Vespasian and later traveling with the army of Titus, Josephus was granted Roman citizenship and a pension in Rome. He never returned to Eretz Yisrael and was hated as a traitor by most of the Jewish community.

Josephus's *The Jewish Wars* is an important account of the first Jewish revolt, with an opening section from the time of the Maccabees through the life of Herod the Great. Although written while subject to Emperor Vespasian (a fact the reader should always keep in mind), Josephus's account is detailed and interesting. In many cases his personal observation of the events is evident as well as his collection of individual stories from other defectors and from prisoners of war. Josephus also appears to have had access to Roman military reports. *The Jewish War* gained Josephus a place of literary stature in the Roman Empire at the young age of forty. It was widely read by both Gentiles and Jews.

Sixteen years later in *The Antiquities of the Jews,* Josephus sought to dispel the rampant anti-Semitism in the Roman Empire by teaching Gentiles the history of Judaism from creation to the Revolt in A.D. 66. Believing that ignorance led to anti-Semitic slander, Josephus in *Antiquities* tries to show both the longevity of religion in Israel and the light Judaism brings to the world. At the close of the first century, Josephus answered the charges of the Alexandrian anti-Semite Apion in the work

Against Apion, and defended himself in his autobiography, *Vita (Life).* Without the works of this Jewish historian we would be missing an important segment of primary and secondary historical source material.

Emperor Hadrian (ruled A.D. 117-138) provoked the Second Jewish Revolt in Judea by his decision to establish a Roman colony on the ruins of Jerusalem. Unable to understand a people who refused to accept the "enlightened" Greco-Roman culture and polytheistic religion he valued so highly, Hadrian visited Judea in 130 and 131. Scholars are divided on whether Hadrian's cruel edicts forbidding circumcision and demanding that a temple to Jupiter be built on the Temple Mount in Jerusalem were proclaimed before or after the rebellion. The result, however, was that Hadrian's Roman forces crushed the Jewish rebels led by Simon bar Kokhba in a three-year campaign (A.D. 132-135), and an entire pagan city, Aelia Capitolina, was built on the ruins of Jerusalem. A temple to Jupiter and Hadrian's statue were constructed on the Temple Mount. A temple to Aphrodite, the goddess of love and beauty, was placed next to the new forum on the west side of the city.

Hadrian declared it a capital offense to study Torah and to practice Judaism. Circumcision was forbidden by reviving an ancient law against "mutilation." A bloody purge of Jewish sages ensued, and the elderly Rabbi Akiva (see below) was martyred. Jews in the area were either enslaved, killed, or fled for their lives. For a time, only Galilee contained a significant Jewish presence in the area. Hadrian's edicts remained in effect until his death in 138 A.D. Gradual improvement in Jewish-Roman relations took place during the long reign of his successor, Antoninus Pius (138-161 A.D.).

Although a Jewish remnant would remain in Judea and Jerusalem for the next eighteen centuries, the Holy Land would be passed among foreign conquerors. Not until 1948 would a Jewish nation again exist in Eretz Yisrael. The exiled Jewish community would spread its creativity, discipline, and spiritual depth among other Jews dispersed throughout the Roman Empire. Together they would influence the direction of Western civilization. Stable areas of Jewish scholarship would continue in the *yeshivot* in Babylon and Galilee. Jerusalem, however, would retain a special place in the hearts of Jews everywhere. Although the Temple was gone and the pilgrimages and sacrifices no longer could be made, the Babylonian Exile had prepared the Jewish people. The synagogue structure maintained the Sabbaths and the festivals. Judaism was alive, and its people believed that God had indeed provided once again a "little sanctuary" (Ezekiel 11:16).

TALMUD

In the pharisaic tradition that became normative Judaism, God is said to have revealed the interpretation of His Torah at Mount Sinai. Torah demands interpretation, and the discussions and insights by Jewish sages during the intertestamental period attempted to rediscover the original meaning of God's Word—the divine framework with which God surrounded His message to humankind.

The vast Oral Tradition and its decipherment dates back to the time of Ezra. The *Soferim* (a word translated "scribes" but literally meaning "men of the book") began to interpret and supplement the written Torah so that it could apply to life in Judea after the Exile. Their clarification and amplification of Scripture to understand its fuller meaning was known as *Midrash*. Ancient biblical precepts and guidelines were applied to new living conditions, and legal conclusions began to build. Once collected, these conclusions began to be taught separately as *halakhah* ("the way one goes"). Oral Tradition was not meant to be a scholastic exercise in legalism, but rather was aimed at creating a pious, humble, and righteous life.

Many scholars believe that the Soferim became founders and members of the Great Synagogue, a primary assembly that continued the work of Ezra in Eretz Yisrael. Because of their activities, the Torah ceased to be the privileged domain of priests and Levites. The Soferim taught any willing student who loved Torah, and scholars and sages arose from all classes. The Soferim were succeeded by the Pharisees, who became the outstanding religious teachers during the two centuries before Jesus' birth. In contrast to the Sadducees, who said that the soul died with the body, the Pharisees interpreted God's Torah to include immortality, resurrection, and a place of future rewards and punishments.

The Pharisees believed that the teachings of Judaism had been communicated in an unbroken chain from generation to generation since Sinai. The chain of tradition was called *Shalshelet Hakabbalah* (*kabbalah* meaning "that which has been received"). The process is described in the Talmud in these words: "Moses received the Torah from Sinai and transmitted it to Joshua, Joshua to the Elders, the Elders to the Prophets. And the Prophets transmitted it to the men of the Great Synagogue."

We have seen that Hillel the Elder became the outstanding pharisaic teacher at the time of Jesus. Hillel contributed to the standardization of the methods and guidelines employed for interpreting Torah and applying Tradition. *Hesed* (see chap. 1) became the normative principle to be applied by a humble spirit in a faithful relationship to God.

The Jewish sages from the period of Hillel to the compilation of the *Mishnah* (see below), a period to approximately A.D. 200, are called *Tannaim*. Johanan ben Zakkai, a disciple of Hillel, was one of those important scholars decades before the destruction of the Temple. He seems to have foreseen the impending crisis for Judaism. He strengthened the pattern of the Tannaim to make the study of Torah the aim of one's life and to spread the knowledge of Torah among the masses. And yet, the necessity of humility is found in his warning to his students: "If you have learned much Torah, do not ascribe any merit to yourself, since it was for this that you were created."

Johanan ben Zakkai called for peace "between nation and nation, between government and government, between family and family." In the middle of the First Jewish Revolt, he realized that the Romans were going to crush the Zealots in Jerusalem and that his calls for peace were literally viewed as traitorous conduct. In approximately A.D. 68 he had his students feign his death and carry him out of the city of Jerusalem to Vespasian's camp. There he asked the general (soon to become emperor) that the Jewish sages of his generation be spared and allowed to establish an academy at Yavneh, a place near the Mediterranean coast, south of modern Tel Aviv.

Yavneh would become a new Tannaim center of Torah and tradition after the destruction of the Temple, regulating the calendar and reorganizing the Sanhedrin. It was here that the textual integrity of the Scriptures was maintained, and decisions at Yavneh reached out to communities in the Diaspora for the next six decades. Hadrian's decrees and the Second Jewish Revolt brought an end to Yavneh's influence on Jewish belief in Eretz Yisrael.

One of the outstanding Tannaim that followed Johanan ben Zakkai was Akiva ben Joseph (c. A.D. 50-135). A poor shepherd in his early years, Akiva was encouraged by his wife, Rachel, to devote himself to the study of Torah. He studied at the academy in Yavneh (among other places), and by A.D. 95 was so highly respected that he led a delegation to Rome to intercede for the Jewish people. Emperor Domitian (A.D. 81-96) had leveled new restrictions against Jews. Domitian was an irascible character, but he died during Akiva's stay in Rome. A kindly lawyer, Nerva (A.D. 96-98), succeeded him. When Akiva returned from Rome in A.D. 97, he was viewed by the Jewish people as a leader as well as a scholar.

It is Akiva who is credited with systematizing the halakhah and the principles that became basic to later rabbinic interpretation. Most of the great scholars of the second century were his disciples, and he is said to have influenced subsequent systems of Jewish hermeneutics, ethics, and theology. Akiva declared that the fundamental principle of the Torah was "Thou shalt love thy neighbor as thyself." In the Talmud, his influence is abundantly evident. He insisted that because Torah comes from God, it is never redundant, and each passage has a definite purpose (even to the letters used in the Hebrew words). "Study leads to practice," he was fond of saying. Akiva was deeply concerned with the plight of the poor.

Akiva's disciples remembered him not only for his scholarship but also for his modesty, his humility, his kindness, and his courage. "Whatever God does is for the best," he believed. "Everything is foreseen, and free will is given." Hadrian's decrees came in Akiva's old age (perhaps his ninetieth year), and he could no longer continue his attitude of pacifism and of good relations with Rome. He supported the rebellion, and when the charismatic Jewish soldier and strategist Simon bar Kokhba won some initial skirmishes against the Romans, Akiva was caught up in the wild contagion of the people. On one occasion he referred to Bar Kokhba ("Son of the Star") as "the Messianic King" who would liberate Judah from its oppressors.

Hadrian drove the Jewish rebels from Jerusalem; Bar Kokhba and his men made their last stand seven miles away at the fortress of Betar. Akiva was imprisoned for teaching Torah in spite of Hadrian's command to desist from such practices. Even in prison, he continued to teach Torah, and when judged guilty of disobeying the emperor's law, Akiva was tortured to death as Roman soldiers literally tore his flesh from his body. As he lay dying, the elderly Akiva intoned in a strong, steady voice the Shema (a practice Hadrian had also forbidden). The Roman general who supervised Akiva's execution marveled at this man. "Are you a wizard," he asked, "or are you utterly insensible to pain?" "I am neither," Akiva replied, "but all my life I have been waiting for the moment when I might truly fulfill this commandment. I have always loved the Lord with all my might, and with all my heart; now I know that I love him with all my life."

Akiva began to repeat the Shema once again, and it is said that he died as he reached the words "The Lord is One."

Akiva's followers were dispersed throughout the world, and by the latter part of the second century there was great concern that the vast Oral Tradition would be forgotten or distorted. With this in mind, Judah ha-Nasi ("Judah the Prince"), a seventh-generation grandson of Hillel, provided the skeletal outline upon which the Talmud is based. Judah was the head of a yeshivah at Bet She'arim, three miles west of the modern settlement in lower Galilee on the Nazareth-Haifa road. Well respected as the "holy teacher" and "patriarch" of the day, Judah met with at least one Roman emperor who came to Eretz Yisrael and circumspectly forged a policy of nonintervention in Roman affairs. Like his great-grandfather, Hillel the Elder, Judah devoted himself to the study of Torah and to spreading its precepts.

Judah ha-Nasi's skeletal outline (c. A.D. 200) of the vast Oral Tradition is known as the *Mishnah* (derived from *shanah,* "to repeat") and is written entirely in Hebrew. It not only codified the halakhah, but also recorded the teachings of the Tannaim. So well respected was the Mishnah that it was regarded as authoritative in both Eretz Yisrael as well as the academies of Babylonia. A new group of Jewish scholars, known as *Amoraim* ("spokesmen, interpreters"), arose in both Eretz Yisrael and Babylonia from approximately A.D. 250-500. They provided an extended commentary on the Mishnah, a commentary on the commentary, which became known as the *Gemara* ("completion," "compilation," or "tradition").

Together, the Mishnah and the Gemara are known as the *Talmud* ("study" or "learning"). There are two Talmuds, reflecting the two great centers of Amoraim scholarship. The Jerusalem Talmud (actually collected in academies in Galilee) is the Talmud produced by the Amoraim in Eretz Yisrael. Less than one-third the size of the Babylonian Talmud (produced by Amoraim in Babylonia), the Jerusalem Talmud is considered less authoritative than the larger Babylonian Talmud. This is not only because of size, but also because the discussions in the Babylonian Talmud are more sophisticated, the writing style is more lively, and the development of themes is more focused. It also has more extensive "tractates," divisions dealing with a variety of subjects. With the compilation of the Talmud, the basic beliefs and values, customs and ceremonies, forms and character of the living *Torah* were written and established.

Thus, the Talmud includes Torah teachings, legal precedents, guiding principles, and personal accounts spanning a period of nearly one thousand years. The rabbis compared it to a sea in which one must submerge oneself. From Sopherim to Pharisees, from Tannaim to Amoraim, the rabbis have derived principles of practice and God's commands for Jewish life in a foreign culture. Jesus was well acquainted with the Oral Tradition, because it was discussed in the synagogues and would have been referred to by the teachers in the Temple courts (cf. Luke 2.46-47). In the Talmud, one notes the attempt to capture that same rich Oral Tradition in the written word.

CHRISTIANITY AND JUDAISM

Christianity was born in a world where Judaism was vibrant and expanding. Population statistics are sporadic, but during the reign of Claudius, the Jewish population of the entire Roman Empire was numbered at approximately seven million (10 percent of the total population of the Empire). It has been suggested that this may have included only Jews who were Roman citizens. In Egypt alone, its population of more than one million Jews was concentrated in Alexandria, where 40 percent of the city seems to have been Jewish. Asia Minor and Syria account for another one million each. Eretz Yisrael may have had upwards of two million Jews. Outside the Roman Empire, Babylonia probably had a million as well. Then there were other communities scattered as far as China. Judaism was increasing in numbers, thousands of converts entering its fold each year. Josephus insisted: "There is not one city, Greek or barbarian, nor a single nation where the custom of the seventh day on which we rest from all work, and the fasts and the lighting of candles are not observed . . . and as God permeates the universe, so the Law [Torah] has found its way into the hearts of all men."

In addition, there is a divergence of views in Judaism that leads to extreme complexity. Although general attitudes in Eretz Yisrael toward the future messiah seemed to favor a political-military leader who would establish an earthly kingdom, the intertestamental period provides a spectrum of beliefs and theologies (as dissimilar as in Christendom today). The gospels record that many Jews believed in Jesus, and the early Christians were certainly Jews.

Most Jews, however, did not live in Eretz Yisrael and were not aware of Jesus' ministry while He lived on earth. Estimates are difficult, but it seems to be safe to say that less than 25 percent of all Jews in the world at the time of Jesus lived in Eretz Yisrael, and Jesus did not travel to all areas in His land. As Paul and other missionaries went out, it was in areas prepared by Judaism that the Christian message flourished. Scarcely a Christian congregation arose in an area where a Jewish synagogue had not preceded it. In Eretz Yisrael, previous "deliverers" had come and had failed, which made Gamaliel's argument very effective before the Sanhedrin (Acts 5).

It is a sad fact, therefore, that the gospel passage that has been used the most by professing Christians and non-Christians throughout history to vilify the Jews as "Christ-killers" has been severed from this historical context. It is absurd that in Matthew 27:25 a mere mob can cry, "Let his blood be on us and on our children," and professing Christians and non-Christians from that time forth could use this verse to ridicule, malign, imprison, torture, maim, and kill Jewish men, women, and children.

I realize that popular preachers teach this today, but may I suggest that the utterance of this crowd was no more binding before God than Pilate's proclamation "I am innocent of this man's blood," recorded in the preceding verse. Pilate agreed to the crucifixion of Jesus and is guilty of that act because his soldiers both tortured and crucified Jesus at his command. But even Pilate did not have the power over Jesus. Jesus proclaims in John 10:17-18:

> The reason my Father loves me is that I lay down my life—only to take it up again. No one takes it from me, but I lay it down of my own accord. I have authority to lay it down and authority to take it up again. This command I received from my Father.

Blaming the Jewish people for Jesus' death is tantamount to denying Jesus' sovereignty and love in laying down His life. Sadly, the "Christ-killer" theme was used more frequently as Christendom expanded in numbers and in power.

Christianity spread rapidly across the Roman Empire. During the first century it was confined mainly to the eastern half of the Roman Empire, an urban movement pushing from city to city. Often the Jewish communities received the first message of the missionaries. By A.D. 150, it was active in the rural areas of Asia Minor, rapidly expanding to the Gentile population of the entire Empire. By the codification of the Mishnah in A.D. 200, Christians could be found in all parts of the Roman Empire, and, although Christianity was an illegal religion according to Roman law, it constituted approximately 10 percent of the Empire population of seventy-five million. This is the same percentage the Jews constituted a century and a half before.

Violence toward Christians until A.D. 250 was more the result of mob action rather than the definite policy of the Roman government. Although Christianity was unlawful, government officials did not seek to expose or persecute Christians unless a disturbance had been raised and names of Christians came to the fore. And yet, sporadic persecution under an emperor or governor who wanted to use Christians as scapegoats appeared from time to time. Nero is an example of such an emperor. The same phenomenon was occurring for the other monotheistic religion of the Empire: the "legal" Jewish religion. Emperor Hadrian persecuted both Jews and Christians during his reign. But this was *not* the normal, "official" policy of the Roman state.

Alas for the Jewish people, their numbers had rapidly declined during the same period of time in which Christendom was expanding. The ravages of two Jewish Revolts and the rebellions throughout the Empire against the Romans had claimed millions of Jewish casualties in death and enslavement. Jewish uprisings in North Africa and Egypt against Emperor Trajan from A.D. 115-117 had been put down with such savagery that Alexandrian Jewry was nearly destroyed. Likewise, Babylonian Jewry had fought against Trajan's expansion of the Empire to their area of Parthia. A great rebellion in Jewish communities broke out behind Trajan's lines, resulting in the death of thousands of Jews. During the fourth century, Emperor Constantine (sole rule A.D. 312-337) accepted Christianity, beginning the process of creating a "Christian Roman Empire." Vehement anti-Jewish legislation ensued from subsequent Christian emperors to such an extent that the Jewish community was further decimated.

The process of Christian anti-Semitism was a gradual one. Relations between Jews and Christians had begun to deteriorate even during the first century. A mutual opposition arose as the Christian church became more gentilized and more Roman. Mainstream Judaism had refused under threat of persecution to worship a Roman emperor who claimed to be "god," and it refused to accept mainstream Christianity's claim that Jesus was God. To become a Christian increasingly meant that a Jewish person would have to apostatize from Judaism. A climate of hostility arose.

The Roman wars against the Jews not only destroyed the Temple and ravaged Jerusalem but also resulted in Jerusalem's relinquishing her position as a center of Christian faith in the Roman world. Gentiles of the Empire had long disdained Judaism and Jewish nationalism. Now, theological and political power moved from Jewish Christian leaders in Jerusalem to centers of Gentile Christian leadership in Alexandria, Rome, and Antioch. The Gentile Christians interpreted the destruction of the Temple and Jerusalem as a sign that God had abandoned Judaism, that He had provided the Gentiles freedom to develop their own Christian theology in a setting independent from Jerusalem's influence.

And yet, the Gentile Christian church found itself in an ambivalent position in regard to the Jewish faith. It realized that Christianity was not a "new" religion and grudgingly accepted its Jewish foundation. Christianity had much in common with Judaism, that is, the God of Abraham, Isaac, and Jacob; a stand against relativism in morals and ethics; the wisdom and proclamation of the prophets; the Torah precept of loving God with all one's being and loving neighbor as oneself; the hatred of war, the spirit of peace, and the hope for the future; the imperishable nature of the human soul; rewards and punishments.

Undergirding all of this was the church's firm belief that the Jewish Scriptures were *her* Scriptures—the Scriptures used by Jesus, Paul, and the disciples. Early church Fathers quoted from the Jewish Scriptures and even defended themselves to the Romans from the Jewish Scriptures. Had the Jewish people at this point disappeared from history, annihilated by the Romans, Christians very possibly would have memorialized them as preparers of God's kingdom. Because Judaism instead remained a vibrant, dedicated Torah faith, which drew converts and was firm in its witness to the one true God, the climate of hostility grew worse.

The Jewish Scriptures being used by the Gentile church required a drastic reinterpretation because, according to those Scriptures, the Jewish people are the chosen people with an immense responsibility to the world. The Gentile church attempted to reconcile this difficulty by reinterpreting those Scriptures to state that the Christian church is the true Israel, the "new" Israel—not just grafted in as Paul stated in Romans 11:17, but totally *replacing* the Jewish people. This triumphalism, the attitude of celebrating a victory over an "enemy," has fanned the flames of religious anti-Semitism ever since.

On his way to martyrdom by the Romans in the early second century, Ignatius, the famed Bishop of Antioch, claimed that Satan "fights along with the Jews to a denial of the cross" and "if any one celebrates the passover along with the Jews, or receives emblems of their feast, he is a partaker with those that killed the Lord and His apostles." This is ironic, because Jesus and the apostles always observed the Passover. Ignatius upheld the prophets and declared, "And the 'Prophets,' let us love them too, because they anticipated the gospel in their preaching." Nevertheless, a few lines later he wrote, "Now, if anyone preaches Judaism to you, pay no attention to him."[1]

---

1. All references from the early church Fathers can be found in Alexander Roberts and James Donaldson, eds., *The Ante-Nicene Fathers: Translations of the Writings of the Fathers down to* A.D. *325,* 10 vols. (Edinburgh: The Ante-Nicene Christian Library, 1885-1896).

The Epistle of Barnabas, which circulated about the same period, explained that the Jewish sacrifices were abolished, their fasts were not acceptable to God, and that Christians, not Jews, were actually the heirs of God's covenant with Abraham. To those who believed that the Jewish people still had a future through the covenant, the epistle harshly stated: "Take heed now to yourselves, and not to be like some adding largely to your sins, and saying, 'The covenant is both theirs and ours.' But they [the Jews] thus finally lost it." This epistle was highly regarded in the church and was even included in some of the early canon lists. Reading between the lines, one notes the existence of Christians who believed that the Jewish people definitely had a future through the Abrahamic covenant and were quite vocal about it.

Unfortunately, many in the church were not content with claiming an interest in the Jewish Scriptures but proceeded to try to make the Old Testament the exclusive domain of the church. Justin Martyr, one of the greatest Christian defenders of the faith, continued this theme. In his *Dialogue with Trypho* (c. A.D. 140), Justin quoted fluidly from the Jewish Scriptures and then proclaimed to Trypho, the Jewish escapee from the Second Jewish Revolt:

> For these words have neither been prepared by me, nor embellished by the art of man; but David sung them, Isaiah preached them, Zechariah proclaimed them, and Moses wrote them. Are you acquainted with them, Trypho? They are *contained* in your Scriptures, or *rather not yours,* but ours. For we believe them; but you, though you read them, do not catch the spirit that is in them.

Later Justin remarked to Trypho: "For the prophetical gifts remain with us, even to the present time. And hence you ought to understand that [the gifts] formerly among your nation have been transferred to us."

The great defender of the faith Irenaeus, Bishop of Lyon after A.D. 177, declared that the Jews were "disinherited from the grace of God" and "would never have hesitated to burn their own Jewish Scriptures." Tertullian of Carthage, the first church Father to use the word *trinity,* wrote in A.D. 200:

> In former times the Jews enjoyed much of God's favor, when the fathers of their race were noted for their righteousness and faith. So it was that as a people they flourished greatly, and their kingdom attained to a lofty eminence.... But how deeply they [the Jews] have sinned, puffed up to their fall with a false trust in their noble ancestors,

turning from God's way into a way of sheer impiety, though they themselves should refuse to admit it, their present national ruin would afford sufficient proof.

According to Tertullian, the Jewish people no longer had any witness or truth. Their only reason to exist was to testify to the misery and degradation that befell a people rejected by God. The curses of the Bible were ascribed to the Jews; the blessings of the Bible to the Christians.

The church Fathers were men of piety, noted for moral excellence in other areas of the Christian life. When it came to the Jewish people, however, they laid a foundation and conveyed a message that Adolf Hitler would duplicate. They declared that the Jews were no longer God's chosen people and that the church had inherited the covenant promises of God—the church was God's chosen people. They insisted that the Jews were "Christ-killers." They believed that the Jewish people deserved persecution and the loss of their land. In A.D. 300 a Christian council in Spain forbade eating with Jews on penalty of excommunication from the church.

THE CHRISTIAN ROMAN REPUBLIC

As a wall of intolerance was being built against the Jewish community, early church Fathers were pleading for religious toleration from the Roman government. They assured the Roman emperors that like their Lord, Jesus Christ, they did not seek earthly power and had no intention of ever wielding such power. They said that they lived in two worlds, but heaven was their true home. They expected Jesus to return at any time to fetch them away from the wickedness that encompassed the world system, and these brave church Fathers reminded the Romans that God would judge them if they did not show tolerance to Christians. The pagan Roman Empire, however, was so "religious" that it actually considered the Christians to be "atheists."

The second-century *Letter to Diognetus* included an entire section that described Christians and their relationship to the world. Explaining that "Christians cannot be distinguished from the rest of the human race by country or language or customs," the Christian writer bemoaned the fact that they were treated as "aliens" because of their religion. He clarified to the Romans that Christians "obey the established laws, but in their own lives they go far beyond what the laws require" in love, purity, and piety. "To put it simply," the writer suggested, "what the soul is in the body, that the Christians are in the world."

The writings of the early Christians faithfully confirm that they sought no Christian state and, in fact, were quite disgusted with those who would accuse them of such. "When you hear that we look for a kingdom, you rashly suppose that we mean something merely human. But we speak of a Kingdom *with* God," Justin Martyr explained in his *First Apology*. "For if we looked for a human kingdom we would deny it in order to save our lives, and would try to remain in hiding in order to obtain the things we look for ... we do not place our hopes on the present [order]. ... We are in fact of all men your best helpers and allies in securing good order." [2]

In spite of being members of an illegal religious movement, Christians had been persecuted mainly as the result of mob action rather than by direct decree of the Roman government. Before A.D. 250, persecution was local and sporadic, rarely as intense as a number of books about martyrs would suggest. Occasionally, an emperor would scapegoat the Christians or initiate a pogrom in a fit of pagan religious fervor, but such was not the policy of the Roman government. In practice during the early third century, existing laws had not been enforced.

Thus, no one was more surprised than the growing Christian community when Emperor Decius (A.D. 249-251) declared that all subjects of the Roman Empire were required to present certificates that stated that they "have always sacrificed to the gods" and to prove loyalty by a current sacrifice in the presence of a royal official. Christians were caught in the dilemma of obeying God rather than men, and the first general persecution of Christians throughout the Roman Empire had begun. For the next six decades, persecution of Christians was the policy of the Roman state.

Although a number of Christians lapsed, it was said that during this period there were times that the prisons were so crowded with Christians that there was not enough room for criminals. Emperor Valerian (A.D. 253-259) also directed the persecution at the heads of the churches —the bishops—in an effort to destroy institutional Christianity. Many of these bishops died; others lapsed. At the turn of the fourth century, Christians were ordered once again to sacrifice to pagan idols or die. It appeared that the fourth century would be one of persecution for Christians.

2. In addition to the translation found in *The Ante-Nicene Fathers* compare Cyril C. Richardson, ed., *Early Christian Fathers* (New York: Macmillan, 1970).

Such was not to be the case. A young commander in charge of his deceased father's troops would claim that he had asked the Christian god to help him defeat Maxentius at the decisive battle of Rome's Milvian Bridge in A.D. 312. In a last-minute decision prompted by a celestial vision, Constantine adopted the Christian insignia for his army. He won the battle to claim the West and within twelve more years was sole ruler of the entire Roman Empire. Questions concerning the legitimacy of his conversion and his reasons for becoming a "Christian" emperor have consumed scholars ever since.

Although Constantine may be an enigma, the impact of his rule on both the status and the attitude of the church is clearly observable. With a "Christian" in control, early Christian attitudes toward the state were being reevaluated. The mission of the church to draw the individual to "kingdom *with* God" changed swiftly to a new idea: conversion of the state. With a Christian state and a Christian leader, church leaders felt confident that God would be glorified and that Christ's kingdom would have dominion over the earth. In the Edict of Milan (313), Christianity became a legal religion (after being illegal for two-and-a-half centuries). In the year 380, Christian Emperor Theodosius I declared Christianity the "exclusive" religion of the Roman state. A "Christian" empire had been realized, but nearly at the cost of Christianity itself.

Certainly, leaders of the church were in part the victims of circumstances. Their ease in succumbing to the lure of state favors and power, however, is instructive as well as a sad commentary on the nature of human depravity and corporate evil. Emperor Constantine showered Christian leaders with "presents." Imperial funds were sent to subsidize churches in the provinces. Clergy and churches were exempted from taxation, and secular power was given to the Roman bishops to judge Christians. The Lateran palace in Rome was given to the Roman bishop, and court ceremonies were instituted. The Christian church was legally allowed to have property willed to her, and her holdings increased greatly. But in spite of her wealth, the church could not adequately teach all her "converts." It was becoming socially acceptable to be Christian, and many "converts" overwhelmed the fragile institution. To accommodate Roman customs, the church adopted trappings of paganism (after rationalizing that she had properly "Christianized" them).

An understanding of Roman religion is needed to perceive how easily Constantine and the emperors who succeeded him could accept a one-religion empire. As with many ancient societies, Rome had merged the religious with the secular. There was no political rule without religious rule, and religion was considered a department of the state. Sacrifices were conducted by state officials at state expense. The emperor was the *pontifex maximus,* the high priest of the Roman religious system, whose divine status was declared in the provinces to encourage loyalty. He was to be worshiped in conjunction with the goddess of Rome. Sun worship was very important in state worship, and the sun was considered an important deity. December 25 was the annual birthday of the sun, and pagan celebrations were plentiful. Sunday was the day of the week devoted to the sun. After the Milvian Bridge triumph, Constantine continued to lead this pagan system, nominating pagan priests and gaining the reputation as the restorer of old Roman traditions. The Christian god could be accepted as long as the pagan traditions and duties of the royal office were not neglected.

Christianity would soon permeate the royal household as well as the aristocracy in Rome. Constantius, Constantine's son and successor, considered himself an amateur theologian and tried to suppress paganism by law and replace it with his brand of Christianity and "Christian" dogma. Often neglecting to consult the bishops of the church, he attempted to make himself the *pontifex maximus* of Christianity.

It would seem that the church would have no more reason to fear Judaism. Ironically, however, the church's paranoia got worse; attacks against the Jewish community became more bitter. In A.D. 325, Constantine as a "Christian" emperor forbade Jews to live in Jerusalem. They were not allowed to engage in any evangelism. At the Council of Nicea it was decided that Easter should not be determined by the Jewish Passover calendar, and that Christians should "have nothing in common with this odius people," the Jews. Emperor Constantius in A.D. 357 confiscated the property of a Christian who dared to convert to Judaism, and Hilary of Poitiers wrote that the Jews were a perverse people accursed by God *forever.* Ambrose of Milan was so upset with Emperor Theodosius I (A.D. 379-395) for ordering the synagogue in Milan to be rebuilt that he wrote: "I hereby declare, that it was I who set fire to the synagogue; indeed, I gave the orders for it to be done so that there should no longer be any place where Christ is denied."

It is during this period that the word *Christian* became associated with fear and persecution in the Jewish mind. Jews felt that a Christian was someone who *professes* the high ideals of love, grace, devotion to God, and peace, but one who rarely *practices* those ideals. "Christian" became synonymous with discrimination, separation, anti-Semitism, and death.

It must be remembered that the church Fathers were men of piety, noted for moral excellence in other areas of the Christian life. When it came to the Jewish people, however, they were found wanting. A classic example of this phenomenon is the most famous preacher of the fourth century, John Chrysostom, known as the "Golden Tongue." A man admired by the common people and a fearless advocate of modest Christian living to the most pompous of royalty, Chrysostom showed complete lack of restraint toward the Jewish people in a series of eight long sermons delivered in Antioch in A.D. 387.[3]

The only reason Chrysostom was so upset was that some Christians were fellowshiping with Jews. That the Christian church had separated herself from the Jewish parent and severed all ties in an irrational paranoia is amply evident in Chrysostom's raging denunciations. The church, firmly in control of Roman society, presented a bold contrast to the Jewish community, which was choked by rules and regulations in a Roman Empire that now claimed to be 95 percent "Christian." Yet Chrysostom deemed it necessary to strike out against the Jewish people. In those sermons one clearly sees where the rhetoric of the early church Fathers led—and even more frightening, where it can go.

Chrysostom began by discussing an "illness" that had infected the church. He declared:

> What is this disease? The festivals of the pitiful and miserable Jews.
> ... There are many in our ranks who say they think as we do. Yet some
> of these are going to watch the festivals and others will join the Jews in
> keeping their feasts and observing their fasts. I wish to drive this per-
> verse custom from the church right now ... if I should fail to cure
> those who are sick with the Judaizing disease, I am afraid that, because
> of their ill-suited association and deep ignorance, some Christians may
> partake in the Jews' trangressions. ... For if they hear no word from me
> today, they will then join the Jews in their fasts; once they have com-
> mitted this sin, it will be useless for me to apply the remedy.

"But do not be surprised that I call the Jews pitiable," he explained. "They really are pitiable and miserable."

3. John Chrysostom, *Discourses Against Judaizing Christians.* This discourse as well as others from the period can be found in Philip Schaff, ed., *A Select Library of the Nicene and Post-Nicene Fathers of the Christian Church,* 14 vols. (Buffalo: Christian Literature Co., 1886-1890).

According to Chrysostom, the Jews were murderers and worse than wild beasts. Their synagogue "is not only a brothel and a theater: it is also a den of robbers and a lodging for wild beasts." "No Jew adores God!" he exclaimed. His proof for this statement: "The Son of God says so." Chrysostom held the whole Jewish people culpable for the killing of Christ, using statements that would be reaffirmed by anti-Semites for the next sixteen centuries. "So the godlessness of the Jews and the pagans is on a par. But the Jews practice a deceit which is more dangerous. In their synagogue stands an invisible altar of deceit on which they sacrifice not sheep and calves but the souls of men. Finally, if the ceremonies of the Jews move you to admiration, what do you have in common with us?" Chrysostom asked his audience.

One can easily see that a Jewish Christian who wanted to hold onto his heritage or a Gentile Christian who wanted to learn more about the parent of Christianity would have found it extremely difficult under this pressure. Furthermore, Chrysostom sought to separate Christianity totally from Judaism. For example, in the fourth sermon he cajoled:

> Let me, too, now say this against these Judaizing Christians. If you judge that Judaism is the true religion, why are you causing trouble to the church? But if Christianity is the true faith, as it really is, stay in it and follow it. Tell me this. Do you share with us the mysteries, do you worship Christ as a Christian, do you ask him for blessing, and do you then celebrate the festival with his foes? With what purpose, then, do you come to the church? I have said enough against those who say they are on our side but are eager to follow the Jewish rites . . . it is against the Jews that I wish to draw up my battle line.

Four more sermons of vitriolic hatred ensued, bringing the number to eight in all; each contained diatribes against Jews, Judaism, and the synagogue: each separated Jesus Christ from the Jewish people who gave Him birth. Chrysostom in the seventh sermon began: "Have you had enough of the fight against the Jews? Or do you wish me to take up the same topic today? Even if I have already had much to say on it, I still think you want to hear the same thing again. The man who does not have enough of loving Christ will never have enough of fighting those who hate Christ." The message is clear, according to Patristic reasoning: those who love Jesus hate Jews—and fight Jews.

Chrysostom ended his eighth sermon by asking his congregation to pay him interest on the "money" (message) he deposited with them, demanding imperative "action on your own part." Tragically, centuries of

anti-Semitic incidents and severed Christian-Jewish relationships resulted. In spite of her high position in the Roman Empire, the Christian
church remained paranoid about Judaism.

THE MEDIEVAL PERIOD

When the Roman Empire "fell," it did not have far to go. Split into
the Eastern and the Western Empires, only the western part succumbed
to the barbarian onslaught. The Eastern Empire survived as the Byzantine Empire, continuing the relationship between church and state established in the fourth century. From Constantinople, emperors such as Justinian (527-565) continued to regard the church as a department of the
state. The Eastern Orthodox church would develop in such a milieu of
oriental "Christian" despotism.

Nevertheless, the church had passed so quickly from "illegal religion" to "privileged patronage" during Constantine's reign, that Eastern
Christianity never developed a policy on the emperor's position in
Christendom. Although concepts of the "divine right" to rule permeated
the theological structure, strong church leaders affected imperial policy,
and strong emperors determined and enforced theological dogma. The
mingling of politics and religion combine with the ever-changing human
drama to caution one against simplistic generalization as to whether
state was over church or church over state. To the oriental mind, the
question would have been superfluous.

What is again clear is the persecution of groups who did not agree
completely with the theology of the church and the state. For the Jewish
people, who stood outside the bastion of Christendom, the consequences were disastrous. Into his famous law code, Justinian wrote not
only the "orthodox" statement of faith, but also laws against Jews, Samaritans, pagans, and nonorthodox Christians. During his reign, a Jew could
not testify against an "orthodox" Christian, and the dictum that the law
could not work for a Jew (only against him) was firmly established in
Byzantine society. Judaism was treated as heresy, and later Byzantine emperors such as Heraclitus, Leo III, and Basil I promoted forced conversions. Leo III (717-741), in fact, outlawed Judaism and commanded that
all Jews in the Empire undergo baptism. It is little wonder that the Jewish
community (as well as many Christians today) fear a "Christian"
constitution.

So horrid was the persecution by the Christian Byzantines that the
Jewish communities welcomed the rise of Islam in the seventh century

and its rapid victories over Christian lands. Although Muslims were ferocious conquerors and Jews were viewed as inferior second-class subjects (often suffering), the Jewish people as non-Muslims were needed for a tax base. Muslims were not allowed to tax their religious brothers, and the Jews were encouraged in their small business ventures to provide needed capital for the Islamic state.

In the West, the Roman Catholic church was growing in power; the Bishop of Rome (the Pope) gained ascendancy over many of the political leaders in Europe from A.D. 500-1500. Although there are exceptions to the trend, the rhetoric of the church Fathers blossomed into pontifical hatred and persecution of the Jewish people. When the Roman Catholic church finally became the social fabric of the Western medieval world, the entire gamut of society, from aristocrat to peasant, was infested with anti-Semitism.

Jews were forbidden by the church to proselytize, and Christians who converted to Judaism were severely punished. Because, for the most part, this was *religious* anti-Semitism, the only option a Jew had to gain acceptance from medieval Christendom was to convert to Christianity. If a Jew chose this path, it meant total alienation from one's people and one's Torah.

The professions of faith required by Jewish converts to Christianity in the medieval period indicate the total separation from Judaism required by the church.[4] "I do here and now renounce every rite and observance of the Jewish religion, detesting all its most solemn ceremonies and tenets that in former days I kept and held," the convert had to affirm in one creed. "I altogether deny and reject the error of the Jewish religion," he proceeded. "[I] shun all intercourse with other Jews and have the circle of my friends only among honest Christians." The convert had to admit that "because of our pertinacious lack of faith and the ancient errors of our fathers" he had been held back from the Christian faith, and therefore he would not "become involved in any Jewish rites or customs nor associate with the accursed Jews who remain unbaptized." He was not to shun "swines' flesh," and for him and his family he must swear, "We will not on any pretext, either ourselves, our children or our descendants, choose wives from our own race; but in the case of both sexes we will always link ourselves in matrimony with Christians."

---

4. Such professions are plentiful and follow the same basic patterns. For a selection, note James Parkes, *The Conflict of the Church and the Synagogue: A Study in the Origins of Antisemitism* (New York: World, 1934), pp. 394-400.

Others were forced to declare that they would never return "to the vomit of my former error, or associating with the wicked Jews. In every respect will I lead the Christian life and associate with Christians." Denunciation of their Jewish families and Jewish heritage was always required. Such denunciation was sometimes very thorough. For example, the church of Constantinople required in part:

> I renounce all customs, rites, legalisms, unleavened breads and sacrifices of lambs of the Hebrews, and all other feasts of the Hebrews, sacrifices, prayers, aspersions, purifications, sanctifications and propitiations, and fasts, and new moons, and Sabbaths, and superstitions, and hymns and chants and observances and synagogues, and the food and drink of the Hebrews; in one word, I renounce absolutely everything Jewish, every law, rite and custom, and above all I renounce Antichrist, whom all the Jews await in the figure and form of Christ; and I join myself to the true Christ and God.

The penalty for eating and feasting with one's Jewish family, or for going astray from the oath in any way, also had to be declared by the Jewish convert to Christianity. In this case, he declared that if he lapsed from his oath, "then let the trembling of Cain and the leprosy of Gehazi cleave to me, as well as the legal punishments to which I acknowledge myself liable. And may I be anathema in the world to come, and may my soul be set down with Satan and the devils."

Church councils continually legislated during the medieval period to prevent contacts between Christians and Jews, and the anti-Semitic rhetoric filtered down to the peasant class. The examples would alone fill a book. For example, when Charlemagne (reigned 768-814) and his son, Louis the Pious (814-840), initiated a period of tolerance toward the Jewish people, clerical forces in the French territories sought to undermine the dialogue. Charlemagne and Louis had respected the help given them by Jewish traders and merchants. They granted Jews in their domain occupational and religious freedom. Both kings had, in fact, appointed Jews to posts in their administration, and a rebirth of culture and learning took place.

Alas, Agobard, Archbishop of Lyons (from 814-840), was one of the churchmen who leveled a steady and passionate barrage against the Jews. That his jurisdiction encompassed some of the most important Jewish settlements in all of Western Europe was no small matter. He wrote six pamphlets against the Jews, including "On the Insolence of the

Jews," "On the Superstitions of the Jews," and "On the Necessity of Avoiding Association with Jews." He complained that Jews had the right to build synagogues and freely worship; he asked Christians to avoid doing business with Jews; and he even attempted to baptize Jewish children. His successor, Archbishop Amulo, forbade Christians from partaking of "Jewish food and drink," explaining:

> Cursing the infidelity of the Jews and seeking to protect the Christian people from contagion, I have three times publicly asked that our faithful draw aside from them.... And I have published several other severe injunctions, in order to tear out the evil by the root and to imitate the example of our pious master, shepherd and predecessor, Agobard.[5]

False rumors of Jewish plots against Christians began to circulate throughout Europe.

Little wonder that two centuries later the Christian Crusaders would plunder and kill the Jews of Europe to finance their "holy" enterprise and, once in Jerusalem, would burn Jewish men, women, and children alive in the synagogue. Such excessive behavior offended even the church leadership; but once such anti-Semitism was ingrained in the masses, it was difficult to control.

The Roman Catholic church, in fact, continued to preach separation and sought to strip the Jewish people of legal rights. At the height of medieval power, under Innocent III (1198-1216), Jews were forbidden to hold public office, "since it would be altogether absurd that a blasphemer of Christ should exercise authority over Christians," the Fourth Lateran Council of 1215 asserted. Jews were also ordered to wear distinctive garments, ostensibly to curtail intimate relationships between Jews and Christians. The distinguishing badge took many forms: in Italy a disk was sewn on the clothing; in German areas a distinctive hat was worn; and in England two strips of white linen or parchment were sewn on a prominent part of the clothing. The Jewish people, as the only significant and visible nonconverted minority in Christian Europe, were a continual embarrassment for a church that considered itself the "new" Israel.

And "Israel" continued in its labor of love over Torah. As the Babylonian academies passed the zenith of their Talmudic commentary and

---

5. For this and many other medieval quotations, refer to Jacob R. Marcus, *The Jew in the Medieval World: A Source Book, 315-1791* (Cincinnati: The Union of American Hebrew Congregations, 1938).

literary activity by the year 1000, centers of Jewish learning sprang up in Germany and northern France. One of the first great German talmudic scholars, Gershom ben Judah (c. 960-1028), formed a yeshiva in Mainz. Using the Scripture and Talmud, he formulated decisions for Jewish conduct in European society. His students spread the learned scholarship of this "Light of the Exile" (as they called him because Jews were expelled from Mainz in 1012) throughout Europe, forming numerous additional academies.

The famed Rabbi Solomon ben Isaac (1040-1105), better known by his initials as Rashi, studied at the German academies for eight years before returning to his hometown of Troyes, France. There he founded a talmudic school of his own, soon rivaling the fame of the German academies. Hundreds of students studied under Rashi, and he opened up to the Jews of Europe the treasures of the Babylonian Talmud. He commented upon most books of the Bible in his extensive commentaries and is noted for being able to explain the most intricate passages in a language that common men and women could comprehend. Most printed texts of the Hebrew Pentateuch and Talmud in the Middle Ages were accompanied by Rashi's commentary, and Rashi's commentary was the first book in Hebrew to be printed on a printing press (in 1475), seven years before the Hebrew Bible itself.

Rashi's dictum was simply: "Let the interpreter keep on interpreting, but we are interested in the simple, natural meaning of the biblical text." As a teacher, he sought to impart learning through love and desire (in contrast to the medieval pedagogy of fear and pain). Rashi noted: "He who does not care for the words of Torah, even reasonable explanations do not appeal to him; but he who desires them, even those parts which he learns with effort and bitterness become sweet to him." Rashi's impact on biblical studies is evident in that hundreds of commentaries have been written on his commentaries of the Bible and Talmud. Because of his work in the French language, some scholars believe his method may have had influence on medieval Christian hermeneutics as well.

It is a sad fact that the First Crusade with its accompanying atrocities began in 1096, a decade before Rashi's death. The Talmud would be burned in Paris in 1242, instigated by a Jewish convert to Christianity. At that time, a Christian prohibition against Jewish study of the Talmud led to the cessation of the academies in northern France inspired by Rashi.

Jews were expelled from England in 1290; from France in 1306 and 1394; from German territories throughout the period. When the Black

Death epidemic occurred from approximately 1348-1351, the Jewish community was blamed for the plague, and was massacred and evicted in many European towns and villages. Hatred of the Jew permeated medieval society. When the Jewish community found tolerance and began to prosper, their position and goods were coveted. When they were downtrodden, they were used as examples of a life without Christ. Sadly, biblical language and Christian jargon were used most often against the Jewish people to rationalize persecution and even murder. The Jew, it was said, was "supposed to wander," "killed Christ," "plotted against Christians," "asked for Christ's blood to be upon them."

To the dispersed Jewish people, the expulsions and accompanying "Christian" rhetoric left an indelible impression on the Jewish mind-set toward themselves and the world. It affected their entire history and, indeed, their course of settlement. In general, Jews today make little distinction between the diverse Christian groups throughout history.

The Jews of northwestern Europe had very early in the medieval period referred to their territory as *Ashkenaz,* a biblical term (cf. Genesis 10:3; 1 Chronicles 1:6; Jeremiah 51:27) given new meaning. Soon it became a term denoting Jews of northern France and the German territories. Today, the term *Ashkenazim* refers to the entire Jewish religious, social, and cultural heritage arising from that area (later spreading to Poland, Lithuania, and Eastern Europe). This designation is used in contrast to *Sephardim* (cf. Obadiah 20), a term used for the descendants of Jews who lived in Spain or Portugal (Iberian Peninsula) before the expulsion of the Jews in 1492. This expulsion occurred after Catholic monarchs had progressively reconquered the territory from the Muslims, expelling them as well as the Jewish people.

THE SEPHARDIM

It was in Muslim Spain during the Middle Ages that Western Jewry experienced a significant "Golden Age." Jews had lived in Spain from ancient times, enduring sporadic sanctions and anti-Semitic acts. The Visigoths, barbarian tribes that conquered the Romans in the area but converted to Christianity, treated the Spanish Jewish community harshly until Arab Muslims conquered Spain in A.D. 711. Islamic forces now stretched from the border of India in the East to Spain in the West, and Spanish Jewry was immediately linked to the rich heritage of Babylonia, including the Babylonian Talmud.

Hasdai ben Isaac ibn Shaprut (c. A.D. 915-997) emerged as the first of the Jewish dignitaries in the service of the caliph of Córdoba, the Muslim ruler of a vast territory encompassing the entire south and central portion of the Iberian Peninsula. Hasdai had studied medicine; had mastered Hebrew, Arabic, and Latin; was adept at philosophy; and diligently pursued Torah and Talmud by the age of twenty-five. He was one of the best and the brightest of a new generation of Jewish scholars, artists, and prosperous businessmen in Córdoba.

A practicing physician and medical researcher, Hasdai became the caliph's personal physician. It did not take the caliph long to discover Hasdai's many other talents, and Hasdai soon was both the diplomat and the architect of the caliph's foreign policy. In his important position and in the midst of his fame, Hasdai never forgot his people. He remained a leader of the Jewish community and generously supported academies throughout the known world. Even more significant, he forged a new home for talmudic scholarship in Spain. Jewish poets, philosophers, scientists, and historians pursued research and an exciting literary activity. Ancient manuscripts were collected and translated. The library in Córdoba was the best in all of Europe, containing more than four hundred thousand volumes. Thousands of students flocked to study in Muslim Spain, and talented Jews from all over the world joined in this "Golden Age of Spanish Jewry."

Tranquility was not to last even in Spain. Islam traditionally viewed the Jewish people as a despicable and infidel race. In 1066 a series of rumors and conspiracies formed against Joseph ha-Nagid, who had inherited his position of rabbi and vizier (prime minister) of Granada from his father. When warring bands from a neighboring area unexpectedly invaded Granada, the rumor spread that Joseph had invited the enemy into the country. A Muslim mob stormed his palace, killed him, dragged his corpse to the city gate, and impaled him there. Fifteen hundred Jewish families in Granada were massacred that day as anti-Semitic hysteria swept the area, the first of several outbreaks on the Iberian Peninsula during the "Golden Age."

As the Christian reconquest of the Iberian Peninsula progressed acre by acre, some Christian kings also took Jewish subjects into their service. Spanish Jewish studies even influenced Christian theologians. For example, philosopher and poet Solomon ben Judah ibn Gabirol (1020-1058) wrote *Mekor Hayyim (The Source of Life)*, which presents his philosophy of life. It was translated into a number of languages and was soon thought by Christians to be written by a church Father. A group of medieval theologians drew upon it, and even the great Thomas Aquinas (1225-1274), who criticized the work, never dreamed that the author was a Jewish philosopher.

Thomas Aquinas, however, was indebted to the greatest Jewish philosopher, scientist, jurist, and codifier of Jewish law of the twelfth century, Moses ben Maimon (1135-1204), "Maimonides" (fondly known as *Rambam,* from the acronym of the first letters of "*R*abbi *M*oses *b*en *Mai*mon"). Born in Córdoba, Maimonides was the son of a renowned Jewish scholar. At the age of thirteen he and his family were exiled when Córdoba fell to the Almohads, a fanatical Muslim group that instituted persecution against the Jewish community (as well as less zealous Muslims). Under the Almohads, many Jews were forced to convert to Islam or die. Maimonides' family wandered for nearly a decade, finally settling in Fez, Morocco, around 1160. Alas, further widespread outbreaks of persecution and anti-Semitism forced the family to flee once again. They traveled across the Mediterranean Sea to Acre. From there, they were able to tour the Holy Land before journeying to Egypt.

Although Maimonides had written treatises as early as sixteen years of age and had continued his studies in Torah and in medicine in Fez, it was in Cairo, Egypt, that Maimonides devoted himself to publication.[6] His first major work, *Commentary on the Mishnah* (1168), explained to the lay reader the underlying principles of the *Mishnah* and the history of the Oral Torah from Moses to the current era. He also discussed the fundamental doctrines of Judaism, which he formulated into the "Thirteen Principles." These thirteen articles of the Jewish faith according to Maimonides were:

1. The *existence* of God. God's existence is perfect and sufficient unto itself. God is the cause of the existence of all other beings.

2. The *unity* of God. God's unity is unlike all other kinds of unity.

3. The *incorporeality* of God. God must not be conceived in bodily terms, and the anthropomorphic expressions applied to God in Scripture (i.e., hand of God, mouth of God, etc.) have to be understood in a metaphorical sense.

4. The *eternity* of God.

6. The following quotations from Maimonides may be found in a number of sources. An excellent treatment is translated and edited by Bernard Martin, namely, Israel Zinberg, *A History of Jewish Literature: The Arabic-Spanish Period* (Cleveland: Case Western Reserve U., 1972). Chapter 6 is entitled "Maimonides."

5. God *alone* is to be worshiped and obeyed. There are no mediating powers able freely to grant the petitions of human beings. Intermediaries must not be invoked.

6. *Prophecy* is the natural, intelligible device by which God secures the existence and perfection of the human species. It is an overflow coming from the Active Intellect of God toward the individual's rational faculty and then toward one's imaginative faculty.

7. *Moses* is unsurpassed by any other prophet.

8. The entire *Torah* was given to Moses by God.

9. The *eternal immutability* of the Torah. Moses' Torah will not be abrogated or superseded by another divine law, nor will anything be added to or taken away from it.

10. The *omniscience* of God. God knows the actions of men and women.

11. The *reward and punishment* from God. God rewards those who fulfill the commandments of the *Torah* and punishes those who transgress them.

12. The coming of the *Messiah*. For Maimonides, the Messiah is an earthly king, descended from the house of David. The Messiah will bring the Jewish people back to their country, but his major accomplishment will be to bring peace and tranquility to the world, thereby making possible full observance of God's commandments.

13. The *resurrection* of the dead. Body and soul will be reunited.

In credal form, preceded by *Ani Maamin* ("I believe with perfect faith that ... "), these Thirteen Principles first appeared in published form in the 1500s. It is a great tribute to the Sephardic Maimonides that the Thirteen Principles (sometimes referred to as the Thirteen Articles) were incorporated into the daily ritual of Ashkenazic Jewry and are found as an appendix to the regular morning service of the Ashkenazi prayer book.

Only after the writing of the *Commentary on the Mishnah* did Maimonides approach his massive, fourteen-volume *Mishneh Torah* (1180). For ten years he worked day and night on this project, because he believed that "the commentaries of the *Geonim* [the post-Talmudic sages and Jewish interpreters] and their compilations of laws and responsa, which they took care to make clear, have in our times become hard to understand, so that only a few individuals fully comprehend them." Maimonides explained at the end of the introduction to *Mishneh Torah*:

On these grounds, I, Moses the son of Maimon the Sephardi have gird-
ed up my loins and, relying on the help of God, blessed be He, intently
studied all these works, with the view of putting together the results
obtained from them ... all in plain language and terse style, so that the
entire Oral Torah might become systematically known to all without
citing difficulties and solutions of differences of view ... I have composed this work in which are collected all the laws and statutes, with
the enactments, customs and decrees that were introduced from the
days of Moses our teacher to the redaction of the Talmud and that are
expounded in the work of our *Geonim* who lived in later generations.
I have given my work the title *Mishneh Torah* because any one who
will first study the Written Torah and thereafter this work will, through
it, become thoroughly familiar with the entire Oral Torah and need
not consult any other book for this purpose.

Maimonides's goal was that in a clear and concise writing style he might
make all the rules that appeared from Moses through his era accessible
to young and old alike. In his task of classifying the entire literary halakhah, he systematically codified Jewish Law in a manner that had never
been attempted before in Jewish history. The *Mishneh Torah* was a model of the Hebrew scientific style of religious literature, with polished sentences and clear and lucid content. It was accepted with great enthusiasm among the Jewish people. A contemporary Jewish scholar wrote
that Maimonides "has led his people out of the sea of foolishness. He has
implanted God's sacred Torah in all hearts."

Although opposition did arise in Maimonides' day among other
scholars (in some cases because of jealousy), Maimonides' stature in
Jewish history only grew greater. His *Guide for the Perplexed* (c. 1190)
made him the most significant Jewish philosopher of the Middle Ages;
and the *Guide* itself has been considered by many scholars as the most
important philosophic work produced by a Jew. Written for the person
who had studied philosophy and was firmly established in Jewish belief
and practice, Maimonides' *Guide* attempted to harmonize reason and
Scripture in an Aristotelian manner. Here Maimonides dealt with the attributes of God, creation, prophecy, divine providence and free will, the
nature of evil, the nature of human beings, and the reasons for Torah.
The *Guide* had a formidable influence on modern Jewish thought, en-
couraging modern Jewish thinkers toward more study and more speculation. Its influence on Jewish philosophy is seen in that numerous commentaries on the *Guide* have arisen from the medieval period to the
present. Emperor Frederick II had *Guide for the Perplexed* translated

into Latin in the early 1200s, whereupon medieval Christian thinkers were heavily indebted to it. Albertus Magnus quoted entire chapters from the work, whereas Thomas Aquinas employed Maimonides' arguments and logical ideas in his *Summa Theologica.*

By the time the *Guide* was published, Moses Maimonides was a famous physician as well as a competent astronomer. The demands on him are most evident in a letter he wrote in his mid-sixties relating his responsibilities:

> I dwell at Misr [Fostat] and the Sultan resides at Kahira [Cairo]; these two places are two Sabbath day's journey [about a mile and a half] distant from each other. My duties to the Sultan are very heavy. I am obliged to visit him every day, early in the morning; and when he or any of his children, or any of the inmates of his harem, are indisposed, I dare not quit Kahira, but must stay during the greater part of the day at the palace. It also frequently happens that one or two of the royal officers fall sick, and I must attend to their healing. Hence, as a rule, I repair to Kahira very early in the day, and if nothing unusual happens, I do not return to Misr until the afternoon. Then I am almost dying with hunger... I find the antechamber filled with people, both Jews and Gentiles, nobles and common people, judges and bailiffs, friends and foes—a mixed multitude who await the time of my return.

> I dismount from my animal, wash my hands, go forth to my patients, and entreat them to bear with me while I partake of some slight refreshment, the only meal I take in the twenty-four hours. Then I attend to my patients, and write prescriptions and directions for their various ailments. Patients go in and out until nightfall, and sometimes even, I solemnly assure you, until two hours or more in the night. I converse with and prescribe for them while lying down from sheer fatigue; and when night falls, I am so exhausted that I can scarcely speak.

> In consequence of this, no Israelite can have any private interview with me except on the Sabbath. On this day the whole congregation, or at least the majority of the members, come to me after the morning service, when I instruct them as to their proceedings during the whole week; we study together a little until noon, when they depart. Some of them return, and read with me after the afternoon service until evening prayers. In this manner I spend that day.

Maimonides died on December 13, 1204, at the age of sixty-nine. Public mourning occurred throughout the Jewish world. In his place of residence, Fostat, three days of mourning were declared. In Jerusalem, a public fast day was observed. As he had wished, Maimonides was buried in Tiberias, traditionally the resting place for Johanan ben Zakkai and Rabbi Akiva. Maimonides had such high regard for the study of the Torah that he suggested that a clever Jewish craftsman should devote three hours a day to his craft and nine to the Torah. Women, though not required to study Torah because of labors at home, would receive extra merit for doing so; and Maimonides highly encouraged such pursuit. During his lifetime, an Arabic verse had circulated comparing him to the famous second century Greek physician Galen: "Galen's medicine is only for the body, but that of Maimonides is for both body and soul."

In spite of the wave of anti-Semitism that forced Moses Maimonides' family into exile, the Sephardim continued to prosper in Spain for three more centuries. Although the *Reconquista,* the reconquest by Christian Europe, bode future ill for the Jewish community in Spain and Portugal, Jews served Catholic kings as well as Muslim caliphs in the thirteenth and fourteenth centuries. Many Jews served as physicians, surveyors, geographers, mathematicians, and astronomers. As persecution increased during and after the time that the Black Death plagued Europe, thousands of Jews converted to Roman Catholicism and were thus technically free from repressive anti-Jewish law codes. Nevertheless, the general population called these Hebrew Christians *Marranos* ("swine"), an indication that Jewish origin was still a stigma.

The marriage of Ferdinand and Isabella in 1469 united their large Spanish domains of Aragon and Castile. As rigorous Catholics, they introduced a series of restrictive measures against Jews, and in 1478 received permission from the pope to appoint inquisitors in every part of their domain. By 1481, the Spanish Inquisition had begun. Marranos who still showed evidence of being "Judaizers" were arrested, imprisoned, and tortured. Under such duress, extracted "confessions" usually meant death. Those Jews who refused to be converted were given a period of "grace" to see the light. If stubborn, they too were convicted of crimes of heresy and were burned at the stake.

Shortly after the Moors (Muslims) were driven out of their last bastion of Granada, Ferdinand and Isabella decided that the remaining Jews on the Iberian Peninsula must be exiled as well. The official reason given was that the existence of a Spanish-Jewish community encouraged the Marranos to persist in Jewish practices. Given three months to leave their Spanish homeland, the Jewish leadership had nearly worked out a financial settlement to stay when the Grand Inquisitor, Torquemada, thundered before the monarchs: "Judas Iscariot sold his master for thirty pieces of silver. Your Highness would sell him [Jesus] anew for thirty thousand." Holding a crucifix high in the air, Torquemada screamed: "Here he [Jesus] is, take him, and barter him away!" The monarchs reconsidered. More than one thousand Jews were expelled from Spain in 1492, on Tisha Be-Av.

Between the centuries of exile from European nations and the expulsion from Spain, relatively few professing Jews remained in all of Western Europe by 1500. Many of the Jews expelled from Spain settled in the Muslim countries of North Africa or traveled to the eastern Mediterranean territories held by the Ottoman Turks. Never before had vocational opportunities and religious liberty been greater for Jewish refugees than in the sixteenth-century Ottoman Empire. By 1551, a European traveler to the Ottoman Empire exclaimed:

> There are so many Jews throughout Turkey and Greece, but especially in Constantinople, that it is a great marvel. They increase daily through the commerce, money changing, and peddling, which they carry on almost everywhere on land and on water, so that it may be said truly that the greater part of the commerce of the whole Orient is in their hand ... In addition, one meets among them many skilled artisans and craftsmen.

In Eretz Yisrael, the Jewish presence was also being felt. A sixteenth-century Jewish traveler wrote:

> How lovely are the tents of Jacob in Jerusalem. From early morning until late evening and from midnight to dawn voices of worshippers and pupils resound in them. The city possesses two synagogues. The smaller belongs to the community of the *Ashkenazim*. ... The other, which is larger, belongs to the *Sephardim*. In its vicinity is a large House of Instruction.

Eretz Yisrael was not to become the new center of Torah study, however. The flight of persecuted Ashkenazim in northern Europe carried many of them to eastern Europe, especially to Poland. From a community of fifty thousand in 1500, Polish Jewry swelled to more than one hundred fifty thousand in 1600; more than one-half million by 1650.

By the time of Adolf Hitler in 1939, world Jewry numbered approximately 16.5 million. Of these, 15 million were Ashkenazim, nearly 3.5

million of them living in Poland. This made Poland one of the largest centers of world Jewish culture. The Nazi Holocaust would kill two-thirds of European Jewry—one-third of the world Jewish population. Less than 5,000 Jews live in Poland today.

MARTIN LUTHER

The church that perpetrated the afore-mentioned anti-Semitism in Europe during the Middle Ages was Roman Catholic, but it is important to remember that the Nazi Holocaust was nurtured in the land of the Reformation. Protestants must also remind themselves that the early Reformers were all once Roman Catholics, and that a legacy of hatred was fostered within Protestantism as well. This Protestant legacy was initiated early by the great Reformer Martin Luther.

Luther appeared to be a breath of fresh air in the midst of a dismal situation. Initially, he had high regard for the Jewish people because he expected them to convert en masse once they were presented with a Christian message free from "papal paganism." In his treatise *That Jesus Christ Was Born a Jew* (1523) the German Reformer demonstrated that Jesus Christ was a Jew, born of the seed of Abraham, and provided a sad commentary on the medieval church's treatment of the Jewish people. He wrote: "If I had been a Jew and had seen such dolts and blockheads govern and teach the Christian faith, I would sooner have become a hog than a Christian." At this time he took a firm stand against the mistreatment of Jews and advocated a new relationship with them. He concluded:

> Therefore, I would request and advise that one deal gently with them [the Jews] and instruct them from Scripture; then some of them may come along. Instead of this we are trying only to drive them by force, slandering them, accusing them of having Christian blood if they don't stink, and I know not what other foolishness. So long as we thus treat them like dogs, how can we expect to work any good among them? Again, when we forbid them to labor and do business and have any human fellowship with us, thereby forcing them into usury, how is that supposed to do them any good? If we really want to help them, we must be guided in our dealings with them not by papal law but by the law of Christian love. We must receive them cordially, and permit them to trade and work with us, hear our Christian teaching, and wit-

ness our Christian life. If some of them should prove stiffnecked, what of it? After all, we ourselves are not all good Christians either.[7]

It is no wonder that Jewish people viewed the Reformation as an opportunity for religious freedom, an opportunity to be treated as human beings.

Alas, Luther became irritated when the Jewish people continued to resist conversion. In 1526 he complained of the Jews' stubbornness, and by the 1530s he was presenting the common medieval stereotypes accorded to Jews. In conversations in *Table Talks* he caricatured Jews as "stiffnecked," "ironhearted," "stubborn as the Devil," and "usurers." In 1543, at the end of his life, he wrote three derogatory treatises against Jews, which anti-Semites would quote for the next four hundred years. So horrible were his statements that Julius Streicher, Hitler's hate-sheet editor and propagandist in *Der Stürmer,* cited Luther at his Nuremberg trial to justify his actions.

One of these treatises is *On the Jews and Their Lies.* In it Luther called the Jews "venomous," "bitter worms," and "disgusting vermin"; he asserted that they were all thieves and should be deported to Palestine. He made numerous suggestions concerning treatment of the Jewish people throughout the treatise, including these:

> What shall we Christians do with this rejected and condemned people, the Jews?... I shall give you my sincere advice. First, to set fire to their synagogues or schools and to bury and cover with dirt whatever will not burn, so that no man will ever again see a stone or cinder of them. This is to be done in honor of our Lord and of Christendom.... Second, I advise that their houses also be razed and destroyed.... Third, I advise that all their prayer books and Talmudic writings, in which such idolatry, lies, cursing, and blasphemy are taught, be taken from them. Fourth, I advise that their rabbis be forbidden to teach henceforth on pain of loss of life and limb.... Fifth, I advise that safe-conduct on the highways be abolished completely for the Jews. For they have no business in the country-side, since they are not lords, officials, tradesmen, or the like. Let them stay at home.... Sixth, I advise that usury be prohibited to them, and that all cash and treasure of silver and gold be taken from them and put aside for safekeeping.... Seventh, I recommend

7. Martin Luther, *That Jesus Christ Was Born a Jew,* 1523; trans. Walther I. Brandt, in *Luther's Works* (Philadelphia: Muhlenberg, 1962), 45:229. See p. 200 for earlier quote.

putting a flail, an ax, a hoe, a spade, a distaff, or a spindle into the hands of young, strong Jews and Jewesses and letting them earn their bread in the sweat of their brow.[8]

Luther's about-face caused extreme bitterness among the Jewish people, some of whom had hailed him as the forerunner of the Messiah and a new age. Jews were forced out of Saxony the same year.

Sadly, in Luther's beloved homeland, synagogues would be burned and homes demolished; Jewish books would be destroyed and rabbis killed. There would be no safe place in Germany (or in most of Europe) for Jews; rich and poor, all would have their money confiscated by the Third Reich. Work gangs of young and old men would provide twelve- and fourteen-hour days of slave labor. Even the great Protestant Reformer Martin Luther could not have foreseen the horrible way in which his words would be used.

THE NEW WORLD

Of those accompanying Christopher Columbus to the New World, the interpreter Luis de Torres, a Jew who had been baptized the day before the expedition set sail, was the first European to set foot on American soil. Other Jews accompanied Hernando Cortes in 1519. Scores of Jews from the Spanish Inquisition ended up in the New World. It was a small band of Jewish refugees from Brazil who in 1654 sought a home in New Amsterdam (later New York). The saga of North American Jewry had begun.

---

8. Martin Luther, *On the Jews and Their Lies,* 1543; trans. Martin H. Bertram, in *Luther's Works,* 47:268-72. The total treatise is found on pp. 137-306.

5

American Jewry

It was the young Jewish poetess Emma Lazarus (1849-1887) who wrote the poem inscribed on the Statue of Liberty: "Give me your tired, your poor, your huddled masses yearning to breathe free." Indeed, the promise of freedom and opportunity drew the Jewish people to the shores of America: the belief that they could be themselves in this young country. And yet, America has changed the peoples who immigrate to her shores, and the Jewish people were no exception. In part 3 (chaps.7-10) we will briefly familiarize ourselves with the three major branches of American Judaism and the other groups affected by this process of change. It is important at this time, however, to survey the history of the American Jewish experience.[1]

THE COLONIAL PERIOD

The Inquisitions in Spain and Portugal had forced a small group of Jews to emigrate to the Dutch colony of Recife in Brazil. The Jewish people had found the Dutch to be more tolerant of their religious beliefs both in Europe and in the New World, and Recife was a prosperous center for the sugar industry in which Jews were heavily involved.

1. Outside of the primary documents cited and quoted in this chapter, printed copies of various quotations may be found in sources listed in the Suggested Reading section of this book. Among these are Jonathan Sarna, ed., *The American Jewish Experience* (New York: Holmes & Meier, 1986); and the *Encyclopedia Judaica*. Please compare a resource work that is not cited, but is a fine work: Paul R. Mendes-Flohr and Jehuda Reinharz, eds., *The Jew in the Modern World: A Documentary History* (New York: Oxford U., 1980).

Anti-Semitism, however, soon followed. A Jew was burned at the stake in Mexico (New Spain) in 1528, and sporadic Spanish and Portugese persecutions and murders of Jews occurred in the Americas for the next century. In the 1630s, a full-fledged inquisition was carried out in South America, and to the fledgling Jewish community's horror, the dreaded Portugese captured their oasis of Recife from the Dutch in 1654. Hurriedly, Jews boarded ships to islands throughout the Caribbean.

Twenty-three of those fugitives took refuge in the cramped and rat-infested holds of a tiny sailing vessel bound for the Dutch community of New Amsterdam. By September, Manhattan Island lay before them, a haven of hope, opportunity, and life. Those Jewish immigrants were technically Dutch subjects and knew that the Dutch had helped them in the past. They believed they had found a safe haven, a home where they could live in peace.

Although most of the populace of Dutch Calvinists seemed undisturbed by the presence of Jews in their community, the governor of New Amsterdam, Peter Stuyvésant (1592-1672), hated them. A staunch member of the Dutch Reformed church, Stuyvesant was determined to keep Jews (as well as Catholics, Lutherans, and Baptists) out of his colony. He had complained to his superiors on several occasions about Jewish merchants who were his competitors. Now, he petitioned the directors of the Dutch West India Company, the group that had established the colony, for permission to ban Jews. He wrote on September 22, 1654:

> The Jews who have arrived would nearly all like to remain here, but learning that they (with their customary usury and deceitful trading with the Christians) were very repugnant to the inferior magistrates, as also to the people having the most affection for you; the Deaconry also fearing that owing to their present indigence they might become a charge in the coming winter, we have, for the benefit of this weak and newly developing place and the land in general, deemed it useful to require them in a friendly way to depart; praying also most seriously in this connection, for ourselves as also for the general community of your worships, that the deceitful race—such hateful enemies and blasphemers of the name of Christ—be not allowed to further infect and trouble this new colony to the detraction of your worships and the dissatisfaction of your worships' most affectionate subjects.

One notes the same anti-Semitic canards about the Jewish people in these brief sentences that have plagued the Jewish experience—Jews are deceitful and worship money; Jews may convert the populace to Judaism and lead Christians astray; Jews are haters of Christ, enemies, Christ-killers; Jews are infectious bacteria; and so on. All of this couched in polite, religious language.

Jews throughout American history would be harassed with such slander. When the canards were not believed, anti-Semites (like Peter Stuyvesant) would point to economic factors, claiming that Jews would most certainly become wards of the Gentile community—financial liabilities. For instance, four centuries later, when Adolf Hitler announced to the free world on January 30, 1939, that they could have the Jews of Europe, public opinion polls showed that although the American people were becoming sympathetic to the plight of the Jews, they believed that the United States's economy was not strong enough to assimilate the refugees. Coast guard ships forced the S.S. *St. Louis* (carrying 907 desperate Jewish refugees) back to Europe in 1939, and New York Senator Robert Wagner found it impossible to get a bill passed in Congress that would have admitted twenty thousand Jewish refugee children from Nazi Germany. Ironically, between 1933 and 1945, two million visas went unused because they were "saved" for other groups.

Peter Stuyvesant thought the Jews "repugnant" because they demanded equality and humane treatment as Dutch citizens. Those Jewish refugees wrote members of their own community, stockholders in the Dutch West India Company, to help them gain the same freedom Gentiles had in the territory of New Netherlands. Throughout modern Jewish history, Jews have been vilified on the one hand as "pushy" if they stood up for their rights and on the other hand as pacifist "sheep to the slaughter" if their rights were taken from them.

The colonial refugees knew their options. In 1655 five thousand Jews were living in a Venice ghetto, surrounded by high walls with bricked-up windows from a foundry (Italian *getto* or *ghetto*) appropriated for this purpose a century before. Two gates were manned by Christian guards, and two boats patrolled the outer canals that encircled the ghetto. And Jews had to pay a tax for this "separation." Jewish ghettos dotted the European continent after the Reformation period. The word *ghetto* would have an ugly meaning for blacks and other minorities in America at a later date.

The Dutch West India Company in Amsterdam, Netherlands, replied to Director General Peter Stuyvesant that in New Netherlands the Jewish people were "to enjoy the same liberty that is granted them in this country ... with respect to civil and political liberties." Jews were also not to be "hindered" from trade. Nevertheless, Jews were *not* "entitled to a license to exercise and carry on their religion in synagogues or gatherings." The "beneficent" company officials noted that the Jews "have many times requested of us the free and public excercise of their abominable religion, but this cannot yet be accorded to them."

Members of the Jewish community continued to petition for rights in New Amsterdam, and new immigrants bolstered their numbers. Asser Levy (died 1681) was one of the few original refugees who remained in the area, and his descendants can be traced throughout the 1700s. A butcher and tanner by trade, Levy became a successful merchant and land developer, fighting for the right to stand guard duty with the militia of Christian burghers (legal citizens of a town). In 1657, Levy became a burgher himself—the first Jewish "citizen" on the American continent.

The Dutch surrendered New Amsterdam to the British in 1664, and the name changed to New York. Jews had been gaining civil rights in Great Britain during the seventeenth century, and these gains were transferred to the New World. Jews were permitted to hold public office, and private homes were used as synagogues. By 1727 the Jewish community had won the right to have the words "on the true faith of a Christian" struck from their public oaths. The first official Jewish synagogue to be built in New York was *Shearith Israel* (The Remnant of Israel). Constructed in 1729-1730, the building has since been replaced and the Sephardic congregation has moved to Central Park West, but Shearith Israel still exists today as the oldest Jewish congregation in the United States.

Jews also were settling in other urban centers during the 1740s, such as Philadelphia, Pennsylvania, and Charleston, South Carolina. Small Jewish communities that did not survive in earlier decades in Newport, Rhode Island, and Savannah, Georgia would be reestablished by the time of the American Revolution. A few Jews moved west during the Colonial Period, but most lived near the East Coast. Jews from New York even founded a new congregation to the north in Montreal in December 1768 (also called Shearith Israel). Approximately 250 Jews lived in the colonies before 1700; by the American Revolution the number had expanded to between two and three thousand.

Never more than one-tenth of one percent of the American colonial population, Jews were heavily involved as merchant shippers and were an important factor in the candle industry (an indispensable commodity before electricity). The majority of Jews were lower-middle-class shopkeepers and craftsmen. They faithfully attended synagogue and were devoted to Torah. Ashkenazic Jews (German-Polish) composed the majority before the Revolution; however, their synagogues followed the Sephardic liturgy.

It was during the Colonial Period that the American Jewish community established patterns that are detectable in the modern period. For instance, they concentrated in urban areas and yet were not adverse to the pioneering spirit. They faced legal restrictions and anti-Semitism but tenaciously struggled for freedom, dignity, and equality. They established social services through the synagogue to take care of their own (and other unfortunates) and to bury their dead (a cemetery was the first acquisition of the Jewish settlers). Education was a priority, both religious and secular, and the Jewish community even subsidized a teacher for poverty-stricken families.

The colonial Jews held fervently to their peoplehood, and yet they became community figures, intensely involved in the emerging American culture. They attempted to unload their Old World prejudices, while contending with Christians and their children who immigrated with millstones of hatred and bigotry hanging around their psyches. For example, early in the 1700s, New York Jewish businessmen generously contributed to the building of an Anglican church. As with many colonial Americans, the quest for religious freedom and individual conscience permeated the soul of the Jewish American. The Jewish colonist firmly believed that he had found more acceptance in his new land than could be found in any other part of the world.

THE EARLY NATIONAL PERIOD

During the Revolutionary War (1775-1783), most Jews fought for the cause of independence side by side with their Christian neighbors. Few Jews supported the British cause in the colonies, because they approved wholeheartedly of revolutionary principles. Jewish merchants helped the warring colonies break blockades and obtain supplies. Polish immigrant and merchant Haym Salomon (1740-1785) was captured by the British, yet managed to pass strategic information to the American army. While operating a business in British-occupied New York, he helped a number of war prisoners to escape back to the revolutionary forces. The personal risks he took and his deep patriotism are representative of many other Jewish patriots during the War.

A considerable number of Jews volunteered for colonial army duty, and many were found in local militias. The French Jew Major Benjamin Nones (d. 1826) served under both the Marquis de Lafayette and George

Washington. Some attained historical distinction. Philadelphia-born Solomon Bush (1753-1795) was seriously wounded and taken prisoner by the British but returned to fight after being released. He obtained the rank of lieutenant colonel in the Continental Army in 1779, the highest rank held by a Jewish officer during the War of Independence. He later joined an abolitionist society to try to end the evil of black enslavement.

David Salisbury Franks (c. 1743-1793) likewise was promoted to the rank of lieutenant colonel in 1780. As an American merchant in Montreal, he aided the colonial attack on Quebec. Returning to Pennsylvania, Franks served as a major in the Continental Army, later becoming a courier to John Jay in Madrid and Benjamin Franklin in Paris. He also served John Adams and Thomas Jefferson and in 1790 became assistant cashier to the newly created Bank of the United States.

The American Revolution brought more colonists in touch with the Jewish community, and many gained a deep respect for a people they found to be much like themselves. Furthermore, the promise of the Declaration of Independence that "all men are created equal" and are endowed with "certain unalienable Rights" was interpreted by the Jewish community in the most positive manner.

The framers of the American Constitution realized the failings of various colonies with respect to religious liberty. They realized that their own personal religious beliefs were threatened under a rigid, intolerant religious code. Both Puritans and Anglicans had required land-holding *and* church membership in "good standing" (their denomination) before a person could vote. Such a system kept out most Gentiles as well as Jews. But those who were not members of the church were still required to pay tithes.

"Is uniformity attainable?" Thomas Jefferson questioned in his *Notes on Virginia.* He concluded, "Millions of innocent men, women, and children, since the introduction of Christianity, have been burnt, tortured, fined, imprisoned; yet we have not advanced one inch towards uniformity. What has been the effect of coercion? To make half the world fools, and the other half hypocrites. To support roguery and error all over the earth."

Little wonder that Jefferson's Virginia was the first state to pass a comprehensive "Bill for Establishing Religious Freedom" in 1785, free of loyalty oaths. New York had extended liberty of conscience regardless of religion in 1777, but required an anti-Catholic test oath for those born abroad. Virginia's Act for Religious Freedom declared in part:

Whereas, Almighty God has created the mind free ... who, being Lord both of body and mind, yet chose not to propagate it by coercions on either, as was in his Almighty power to do; that the impious presumption of legislators and rulers, civil as well as ecclesiastical, who being themselves but fallible and uninspired men, have assumed dominion over the faith of others, setting up their own opinions and modes of thinking as the only true and infallible, and as such endeavoring to impose them on others....

Be it enacted by the General Assembly, That no man shall be compelled to frequent or support any religious worship, place or ministry whatsoever, nor shall be enforced, restrained, molested or burthened, in his body or goods, nor shall otherwise suffer on account of his religious opinions or belief; but that all men shall be free to profess, and by argument to maintain, their opinions in matters of religion, and that the same shall in no wise diminish, enlarge or affect their civil capacities.

The Virginia Act of 1785 concluded that "if any act shall be hereafter passed to repeal the present, or to narrow its operation, such act will be an infringement of natural right."

That Article VI of the *Constitution of the United States of America* (1789) proclaimed that "no religious Test shall ever be required as a qualification to any Office of public Trust under the United States" and the First Amendment to this Constitution added that "Congress shall make no law respecting an establishment of religion, or prohibiting the free exercise thereof" was not only making religious liberty federal law, but also was a declaration against the United States becoming a "Christian state" (as happened in the Roman Empire).

The lessons of history were considered, and the verdict was inescapable. The commencement of the American governmental and social experiment (although incomplete in practice with regard to blacks, Jews, Catholics, and women) was to serve as an example to the rest of the world. Many believe that the French National Assembly used the Virginia Act of 1785 as an authoritative precedent for its "Declaration of the Rights of Man and of the Citizen" (1789).

Alas, both in Europe and the United States, there was still much to do. Anti-Semitic stereotypes and suspicion continued. The Jewish people found that legal freedom did not necessitate social freedom. Besides, although federal law granted Jews religious liberty, state legislatures enacted laws as they saw fit. New England, Maryland, North Carolina, New

Hampshire, and New Jersey granted religious liberty *only* to Protestants. If Jews did not avow their faith in Protestantism, they could not hold public office.

The Jewish community, however, had fought in the Revolutionary War and had given their lives for freedom and independence. They now joined others in fighting for complete religious liberty, and by 1830 the majority of the above states had granted Jews full rights. To its discredit, New Hampshire had anti-Jewish legislation on its books until 1877.

Nevertheless, the early national period was an exciting time for the American Jewish people, and they felt quite comfortable in American society. They loved their new nation, and they strove diligently to be a part of its culture. When President George Washington visited Newport, Rhode Island, in 1790, Moses Sexias, Warden of the Hebrew Congregation, was authorized to write: "Permit the children of the stock of Abraham to approach you with the most cordial affection and esteem for your person and merits and to join with our fellow-citizens in welcoming you to New Port."

Moses Sexias compared "the God of Israel's" deliverance of George Washington and the revolutionary forces to that of His deliverance of David, and "the same Spirit" that rested on Daniel to that which rested on Washington. He then conveyed deep-seated feelings to the president which no doubt permeated the Jewish community. He wrote:

> Deprived as we have hitherto been of the invaluable rights of free citizens, we now, with a deep sense of gratitude to the Almighty Disposer of all events, behold a government, erected by the majesty of the people, a government which to bigotry gives no sanction, to persecution no assistance, but generously affording to all liberty of conscience and immunities of citizenship, deeming every one, of whatever nation, tongue or language, equal parts of the great governmental machine. This so ample and extensive federal union whose basis is philanthropy, mutual confidence, and public virtue, we cannot but acknowledge to be the work of the Great God, who ruleth in the armies of heaven and among the inhabitants of the earth, doing whatsoever seemeth him good.

> For all the blessings of civil and religious liberty which we enjoy under an equal and benign administration, we desire to send up our thanks to the Ancient of Days, the great Preserver of Men, beseeching him that the angel who conducted our forefathers through the wilderness into the promised land may graciously conduct you [President Washington]

through all the dangers and difficulties of this mortal life. And when
like Joshua, full of days and full of honor, you are gathered to your
fathers, may you be admitted into the heavenly paradise to partake of
the water of life and the tree of immortality.

Quite pleased with his welcome in Newport, George Washington responded with his own allusions to Scripture, underscoring that "the government of the United States, which gives to bigotry no sanction, to persecution no assistance, requires only that they who live under its
protection should demean themselves as good citizens, in giving it on all
occasions their effectual support . . . every one shall sit in safety under his
own vine and fig tree."

Receiving similar support from Jewish congregations in New York,
Philadelphia, Charleston, and Richmond, President Washington wrote,
"The affection of such a people [the Jews] is a treasure beyond the reach
of calculation." President John Adams wrote the greatest Jewish leader of
the time period, Mordecai Manuel Noah (1785-1851), that although the
United States "has done much" he wished "it may do more; and annul
every narrow idea in religion, government and commerce." And yet,
when Noah received the first consular appointment ever given to a Jew
by the United States government, it was to Tunis, a Muslim hotbed of pi-
racy with which the U.S. had hostile relations. Secretary of State James
Monroe curtly dismissed Noah on the grounds of "the Religion which
you profess." Jews did not often seek elective office during the pre-Civil
War years.

By the 1820s, most Jews were second-generation or third-genera-
tion Americans who spoke fluent English. They shared in the prosperity
of the nation and wanted to immerse themselves in its culture. For
some, this meant intermarriage and total assimilation. Most tried to adapt
to society while maintaining the basic traditions of Judaism. Demands for
religious reform occurred during this period (see chap. 8), and Jews
moved westward, making traditional practices all the more difficult.
Charleston, South Carolina, became a center of reform, boasting an educated and literary-minded community, at home in the classics and modern European literature, devotees of music and poetry. Penina Moise
from Charleston became a prolific writer and composer of hymns. These
hymns were incorporated into the Reform synagogues and are still to be
found in the Reform Union Hymnal today.

The extraordinary Mordecai Manuel Noah exemplifies the Jewish
belief in America's potential, commitment to pluralism, quest for suc-

cess, adaptation to culture, devotion to tradition, and synagogue-centered faith in the Early National Period. Born in Philadelphia to a bankrupt merchant and Revolutionary soldier, Noah was apprenticed as a carver and became a clerk in the U.S. Treasury. In 1808 he worked in Philadelphia for the presidential campaign of James Madison and moved to Charleston the next year. In Charleston he edited the *City Gazette,* strongly supported the War of 1812 and in 1813 was appointed consul to Tunis. Recalled two years later, he established himself in New York City and became editor of the *National Advocate* newspaper.

In the 1820s, Noah was appointed to the office of High Sheriff, becoming an influential political leader. He also wrote many plays, most depicting his patriotic fervor, and was a popular Jewish speaker. A strong supporter of the synagogue (in New York he belonged to Shearith Israel) and Jewish tradition, Noah tried to establish the Jewish colony of Ararat on Grand Island in the Niagara River near Buffalo, New York. According to Noah, this asylum was for Jews throughout the world, a place "where they can enjoy that peace, comfort and happiness which have been denied them through the intolerance and misgovernment of former ages." Although this colony failed, the experience turned Noah's attention toward Eretz Yisrael, and he openly advocated a national home for the Jewish people in the Holy Land a half century before Theodor Herzl's political Zionist movement. He also was a key spokesman in America in protesting the Damascus Affair of 1840.

Jews in America joined Jews throughout the world in petitioning their respective governments to intervene to stop the blood libel atrocity that was occurring in Damascus, Syria. When an Italian Capuchin friar named Thomas disappeared in Damascus with his Muslim servant on February 5, 1840, the other Catholic monks spread the rumor that the Jews had murdered these men to obtain their blood for Passover. The monks provided forged passages reputed to be from the Talmud to support their contention. High government officials in Syria accepted this lie, while Christian and Muslim mobs ravaged the Jewish community in Damascus. Wholesale arrests of Jews took place. A number of Jews were tortured by Syrian officials into "confessions," and sixty-three Jewish children were imprisoned to force their mothers to reveal the supposed "hiding place" of the corpses.

Some bones were later found in a sewer in the Jewish quarter and immediately were declared to be those of the friar. Although there was no proof for this, the monks buried them with great fanfare. The inscription on "Thomas's tomb" stated that he was a saint tortured by Jews.

Scores of Syrian Jews were slated to be hanged, but the Jewish outcry from abroad prevented more from dying in this affair. Jews worldwide, including those in France, Britain, and the United States, were reminded that medieval anti-Semitism was not dead in their "enlightened" and "modern" times. Although the Ottoman Empire issued an edict against the blood libel, the Catholics in Damascus continued for years to tell foreign tourists about the "saintly friar" who had been tortured and murdered "by the Jews"—who had been saved from their just fate of hanging by the conspirers to control the world, "international Jewry." Such falsehoods served to fan the flames of anti-Semitism and, even in America, Jewish people would feel the repercussions.

By 1826, six thousand Jews were scattered thoughout the United States; by 1840, nearly fifteen thousand. Although the American Revolution had bankrupted most of the merchant shippers, Jew and Gentile alike, new avenues of trade were expanding in the fur industry, government service, retail stores, and land speculation. When the Louisiana Territory was purchased in 1803, Jews were there. An English Jew, Joseph Philipson, had a general store in St. Louis. In the Northwest Territory, Joseph Jonas was the only Jew in Cincinnati in 1817 among a few Christian settlers. Within seven years there were enough Jews in Cincinnati to form a congregation. They felt the need to have orthodox tradition modified, and Cincinnati Jews were very receptive to the Reform movement.

THE GERMAN PERIOD

Economic turmoil and civil unrest in German-speaking Central Europe initiated a large emigration movement from Europe to the United States in the 1840s. This emigration soon included masses from Poland, Austria, Bohemia, Hungary, and other areas, but in Jewish American history the influence of the German Jew is so dominant that 1840-1880 is generally known as the "German Period."

At the turn of the nineteenth century, the Jews in German territories were struggling under an assessment of special taxes and a multitude of restrictions. Bavaria sought to control its Jewish population by legally limiting the number of marriages among Jews. Prussia blamed the Jews for its humiliating defeat to Napoleon, accusing them of plotting secretly with the great French general. Johann Gottlieb Fichte, professor of philosophy at the University of Berlin, in 1807 described Jews as members of a decadent, mongrel race. In spite of his deep respect for the Bible and even for some individual Jews, Fichte wrote: "A mighty state stretches across almost all the countries of Europe, hostile in intent and in constant strife with everyone else. . . . This is Jewry." Fichte insisted that the "pure" Germanic peoples could create a new era in the midst of their current unemployment and famine. At the same university, history professor Christian Friedrich Ruehs emphasized that Jews should not be citizens of the "Christian" German state and that allowing Jews to prosper had brought decline and decay.

In 1816, a year of severe famine and unemployment in Germany, Jakob Friedrich Fries, an anti-Semitic philosopher who lectured at both Jena and Heidelberg universities, led demonstrations of ultranationalist students against Jews, urging that the Jewish people be "destroyed root and branch." In 1819, riots against Jews did break out in Germany and spread to neighboring countries. Crying, "Hep! Hep! Hep! Death and destruction to all the Jews," mobs smashed windows and looted businesses and homes of Jews. Scattered throughout the countryside and villages as craftsmen, small traders, and merchants, Jews were not only humiliated, but fearful. Knowing that business and life under such circumstances was difficult (if not impossible), they emigrated by the thousands. The American Jewish population more than doubled to fifteen thousand in 1840, fifty thousand in 1850, and one hundred fifty thousand in 1860. By the Civil War, the American Jewish community was almost entirely an Ashkenazic community, deeply influenced culturally by German Jewry.

Many of these German immigrants traveled to small towns in the Midwest and South. Quite a few became itinerant peddlers, finally settling in towns where they established general stores, dry goods shops, and clothing outlets. From these humble beginnings, a number of large department store chains emerged. For example, Bavarian Adam Gimbel (1817-1896) peddled dry goods along the Mississippi in the late 1830s before opening his first general store in Vincennes, Indiana, in 1842. The Gimbel Brothers department store chain was founded by his seven sons, who opened stores in Milwaukee, Philadelphia, and finally New York City. In New York, Gimbels became one of the city's largest retail establishments, catapulting it into national prominence. In a similar manner, famed Levi Strauss (1829-1902) was a German Jew who arrived in New York on the brink of the California gold rush of 1849. Traveling West, he built a strong business on sturdy blue denim trousers that were reinforced with copper rivets. *Levis* is still a household word nearly a century and a half later, popular throughout the world. Noted for his charitable spirit, Levi Strauss gave large sums of money to Jewish, Protestant, and Catholic orphanages, as well as to other philanthropic endeavors.

Through another family of German Jewish department store merchants, one can view the correlation between economic success, public service, and philanthropy. Lazarus Straus (1809-1898) immigrated alone from Germany to Georgia in 1852. His wife and three sons joined him two years later. Moving his family to New York City in 1865, he became a successful crockery importer. His sons, Isidor (1845-1912, who died in the sinking of the *Titanic)*, and Nathan (1848-1931), became partners in the R. H. Macy Department Store in 1874, where they had rented the basement to display their father's glassware. By 1887, they were sole owners of Macy's.

Isidor was elected to fill an unexpired term for a deceased congressman (1894-1895) and served on the New York and New Jersey Bridge Commission. Nathan served as New York Park Commissioner and as Health Commissioner. He was instrumental in establishing a milk pasteurization laboratory in New York and emergency relief centers to distribute coal and food and to give lodging to the poor. The entire Straus family was deeply involved in philanthropic endeavors and Jewish affairs in the United States as well as in Eretz Yisrael.

While the family business was being expanded, Lazarus's youngest son, Oscar (1850-1926), was educated in law at Columbia University. Becoming a reformer and political activist, Oscar fought during his lifetime for open immigration policies, civil service reform, sound money, low tariffs, the direct primary, and regulation of trusts. Appointed as minister to Turkey by President Grover Cleveland in 1887, Oscar Straus worked to secure Christian missionaries some rights in the Islamic country. President Theodore Roosevelt appointed Oscar as a jurist to the International Court of Arbitration at The Hague, and he became Roosevelt's Secretary of Commerce and Labor from 1906 to 1909. This made Oscar Straus the first Jewish person to hold a cabinet post in the United States, and he interceded for Jews who were being persecuted and murdered in Russia and Romania.

In 1906 Oscar helped found the American Jewish Committee, in which his brothers and family would become involved. Oscar was also the first president of the American Jewish Historical Society. As a writer, he published *The Origin of the Republican Form of Government in the United States of America* (1887 and 1925). He named his son, Roger Williams Straus, who was born in 1893, after the great Baptist reformer he admired and published *Roger Williams, the Pioneer of Religious Liberty in the United States* in 1896. A Reform Jew, Oscar Straus found great similarities between the mission of America and the mission of Judaism. His autobiography, *Under Four Administrations* (1922), appeared four years before his death.

German-Jewish doctors, lawyers, butchers, and craftsmen also spread across the continental United States before the Civil War. They opened up the Midwest, establishing communities and founding synagogues. Their synagogues were characterized by Reform Judaism, although few openly were founded upon Reform principles. Usually an Orthodox congregation would change a few of its rituals or adapt some English liturgy into the Hebrew service. The immigration of Reform rabbis led to more radical changes (note chap. 8). Rabbi Isaac Mayer Wise, an immigrant from Bohemia in 1846, settled in Cincinnati in 1854, becoming the spokesman for the Reform movement in the United States. By the time of the Civil War, dozens of congregations had taken steps toward Reform, and large-scale expansion of the Reform movement occurred in the 1860s and 1870s.

Many of the ten thousand Jewish soldiers who fought for their respective regions during the Civil War (1861-1865) were recent German-Jewish immigrants. The Northern army was forced to rescind its restriction that only Christian clergymen could serve as chaplains, and the first Jewish chaplains were appointed in 1862. As the Confederate Army began to lose the war, anti-Semitism arose more frequently in the South. Judah Benjamin (1811-1884), a prominent Southern lawyer and the first professing Jew to be elected to the United States Senate, was barraged with anti-Semitic slander. A friend and confidant of Confederate President Jefferson Davis, Benjamin served under him as Attorney General, Secretary of War, and, later, Secretary of State. Judah Benjamin was the only leading Confederate to choose exile rather than to live in the defeated South. He went to England, forging a more distinguished legal career that progressed into his being appointed Queen's Counsel.

It was in the North, however, that the single most public anti-Semitic act ever taken by a high official of the United States government occurred. An action taken by Union Army general Ulysses S. Grant (1822-1885) underscored the anti-Jewish prejudice rampant among military officials during the Civil War. On November 10, 1862, General Grant ordered that "no Jews are to be permitted to travel on the railroad south from any point." He explained that the Jews "are such an intolerable nuisance that the department must be purged of them." Then, on December 17, 1862, Grant issued General Order Number 11 from his headquarters. Whether he was influenced by subordinates, Gentile cotton buyers, officials in the War Department, or his own family is a matter of historical debate; but this order is the harshest federal edict against Jewish people in all of American history. General Order Number 11 stated:

> The Jews, as a class violating every regulation of trade established by the Treasury Department and also department orders, are hereby expelled from the [military] department within twenty-four hours from the receipt of this order. Post commanders will see that all of this class of people be furnished passes and required to leave, and any one returning after such notification will be arrested and held in confinement until an opportunity occurs of sending them out as prisoners, unless furnished with permit from headquarters. No passes will be given these people to visit headquarters for the purpose of making personal application for trade permits.

On the same day, General Grant acknowledged to the Assistant Secretary of War, "I instructed the commanding officer of Columbus (Mississippi) to refuse all permits to Jews to come South, and I have frequently had them expelled from the department." He also caricatured, "The Jews seem to be a privileged class that can travel anywhere."

President Abraham Lincoln insisted that the order be revoked immediately. A delegation of Jews from St. Louis who later traveled to Washington, D.C. to thank Lincoln, reported that Grant had written a note to the President asserting that "these people [Jews] are the descendants of those who crucified the Saviour and from the specimens I have here, the race has not improved."

During his own presidential campaign, Grant apologized, and the majority of Jews (who had become Republicans, adopting the party of Lincoln) voted for him. During his presidency from 1869-1877, Grant appointed a number of Jews to important posts in his administration. In fact, in the post-war Reconstruction Era, the majority of the Jewish community fared well. Peddlers were able to branch out into their own retail stores and small shops. Successful merchants were able to enter the developing fields of finance and investment banking. In the South, Jewish storekeepers were noted for addressing black customers with respect, using "Mr." and "Mrs.," and unintentionally garnering additional customers over more bigoted storeowners.

German Jews held tenaciously to family solidarity and unity. Even the large merchant families made the Friday evening meal a special time of fellowship as children and grandchildren gathered at the "patriarch's" home. They also broadened the framework of organized Jewish life. The

Sephardim had centered all Jewish communal life in the synagogue. The Ashkenazic German Jews founded independent fraternal societies and charitable organizations. An enduring example is B'nai B'rith. On October 13, 1843, the fraternal order of B'nai B'rith (Sons of the Covenant) was established as an organization to unite Jews to help humanity, promote moral character, support science and art, to aid the sick and poor, to combat prejudice and persecution, among many activities. Today, it is the world's oldest and largest Jewish service organization.

Both traditional and reformist Jews could gather in such organizations. Jewish Sunday schools were developed; secular and religious schools for the poor were begun; and benevolent activities flourished. The Hebrew Ladies Benevolent Society in Atlanta was chartered in 1870 and is only one of scores of women's clubs founded in the latter decades of the nineteenth century to supply immigrants with food, coal, and clothing. Jewish social clubs were also established because even wealthy Jews were prohibited from upper-class Gentile clubs on account of "religion" and "race."

Anti-Semitic stereotypes and caricatures permeated these decades, even reaching the press. Cartoons featuring Jews in unfavorable light and with grotesque features began to appear in magazines and newspapers. The *Boston Saturday Evening Gazette* in 1875 openly complained about Jews: "It is strange that a [Jewish] nation that boasts so many good traits should be so obnoxious." In 1877 a Jewish lawyer was blackballed by the New York Bar Association on the grounds that the association did not want Jews as members. A year before, a hotel in New Jersey published in the newspaper that it would not admit Jews, and in 1877 Joseph Seligman, a Pennsylvania German-Jewish peddler turned prosperous New York banker (J. & W. Seligman and Company, with branches in London, Paris, and Frankfurt) and his family were refused lodging at the fashionable Grand Union Hotel in Saratoga Springs, New York, because of their "race."

And yet, the decade after the Civil War was the greatest period of synagogue construction that the United States had known up to that time. By 1875, one quarter of a million Jews were in this country; and German-Jewish influence and success was evident in a growing number of writers, professors, artists, and professionals that prospered in the last two decades of the nineteenth century. In December of 1890, the Census Bureau published a report on the social status of ten thousand German-Jewish families who had immigrated to the United States from 1850-1880. Approximately 50 percent were in business; 20 percent were accountants, clerks, bookkeepers, and assorted white-collar workers; 12 percent worked manually, but included jewelers, watchmakers, tailors, and printers; 5 percent were financiers; 2 percent professionals; 2 percent farmers and ranchers; less than 2 percent were peddlers, unskilled laborers, or domestic servants. American-Jewish scientists were relatively few at this time, but Jewish physicians were growing in numbers and prestige. Abraham Jacobi (1830-1919), a refugee from the 1848 revolution in Germany, invented the laryngoscope (another beat him to the patent office) and later became famous as the father of American pediatrics.

Perhaps the greatest influence of the German-Jewish community was felt in the religious sphere, where "progressive religion" seemed to be the wave of the future. The Union of American Hebrew Congregations was founded in 1873, and by 1890 the census gave Reform Judaism more than half of the congregational memberships and synagogue buildings in this country. The rabbi's sermon had become an important part of the weekly service, similar to the nineteenth-century Protestant's Sunday pulpit.

Nevertheless, a new surge of traditional Judaism accompanied one of the greatest challenges America was to face. Between 1880 and 1930, 27 million immigrants would travel to America's shores, the large majority from Eastern Europe. Of these, more than two million were Eastern European Jews, by 1930 constituting more than 3 percent of the total population of the United States. They would infuse an Old World spirit into Jewish religion and culture, creating a complex entity that would overwhelm the German-Jewish community. The Eastern European Jews would also affect geographical distribution and politics, providing a marked contrast to the social status and institutions of German-American Jewry.

EAST EUROPEAN JEWRY

In stark contrast to most new immigrants, who were males (single or leaving their families behind), the massive Jewish immigration to America from 1880-1930 was a movement of families. They had little incentive to return to their former countries and were determined to make the United States their home. Among the new arrivals to America between 1880 and 1910, Jews were second in numbers only to the Italians. Because of the East European (areas of the Russian Empire, Austria, Poland, Hungary, Romania, etc.) migration, the Jewish population soared from a primarily German Jewish 280,000 in 1880 to more than 4.5 million in 1930. By 1919, the Jewish community of the United States was the largest in the world.

Jews had been immigrating from Eastern Europe since the Colonial Period, but their numbers were small. After the Civil War, an increase in anti-Semitism around the world helped these numbers to grow somewhat. In 1881 the Russian Czar Alexander II (czar from 1855-1881) was assassinated, and Jews emigrated in droves from Russia, nine out of ten coming to the United States. Alexander II had been beloved by the Jews of Russia because he had moderated the repressive measures leveled on the Jewish people in the nineteenth century by former czars—men who viewed the Jews as a group of leeches and parasites on the Russian state. Jews had been limited by those czars in vocations they could enter, places they could live, and land they could own. At the same time, the former czars initiated a full-scale attempt to convert the Russian Jewish population to Russian Orthodox Christianity—an effort to eradicate Judaism.

Although Alexander II continued the cultural "reeducation" effort of his predecessors toward the Jews, especially attempting to assimilate the upper-class Jews, he did ease restrictions on vocations and areas of settlement. Jews viewed him as a more helpful and enlightened leader than his predecessors. His death gave way once again to outbreaks of violence against Jews, harsh laws against the Jewish community, and expulsion of Jews from their homes in many areas. The ridiculous rumor had been spread that the Jews themselves had killed Czar Alexander II, and the Russian government permitted Jews to be murdered and their homes to be looted (often during Christmas and Easter). The czarist Russian government initiated a program of systematic discrimination against Jews that would last for decades. Jewish children were expelled from schools; Jews were even expelled from Moscow in 1891-1892.

A second wave of *pogroms* (a Russian word meaning attack and massacre) began in Kishinev in 1903 during Passover. Forty-five Jews were killed, hundreds injured, and fifteen hundred homes and businesses were looted. Pogroms continued regularly for the next few years. In Odessa in 1905, more than three hundred Jews were killed, and thousands were brutally beaten. In Bialystok in June 1906, eighty Jews were murdered as their homes and businesses were looted and burned. The Russian police and military forces stood by and watched this pogrom, at times opening fire themselves on the terrorized Jewish people.

When the czar was overthrown by the Bolsheviks in 1917, conditions did not improve for the majority of the Jewish populace. The Red Army killed hundreds of Jews in 1918, while the newly liberated Ukrainian soldiers killed thousands. It is estimated that from the death of Czar Alexander II to 1920-1921 when the Red Army regained control of the Ukraine (killing thousands of Jews "for revenge"), approximately eighty thousand Jews were murdered and many times that number badly beaten and wounded.

The Eastern European Jews developed self-defense organizations to protect themselves as much as possible, and a large movement was rallied to create a homeland for the Jewish people in Eretz Yisrael. It was the recently arrived Russian Jewish immigrants in America who would support Theodor Herzl's political Zionist movement in the early decades of the twentieth century; most established German Jews would initially oppose Zionism.

Zionism

Zionism comes from the word *Zion*, an early synonym for Jerusalem. In pre-modern times, Zion was tied to the Messiah, His deliverance, and a return from exile to the Land of Promise: Eretz Yisrael. The Zion idea was enshrined in the hearts of Jews throughout the world and was firmly tied to the Jewish religious experience throughout the centuries of dispersion. A small number of Jews had always remained in Eretz Yisrael, and their numbers were augmented by refugees of the expulsions from Europe, culminating in the Spanish Inquisition.

The advent of the nineteenth century found Eretz Yisrael under the control of the Ottoman Empire, the group of Turks that at one time subdued the entire Middle East and was knocking at the door of Europe. As we have seen in chapter 4, during the sixteenth century the Jewish people had fared well in this empire. By the nineteenth century, however, the Ottoman administration was extremely corrupt, and Eretz Yisrael was in a state of decline. The area's total population was under 250,000 in the early decades of the 1880s, and only a small portion of the land was utilized for agriculture. Local chieftains fought each other for supremacy in the mountainous rural areas, and Bedouin tribes roamed the desert areas to the east and south. Security was minimal, and entire villages were destroyed by warfare or abandoned. Egypt conquered and controlled the area from 1832 to 1840, but the Ottomans regained control.

After 1840 both Jewish and Arab immigration increased. Representatives of Christian churches from Europe and America, as well as Muslims and Christians from the territories of Syria, Lebanon, Egypt, North Africa, and Turkey, all came to Eretz Yisrael. The Russian pogroms of the latter 1800s brought numerous Jewish settlers, and groups such as *Hoveve Zion* (Lovers of Zion) were organized in the 1880s to raise money and to send Jewish settlers to the Holy Land. In the United States, philanthropic Reform German Jews even contributed funds to help the settlers.

Nevertheless, by 1895 only 10 percent of Eretz Yisrael was cultivated. Absentee landlords purchased hundreds of thousands of acres from the financially strapped Ottomans and settled Jewish and Arab tenant farmers on some of it (for example, Sursuk, a Greek entrepreneur from Beirut, owned more than 60,000 acres). By the end of World War I, 144 wealthy landowners owned approximately 750,000 acres in Eretz Yisrael. Concurrently, Jews owned and had reclaimed from marsh areas and deserts more than 100,000 acres. Urban areas also expanded (in 1909 a group of Jaffa Jews founded Tel Aviv, destined to become modern Israel's largest city).

The actual term *Zionism* was not used until the 1890s. It grew to prominence when Theodor Herzl (1860-1904) founded a modern Zionism based on political and economic theory. Herzl was born in Hungary and studied law at the University of Vienna. He became a journalist and a playwright during the latter part of the nineteenth century and witnessed the rising anti-Semitism in France, Germany, and Austria. Herzl had wrestled with the problem of anti-Semitism for years, but the climax of Jew-hatred was reached during the trial and subsequent public degradation of Captain Alfred Dreyfus during 1894 and 1895. The French government charged Dreyfus with treason, but Herzl knew that his real crime was being a Jew. As a Paris correspondent for the *Neue Freie Presse (New Free Press)*, Herzl felt the bitterness of the French people against the Jewish people and knew that this one Jew was being tried and condemned for all Jew-hatred. The nation had judged the Jewish people unworthy of life as equals, in spite of the declarations of freedom and liberty in 1789.

With the Dreyfus affair igniting thoughts that had been latent in Herzl's mind, he began to sketch plans for a solution. In mid-February 1896 he published a small booklet entitled *Der Judenstaat (The Jewish State: An Attempt at a Modern Solution of the Jewish Question* in the English translation). His main thesis was that anti-Semitism was inevitable as long as the majority of Jewish people lived outside their own homeland. He expounded political, economic, and technical efforts that he believed were necessary to create a functioning Jewish state. He called the First Zionist Congress to meet in Basel, Switzerland, in August of 1897, and more than two hundred delegates from all over the world attended. Herzl was named president of the newly formed World Zionist Organization.

Thus, the political Zionist movement was indeed "launched." The platform drawn up at this congress guided the Zionist movement for the next fifty years. The Basel program read:

> Zionism seeks to create for the Jewish people a home in Palestine secured by public law. The Congress contemplates the following means to attainment of this end.
>
> 1. The promotion by appropriate means of the settlement in Palestine of Jewish agriculturalists, artisans and manufacturers.
> 2. The organization and binding together of the whole of Jewry by means of appropriate institutions, both local and international, in accordance with the laws of each country.
> 3. The strengthening and fostering of Jewish national sentiment and national consciousness.
> 4. Preparatory steps toward obtaining the consent of governments where necessary, in order to reach the goal of Zionism.

The World Zionist Organization had a plan and a purpose. Theodor Herzl died at the age of forty-four, exhausted from negotiations and conferences all over the world. But the Zionist movement continued to grow.

Herzl's thinking was purely practical, secular, and academic. The majority of his followers, though, were traditional religious Eastern European Jews whose link with Theodor Herzl was the desire for restoration of a Jewish state in Eretz Yisrael. Most Reform German Jews initially opposed such a state. At the Pittsburgh Conference of American Rabbis in 1885, they affirmed in a statement of belief: "We consider ourselves no longer a nation but a religious community, and therefore expect neither a return to Palestine nor a sacrificial worship under the sons of Aaron nor the restoration of any of the laws concerning the Jewish State."

The Central Conference of American Rabbis (the Reform rabbinical organization formed by Isaac Mayer Wise in 1889) passed a resolution in July 1897 that was sharply critical of Zionism. It stated:

Resolved that we totally disapprove of any attempt for the establishment of a Jewish state. Such attempts show a misunderstanding of Israel's mission which, from the narrow political and national field, has been expanded to the promotion among the whole human race of the broad and universalistic religion first proclaimed by the Jewish prophets.

Many Jews, however, including some in the reformist ranks, could not "broaden" as much as this statement indicated, either in relation to traditional practices or with regard to Eretz Yisrael. This would give rise to Conservative Judaism (see chap. 9), a compromise group that said, "We cannot live and work in America and be totally Orthodox, but we do not want to liberalize as much as Reform Judaism." In the early decades of the twentieth century, many Eastern European Jews would join the ranks of or be in sympathy with Conservative Judaism.

THE NEW IMMIGRANTS

Eighty percent of the 27 million new immigrants to America had settled in the northeastern section of the United States, mainly in cities. Few of these men, women, and children went to the South. Jews followed this pattern, the majority settling in New York City. Unlike most other immigrant groups who were unskilled and often illiterate, nearly 67 percent of the Jewish male immigrants were classified as skilled workers, and the large majority of Jews were literate. Some worked as carpenters; most used their skills in the garment industry of New York City. In fact, by World War I, Jews made up 70 percent of all workers in New York's clothing industry.

Other Jews worked in factories and in the printing industry. Some pushed peddler carts again, later opening their own neighborhood stores. It is estimated that one-half of the actors, actresses, and popular songwriters in New York in the early decades of the twentieth century were Jewish. For example, comedian George Burns (1896-) was born Nathan Birnbaum and sang for pennies on the street corners of the Lower East Side at the age of seven, before teaming up with his future wife, Gracie Allen, in 1923. Composer George Gershwin (1898-1937), who achieved fame writing music for plays, films, and operas, was born in New York and wrote his first songs while working as a pianist with a music publishing firm.

The factories of this time were dangerous and enslaving. The average immigrant worked ten- to twelve-hour shifts, six days a week. In some areas, whole families (including small children) sewed clothes in their ghetto flats for a pittance. At times, garment workers earned a mere 10 cents an hour. Sometimes they were locked in a room so that they would be at their machines for the duration of their shift. A highly publicized fire at the Triangle Shirtwaist Company in New York City in 1911 brought to the fore the plight of the immigrant laborer. Locked in their upper story room, 146 mostly young Jewish and Italian girls died, scores leaping to their deaths to escape the flames. "They hit the pavement just like hail," one fireman explained. "We could hear the thuds faster than we could see the bodies fall." And yet, those factories were not the worst. In 1913, nearly 80 percent of the clothing firms averaged only five employees. Those were the notorious "sweatshops," where employees during rush periods might work sixteen hours a day in hot, unventilated cells.

Little wonder that Jewish involvement in labor unions was active, committed, and self-sacrificing. Clothing workers in New York and Chicago went out on strike in 1910 and after a long struggle won the right to collective bargaining. Unions such as the ILGWU (International Ladies Garment Workers' Union) fought for shorter hours, higher pay, and safety codes. In 1924, Jews constituted 64 percent of the ILGWU membership, the large majority of Eastern European origin. Others publicized the plight of the immigrant worker. As early as 1884, Felix Adler (1851-1933), a German-born professor at Cornell University and a son of a Reform rabbi, aroused public indignation at the horror of the ghetto tenement buildings. He worked for social and labor reform, including child welfare and medical care for the poor. Julian Mack (1866-1943), professor of law at Northwestern University and the University of Chicago before being appointed a federal judge, had an intense interest in social reform, including the welfare of immigrant children. Lillian Wald (1867-1940), a social worker born in Cincinnati to German-Jewish immigrants, brought nursing care to the East European immigrants of the Lower East Side of New York, supported the trade union movement, and campaigned for the end of child labor and for social reform.

Certainly, it was natural for the traditional East European Jews to congregate together in a "Jewish section," where they could obtain kosher food, read and speak Yiddish (a language derived from medieval High German, written in Hebrew characters with vocabulary borrowings from languages such as Russian, Polish, English, and Hebrew), walk to synagogue, and receive community moral support. In every major American city, a Jewish quarter evolved. In New York it was the Lower East

Side, in Chicago the West Side, in Boston the North End, in Philadelphia the downtown district. In New York's Lower East Side of Manhattan, Russian Jews were crammed into five-story tenement buildings, where rapid congestion, poverty, and hunger abounded. Soon the lower-middle-class German Jews they joined there moved half-way up the east side of Manhattan toward the area of settlement of more prosperous Jews. By 1920, Jews made up 29 percent of the total population of Greater New York City (more than 1.6 million of the 5.6 million residents of the city).

Yet, even in the midst of poverty and backbreaking labor, the Jewish quest for culture and education persisted. Between 1885 and 1915, East European Jews started more than 150 Yiddish-language newspapers and journals. A number of Hebrew periodicals appeared in New York City in the 1880s and 1890s. In 1909 an attempt was even made to publish a Hebrew daily newspaper. Yiddish theaters and lectures (later films and radio) entertained and informed the populace. By 1915, Jews made up one-sixth of the student body at Columbia University, one-fifth at New York University, and a phenomenal 85 percent at New York's City College. New York City's Educational Alliance (which taught English classes) had a daily attendance exceeding five hundred and a waiting list twice as long. A 1908 study showed that although Jews constituted 2 percent of the U.S. population, they represented nearly 9 percent of the college population in the United States, 13 percent of all law students, 6 percent of all dental students, and 18 percent of all pharmaceutical students. Medical schools had stringent population-based quotas, but Jews even managed 3 percent of all medical students that year.

At first, the more Americanized, clean-shaven, English-speaking German Jews were appalled at the hordes of bearded, earlocked Russian and Polish Jews entering the Ellis Island immigration depot. In New York City, German Jews had been two-thirds of the Jewish population in 1870. They rightly feared the increase in prejudice that accompanied all new immigrants. Indeed, American Henry Brooks Adams (1838-1918), the well-known Harvard historian and philosopher (who wrote a nine-volume *History of the United States)*, reflected the common Anglo-Saxon bias among even the intelligensia of America when he wrote from Warsaw, Poland, in 1901 on a European tour: "Warsaw is a big, bustling city, like all other cities, only mostly Jew, in which it is peculiar to Poland. I see little to remark in the streets, nothing in the shops. The people are uglier than on Pennsylvania Avenue which is otherwise my lowest standard. Like all other cities and places, it is evidently flattened out, and has lost most of its characteristics. The Jews and I are the only curious antiquities in it. My only merit as a curio is antiquity, but the Jew is also a curiosity. He makes me creep." A 1913 *Life* magazine cartoon featured a danger sign turned upside down to look like Hebrew letters. The caption read: "Say fellows, them Jews is crowding everybody out! Now they're claiming the whole pond." In fact, four years later *Life* referred to New York City as "Jew York." In 1913, B'nai B'rith formed the Anti-Defamation League, an autonomous organization that aggressively has combated such racial and religious prejudice to the present day.

German Jews soon realized that anti-Semitism was no respecter of culture, assimilation, wealth, or Americanization. They began to help their East European brethren. By 1909 there were more than two thousand Jewish charities in the United States, and Jewish philanthropists in that year contributed more than $10 million to their people alone (not to mention the millions of dollars contributed to other groups and charities). Education paid off as well, and many second-generation Jews became independently employed. By the 1930s, Jews made up more than one-half of New York City's lawyers, physicians, and dentists. Immigration historians have constantly noted that no twentieth-century "minority" has risen as quickly socially or economically as the descendants of the East European Jewish immigrants.

In Chicago, the Jewish population grew from approximately ten thousand Jews in 1880 to more than a quarter of a million Jews by 1930 (8 percent of the total population of Chicago). Immigrants of East European origin accounted for 85 percent of this Jewish community after World War I. Chicago's German Jewish philanthropist, Julius Rosenwald (1862-1932), helped not only his own people but others as well. Rosenwald was born in Springfield, Illinois, to German Jewish immigrants. He worked his way from clerking in his uncle's New York clothing store to manufacturing lightweight summer clothing. In 1895 he bought one-quarter interest in a new mail order firm called Sears, Roebuck, and Company. He introduced the famous Sears "money-back guarantee," and he became its vice-president, expanding Sears marketing and factories. By 1925, Rosenwald was chairman of the board at Sears, and forty million copies of the Sears catalogue were being distributed annually. His $37,500 investment now was worth $150 million!

Julius Rosenwald established thousands of rural schools in the South for the poor and funded YMCA buildings for blacks in twenty-five cities. He was a trustee of the all-black Tuskegee Institute as well as the predominantly white University of Chicago. In Chicago, he donated $2.7 million to construct housing for blacks as well as $3 million for the Chicago Museum of Science and Industry. His employees benefited from his profit-sharing plan and company recreational facilities. With other Jewish philanthropists, Rosenwald even loaned money to the International Ladies Garment Workers' Union.

Like the Straus family, Julius Rosenwald would contribute to various projects in Eretz Yisrael although holding no affection toward the Zionist movement. Nevertheless, even within Reform Judaism the commitment toward Zionism was growing. Reform rabbis in the United States, such as Stephen S. Wise (1874-1949), Judah Magnes (1877-1948), Louis Newman (1893-1972), and Abba Hillel Silver (1893-1963), would even be leaders in the Zionist movement. Stephen S. Wise founded the New York Federation of Zionist Societies the same year Herzl called together the First Zionist Congress, and he met Herzl at the Second Zionist Congress in 1898. At that time, Herzl appointed Wise the American secretary of the World Zionist Organization. Rabbi Wise also served as vice-president (1918-1920) and president (1936-1938) of the Zionist Organization of America, and he sounded the first warnings of the dangers of Nazism to both the Jewish and Christian communities.

In fact, it was the rise of Adolf Hitler and, ultimately, the Holocaust that turned most of Reform Judaism to the Zionist cause. Reform laymen officially endorsed the principle of Jewish settlement and the reconstruction of Eretz Yisrael in the 1920s. In 1905 a pro-Zionist professor had been dismissed from Reform Judaism's Hebrew Union College (HUC), but by the 1920s a strong Zionist student movement was found in the same institution.

In 1928 HUC awarded the honorary degree of Doctor of Hebrew Letters to the president of the World Zionist Organization, Chaim Weizmann (1874-1952). Weizmann had won a number of influential British leaders to the Zionist cause, and his development of a crucial new process for the production of acetone (a solvent critical in the production of munitions during World War 1) aided in the British decision to issue the Balfour Declaration in 1917. Chaim Weizmann, a Jew born in the hostile world of nineteenth-century western Russian domain, became the first president of the state of Israel in February 1949.

THE BALFOUR DECLARATION

The Balfour Declaration was an important turning point in the restoration of the Jewish people to the Holy Land. During the nineteenth century both Jewish nationalist and Arab nationalist movements expanded, and both opposed the Ottomans. When the Ottoman Empire became the ally of the Germans in World War I, the British sought and gained the support of both Arabs and Jews. During World War I, the British promised to support the founding of an Arab state in the Middle East. This state was to include areas of present-day Syria (east of Damascus), Iraq, and Saudi Arabia. Through the Balfour Declaration of November 2, 1917, the British promised the Jews a national home in Palestine after the war. This declaration was communicated to Lord Rothschild by Arthur J. Balfour (1848-1930), a former prime minister who served as foreign secretary in prime minister David Lloyd George's coalition government of Britain. The official letter read as follows:

Foreign Office
November 2nd, 1917

Dear Lord Rothschild,

I have much pleasure in conveying to you, on behalf of His Majesty's Government, the following declaration of sympathy with Jewish Zionist aspirations which has been submitted to, and approved by, the Cabinet.

"His majesty's Government view with favour the establishment in Palestine of a national home for the Jewish people, and will use their best endeavours to facilitate the achievement of this object, it being clearly understood that nothing shall be done which may prejudice the civil and religious rights of existing non-Jewish communities in Palestine, or the rights and political status enjoyed by Jews in any other country."

I should be grateful if you would bring this declaration to the knowledge of the Zionist Federation.

It must be remembered that neither the Arabs nor the Jews had a state in the Middle East and that only hindsight affords us the luxury of viewing the storm clouds forming on the horizon. After defeating Germany and the Ottoman Empire in World War I, the French and British moved into the area and carved out "mandates": the French were to control the Syria-Lebanon area; the British the Palestine and Iraq area.

Moderate Arabs and Jews appeared in good rapport when the Ottomans were defeated. Emir Faisal (head of the Arab delegation to the World War I peace conference in Paris and a moderate leader of the Arab movement who had declared himself king of Syria) wrote to British statesman and philosopher Herbert Louis Samuel (1870-1963), a Jew born in Liverpool who began helping Chaim Weizmann when Britain declared war on the Ottoman Empire in 1914:

> I am in the receipt of your letter of Nov. and very much regret to know of the opposition of the Damascus Press to Zionism.
>
> I personally deprecate any difference between the Arabs and the Jews who ought to unite their efforts in word and deed for promoting the development and happiness of our country.
>
> Mr. Sokoloff with whom I had a long conversation will, I hope, convey to you my views about this matter and assure you of my unabated efforts, and the means I am taking for safeguarding our common interests and strengthening the old bonds of friendship and co-operation between Arabs and Jews. Believe me.

This letter was dated November 1919 and had a long history of negotiations behind it. Weizmann and Faisal had met in January of 1919 and had reached a formal agreement that posited a Jewish state in Palestine and cooperation between Arabs and Jews to develop the area. When the French kicked Emir Faisal out of Syria, the British quickly moved to make him king of Iraq. They also created Trans-Jordan out of their Palestine Mandate area west of the Jordan and made Faisal's brother, Abdullah, king of that territory. (Abdullah was considered a moderate and was finally assassinated by more radical Arabs in 1951.) The League of Nations approved these actions in 1922. Article IV of the League of Nations Mandate made special provision for the recognition of a "Jewish agency" to advise and cooperate with the administration of Palestine as representative of the Jewish people.

The rise of the radical Mufti of Jerusalem, Hajj Amin al-Husseini, the right-wing chairman of the Supreme Muslim Council and the greatest Arab nationalist leader until Gamal Abdul Nasser's rise in the 1950s, spelled doom for moderate Arabs as well as the Jewish people in Eretz Yisrael. Under his direction, anti-Jewish riots and massacres occurred in the Holy Land in 1929 and 1936, and even Arab scholars today admit that the Mufti was a fascist collaborator with Adolf Hitler.

American Jews helped pave the way for President Woodrow Wilson's acceptance of the Balfour Declaration and his work toward Jewish self-determination in Eretz Yisrael. The dedication of most American Jews to the Republican Party was shaken in 1912 when Theodore Roosevelt broke from the party, William Howard Taft proved insensitive to some Jewish concerns, and Democratic candidate Woodrow Wilson, a former professor and idealistic intellectual, had a popular platform, the New Freedom. Jews turned toward the Democratic Party in ever-increasing numbers until during the 1930s more than 80 percent of the Jewish vote was Democratic. Three Democratic Jewish governors were elected in the early 1930s; and the Jewish community rallied behind President Franklin D. Roosevelt (president, 1933-1945), becoming known as one of the most solid Democratic voting groups in the modern era.

Jews and Christians alike were thrilled that Woodrow Wilson depended on the brilliant "people's lawyer," Louis D. Brandeis (1856-1941). The Jewish Brandeis had devoted himself to public causes and the defense of the defenseless. Once elected president, Wilson turned to Brandeis for help in translating his ideas of political and social reform into a legal and viable framework. In 1916 President Wilson nominated Brandeis to be a justice of the Supreme Court, the first time a Jewish person had been nominated. The conservative Senate battled for four months before confirming a Jewish lawyer of the reformist bent. It was Brandeis, Rabbi Stephen S. Wise, and another Wilson Jewish appointee, Felix Frankfurter (1882-1965, Eastern European immigrant, Harvard Law School professor, legal officer for Wilson's President's Mediation Commission, and a man who would become the second Jewish justice on the Supreme Court, from 1939-1962), who impressed the importance of the Balfour Declaration and the Jewish restoration to Eretz Yisrael upon the very devout son of a Presbyterian minister, President Woodrow Wilson. Brandeis dictated a memorandum on May 6, 1917, that noted: "The President assured me that he was entirely sympathetic to the aims of the Zionist movement.... Further, the President expressed himself in agreement with the policy, under England's protectorate, for a Jewish homeland." Toward the end of his life, Wilson saw his involvement in the Middle East and his acceptance of the Balfour Declaration as an important personal achievement. He wrote: "To think that I, the son of the manse, should be able to help restore the Holy Land to its people."

FORTY-FIVE YEARS AFTER THE HOLOCAUST

American Jewry would face an onslaught of anti-Semitism and anti-Semitic groups in the 1920s and 1930s that continues to this day. The Jews of America would also come face to face with the horrors of the Holocaust in Europe; and the need for a Jewish homeland would grow ever more imperative in view of Nazi extermination squads, Auschwitz-Birkenau and thousands of other camps, the inability of the "decent" nations of the earth to rescue a persecuted and dying people, and the call of the Mufti to "borrow" Adolf Eichmann to "solve the Jewish problem in the Middle East" after the global Nazi victory. The lessons of the Holocaust were not lost on the modern Jewish community—nor should they be lost on us. And only an overview of the four-thousand-year history of the Jewish people (culminating in the loss in seven Nazi years, 1939-1945, of more Jewish lives than under *all* the anti-Semitic riots, massacres, and pogroms in the preceding thousands of years of Jewish history) could reveal the feeling of most Jews at the establishment of the state of Israel on May 14, 1948. The First World War made a Jewish state possible; the Second World War rendered it indispensable.

Because of the destruction of European Jewry, the American Jewish community felt a greater responsibility to become the cultural and religious center of the modern Diaspora—as the richest, largest, and most emancipated Jewish community in the world to hold the banner of Torah and tradition high; to strive to maintain Jewish identity in the midst of a sea of assimilation; and to rally around Eretz Yisrael as its historical and spiritual center, a homeland that would always welcome its people. Louis Brandeis seemed to sense these important thrusts of modern American Jewry, although he did not live to see the state of Israel come to fruition in 1948. He explained to his fellow American citizens:

> Let no American imagine that Zionism is inconsistent with Patriotism. Multiple loyalties are objectionable only if they are inconsistent. A man is a better citizen of the United States for being also a loyal citizen of his state, and of his city; for being loyal to his family, and to his profession or trade; for being loyal to his college or his lodge. Every Irish American who contributed towards advancing home rule was a better man and a better American for the sacrifice he made. Every American Jew who aids in advancing the Jewish settlement in Palestine, though he feels that neither he nor his descendants will ever live there, will likewise be a better man and a better American for doing so. . . .

> There is no inconsistency between loyalty to America and loyalty to Jewry. The Jewish spirit, the product of our religion and experiences, is essentially modern and essentially American. Not since the destruction of the Temple have the Jews in spirit and in ideals been so fully in harmony with the noblest aspirations of the country in which they lived.

> America's fundamental law seeks to make real the brotherhood of man. That brotherhood became the Jewish fundamental law more than

twenty-five hundred years ago. America's insistent demand in the twentieth century is for social justice. That also has been the Jews' striving for ages. Their affliction as well as their religion has prepared the Jews for effective democracy. Persecution broadened their sympathies. It trained them in patient endurance, in self-control, and in sacrifice. It made them think as well as suffer. It deepened the passion for righteousness.

"The Jewish spirit, so long preserved, the character developed by so many centuries of sacrifice, should be preserved and developed further," asserted Brandeis, "so that in America as elsewhere the sons of the race may in future live lives and do deeds worthy of their ancestors."

Brandeis worried about "demoralization" in the Jewish community —that the freedom in America could leave a new generation of Jews without the "necessary moral and spiritual support." Indeed, the problem of assimilation has worried Jewish leaders ever since. By the 1970s, one out of four Jews was marrying outside the Jewish faith, and more than 9 percent of all married Jewish persons were intermarried. At one time, this act would have resulted in estrangement from one's family. Although this may still occur in Orthodox circles, Conservative and Reform Jews have turned their efforts to maintaining the Jewish spouse's position in the community, educating the children in a Jewish fashion, and perhaps drawing the non-Jewish spouse into the fold of Judaism. When the wife is Jewish, the children of such a relationship usually are raised Jewish. And spouses who convert to Judaism often are some of the strongest adherents of Jewish tradition.

Nevertheless, any successful group in America is going to battle between assimilation and the maintenance of a distinct identity, and in the past forty years, the Jewish people in America have been blessed with a phenomenal success. Numbering close to 6 million (more than 40 percent of world Jewry) and approximately 2.5 percent of the U.S. population, American Jews are more than two times as likely as any other religious or ethnic group to be found in *Who's Who in America*. Jewish representation among successful entrepreneurs is staggeringly high (perhaps 20 percent). Most of this is achieved through privately created enterprises rather than through established corporations where prejudice may remain. Jews appear to be on the cutting edge of business, creative in commerce and industry, as well as in intellectual and cultural life. Nearly half of the Jewish professors teach at top-ranked educational institutions, making up nearly 20 percent of those teaching at elite universities. Jewish men and women constitute 10 percent of all college professors, and are far more likely to publish articles in scholarly journals than their non-Jewish counterparts. In the last few decades 30-40 percent of the American Nobel laureates in science have been Jewish, rising to prominence at the very same time that science began to explode within the cutting edge of human knowledge. Jews have nearly half of the Nobel Memorial Prizes that Americans have won in economics.

Ironically, Jews who for decades have been accused of "controlling the press" are only now rising to prominence there in increasing numbers. They are more than 5 percent of the national press corps, but perhaps 25 percent of the media elite. The names of Jews like Barbara Walters, Ted Koppel, Mike Wallace, Marvin Kalb, and Morley Safer have become household words. The *New York Times,* which is Jewish-owned but rarely promoted Jews to top editorial positions for fear of being castigated as a "Jew paper," has finally allowed talented Jewish editors to move into key positions. A large percentage of Jews are still involved in the entertainment industry, although some of the most famous are hidden because of the name changes endemic to that trade.

The Jewish community remains a heavily urban community, more than 95 percent living in a city or its suburbs. One out of three Jews still lives in New York City, and four out of five congregate in only ten urban centers in the United States. Los Angeles is second to New York; Philadelphia and Chicago follow in Jewish population. Jews are concentrated in the states of New York, Florida, California, Ohio, Pennsylvania, and Illinois. Although most of the children and grandchildren of the Eastern European Jewish immigrants are firmly entrenched in the middle class, close to 15 percent of the New York Jewish community lives at or near the poverty level. Statisticians report that the same percentage is approximately accurate for Jewish communities across the United States.

Around one-half of the American Jewish population report no synagogue affiliation, and of the other half, nearly 50 percent claim to be "Conservative," 30 percent claim to be "Reform," and 20 percent claim to be "Orthodox." Membership, however, does not preclude poor synagogue attendance. Outside of the High Holy Days, perhaps only one or two out of every ten Jews attend synagogue services regularly. And yet, even among Jewish young people, a return to traditional Jewish practice and a devotion to the Jewish peoplehood is very evident. There are some indications of a Jewish transformation and revival taking place in American Judaism in the 1980s that will translate into an even more devoted community in the 1990s. This might well lessen the incidence of "cardiac Jews," a term Jewish leaders have used to describe those Jews who say they have no need of tradition and no desire to contribute to Jewish causes because they feel their Jewishness "in the heart." The key, however, is to realize that in person, practice, and belief each Jew is quite special and unique. Statistics, although informative, can never substitute for personal encounter.

In the past two decades, a number of events have increased the tension and anxieties of American Jewry. When Egyptian President Gamal Abdul Nasser in May 1967 ordered United Nations Secretary General U Thant to withdraw the U.N. buffer zone troops from the Sinai and proceeded to amass one hundred thousand Egyptian combat troops and more than one thousand tanks on the border with Israel, it appeared that the twenty-year-old Jewish state was about to be destroyed. In fact, on May 26, Nasser declared that he would settle for nothing less than the total destruction of Israel. An Islamic *jihad* (holy war) was proclaimed, as Syria and King Hussein's Jordan mobilized their armies, while other Arab states (including Iraq, Kuwait, and Algeria) sent troops to help. The oil-rich Saudis guaranteed financial support.

Soon, more than a quarter of a million Arab troops, seven hundred bombers and fighter planes, and more than two thousand tanks posed to destroy Israel. Ahmed Shukeiri, leader of the Palestinian "Liberation Army," exulted that when the Arabs had wiped out the Jewish state, they would help any surviving Jews return to their native countries. He added, however, that he figured "there will be very few survivors." In Western countries, most leaders were silent toward the Jewish plight; some warned Israel not to lash out at the Arabs. Most church organizations remained silent as well. With such encouragement, Arab nations refused to negotiate with Israel. Indeed, another Holocaust appeared to be in the making.

Israel's complete victory in the June 1967 Six-Day War was a relief for American Jewry, but they never forgot what might have occurred and the supposed "friends" who remained silent during their plight. Holocaust studies began to flourish in America during the 1970s as the Jewish community realized the striking parallels to their present dilemma. Many church leaders, in fact, castigated Israel for her victory; the National Council of Churches treated Israel with contempt. Ahmed Shukeiri was replaced as head of the PLO, and the PLO was reorganized (almost every Palestinian terrorist and guerilla organization joined it). Ironically, because Israel was victorious, she was now portrayed in the press and in propaganda as the Goliath rather than the David.

Even the Arabs' fierce outright attack in 1973 did not dispel this world opinion. When the Yom Kippur War broke out in October of 1973, Israel did not launch a preemptive strike. Although ultimately victorious, Israel suffered heavy casualties. More than 2,500 Israeli soldiers died and many others were wounded. The Arabs had hoped to catch the Jewish people unaware on their holiest day of the year (a tactic utilized by Jewish opponents throughout history). However, the fact that all Israeli troops were either at home or in synagogue services helped Israel to mobilize her forces quickly, thus saving many precious hours. When the U.N. Security Council called for a cease-fire, Israel responded even though she was in Egyptian territory and had the Egyptian Third Army (20,000 troops) totally surrounded.

To American Jewry's horror, Israel was not portrayed as the victim of the 1973 war—a fact that should have been clearly evident to all. The United Nations and individual countries instead castigated Israel for nearly two years, culminating in an infamous U.N. resolution. Under Secretary General Kurt Waldheim (the accused Nazi who would later become Austria's president and would be banned from the United States because of the evidence against him), the United Nations General Assembly on November 10, 1975, passed a resolution stating that Zionism was racism. It even tried to ban Israel from the U.N. organization. This Arab and Russian campaign to destroy the Jewish state and the Jewish peoplehood alarmed the American Jewish population with its repeated public humiliations and propaganda successes. In the United States, Jews gave even more sacrificially and consistently to Israel, often through the United Jewish Appeal. An Israel Emergency Fund was also set up during both the 1967 and 1973 wars. In some years since 1967, contributions of the American Jewish community have approached half a billion dollars! Israel remains close to the heart of American Jewry. Close to 95 percent of the Jewish people polled in the United States in the 1980s stated that they pay special attention to articles about Israel in newspapers and magazines. In addition, one-third of the Jews in America have relatives in Israel today.

Unfortunately, even in this American democracy and haven for the Jewish people, anti-Semitism still exists—a constant reminder to the Jewish people of their perilous history and uncertain future. I have collected hate literature aimed at the Jewish community in the last ten years. My heart nearly broke at the experience of a young Jewish girl in Maryland who saw the display of swastikas, slogans of hate toward Jews, and the eight-foot Nazi eagle that defaced her family's synagogue in 1982. One month later this child viewed a similar defacement of her elementary school. This time the perpetrators of hate drew gas chambers and painted slogans such as "Hitler was right," "Death to Jews," and (next to the gas chamber) "Silent but deadly genocide." The little Jewish girl turned to her mother with questioning eyes and said, "I thought they caught those guys." Her mother responded that this was done by "other guys" and that "there are *more* of them."

In 1977 the Illinois Appellate Court ruled that the Nationalist Socialist Party of America, Nazis led by Frank Collin, could march in predominantly Jewish Skokie, Illinois, *if* they did not wear their swastika armbands. Skokie has a large percentage of Jewish Holocaust survivors. The dread felt by those survivors and other members of the Jewish community in America was carried in newspapers across the United States. One decade later, in June 1987, the same newspapers showed a picture of a defaced Holocaust victims' monument in Skokie. Less than a day after the residents of the Chicago suburb had reverently dedicated their monument, swastikas and the words "Jews Lie" and "Liars" were spray-painted in large letters on the memorial. The *Chicago Tribune* reported that in a light rain, young and old visited the defaced monument and "many wept."

In spite of the intent of such perpetrators of hate, our Jewish neighbor in America is very much alive today. A vibrant American Jewish community is continually faced with Torah and tradition, history and the Holocaust. For those who feared that American Jewry would be totally assimilated and its community a relic of the past, or for those who attempt the elimination or eradication of Jews and Judaism, a lesson in history would serve as a warning. In 1964, *Look* magazine published an article entitled "The Vanishing American Jew." Nearly twenty-five years later, the one to have vanished was *Look* magazine.

6

The Israeli Jew

On the twentieth anniversary of the Arab-initiated Six-Day War, a number of news programs, magazines, and newspapers marked the occasion by totally concentrating on Israel's problems. One prominent news anchor examining the legacy of this Arab-Israeli war entitled his hour-long program, "A Dream Is Dying." His presentation and his selection of interviews were indicative of both past and present predictions of Israel's demise and, indeed, accusations against the Jewish state. Every year, Israel has had to go through a humiliating vote at the United Nations on a motion to exclude her from the international organization.

For example, in 1986 Oman, the chair of the Group of Arab States, again introduced an amendment in the United Nations to exclude "the credentials of Israel." Twenty Arab nations had sponsored the resolution, including Jordan, Saudi Arabia, Kuwait, Syria, and Morocco. In attempting to expel Israel, this Arab bloc was joined and encouraged by the Soviet Union and a number of communist bloc nations, including Cuba, Nicaragua, East Germany, and Czechoslovakia. Only Egypt in the Arab bloc and Romania in Eastern Europe clearly voted against ejecting Israel. Ironically, many of the nations who voted to expel Israel were at the same time calling for an international peace conference on the Middle East. The motion to expel Israel was tabled by an 86 to 41 vote; the anti-Semitic rhetoric became a matter of record.

Another book will be needed to detail the complicated history and relationships between Israel and her Arab neighbors. In this chapter, however, I want to focus briefly on the perceptions of the Israeli Jew today, taking for granted the existence of Israel. As the host of a leading television interview program in June of 1987 stated to a high ranking Catholic official about the Vatican's reluctance to acknowledge officially the existence of the state of Israel: "Isn't it about time that we recognize that modern Israel is a nation that has existed for forty years?"

DEMOCRACY

Israel is the only democracy in the Middle East, and Israeli Jews are for the most part *fiercely independent*. They often are quick to speak their mind and air their problems frankly and forthrightly. From such statements, the editorial department of a television news organization could quickly weave any perception of the Israeli Jew that it wished. In Israel the old Jewish dictum "Where you find *two* Jews, there you will find *three* opinions" is abundantly applicable.

Israel's parliament, or *Knesset* (Hebrew for "assembly"), is a wild organization reflecting the Israeli mind-set. Arguments are fierce; booing and jeering may take place; positions on matters are rarely uniform. For a four-year period, the Knesset is the supreme authority in Israel, and it can only dissolve itself and call new elections before the four-year term is up if the majority of its members "lose confidence" in the way the government is being run, that is, lose confidence in their own Knesset. The 120 representatives to the Knesset (MK's—members of the Knesset) are elected for four-year terms and must be twenty-one years of age. Judges, civil servants, rabbis paid by the state, active army officers, and other officials are not permitted to run for office.

Every citizen over the age of eighteen is eligible to vote, and the country is treated as one district. Any political party, group, or individual may submit a list of candidates for the Knesset, provided the group or individual obtains the signatures of 750 citizens. Voters choose from national "lists" of 120 such candidates. The 120 Knesset seats are distributed according to the percentage of votes each list obtains. For example, if the Labor Party receives 40 percent of the national vote for its list of candidates, the first 48 names (40 percent of 120) on its list become members of the Knesset. If one of those members resigns or dies, the next person on the list automatically takes his or her place.

As one might expect, this system encourages a large number of parties, and it is not uncommon during elections for citizens to vote upon twenty lists. In addition, the Israeli's fierce independence makes it nearly impossible for one list to gain a majority in the Knesset. Therefore, coalitions have been common since the founding of the state of Israel.

In Israel, a president is elected by the Knesset, but he is mainly a ceremonial figure. The key leader is the prime minister. When a new Knesset is elected, the entire former Knesset submits its resignation to the president. He, in turn, consults the newly elected representatives of the parties to determine the member of the Knesset who will form the new government. This prime-minister-elect makes sure he or she has a majority coalition, subsequently proposing a cabinet. A vote of confidence is then taken in the Knesset. If the vote is positive, he or she becomes the prime minister of Israel. If such a vote is negative, the process must begin over again. Parties not represented in the government majority coalition are referred to as the "opposition" parties.

Arab and other non-Jewish delegates of the Knesset are provided translation from Hebrew of speeches and bills into their respective languages. And there are Arab representatives elected to the Knesset. Arab and Muslim citizens are accorded the vote in Israel, whereas in the Arab nations of the Middle East, Jews are not regarded as citizens and are not allowed to hold office. Nevertheless, one of the problems Arabs have in Israel is that if they accept citizenship, they are looked upon as traitors to the Arab cause, which is the annihilation of the Jewish state of Israel.

This became evident on the local level in Jerusalem. Jerusalem's Arabs can opt for Israeli citizenship, but few do. Most continue to hold Jordanian passports and Israeli identification cards (which still gives them municipal voting rights). In 1987, when Jerusalem resident Hanna Siniora, an avowed supporter of Yasser Arafat and the editor of the pro-Palestinian daily *Al Fajr,* announced that he might use the Israeli election system and run for a seat on the Jerusalem City Council, Jewish Mayor Teddy Kollek welcomed the move. The Palestine Liberation Organization (PLO) and a number of Palestinian leaders, however, condemned such a move and labeled him a traitor. Both of Siniora's cars were set on fire, and he was ostracized in many Arab circles. The 135,000 Jerusalem Arabs were divided on his possible actions. As one Arab flower shop worker stated: "Everyone is waiting to see if he'll actually do it . . . I think it's a good move if he can give us services. *It's not so good if he gets killed.*" On the West Bank, many residents will not serve as mayors—such "collaborators" are regularly assassinated by the PLO.

"This is not a question of civil or human rights, but national rights," Elias Zananiri, the editor of Jerusalem's Arab weekly *Al Awdah,* insisted regarding his opposition to Hanna Siniora's thoughts of running for city council. "Palestinians getting involved in Israeli domestic politics negates the fact that we are occupied," he said. In his view, which is representative of many other Arabs, Arab nations, and Arab terrorist organizations, Jerusalem must be taken out of Jewish hands—and, ultimately, Israel must become an "international" (rather than "Jewish") state.

In Galilee, however, non-Jews outnumbered Jews at the end of 1985 by more than two thousand, and Arab leaders who were elected to MK positions (such as Abdel Wahab Darousha of the Labor Party) were insisting that they must be given senior positions in the government or civil service. Darousha points to the Arabs' 17 percent of Israel's population and notes that integration of the Arab community into national and international Israeli posts (embassies, etc.) is essential. "Integration of this nature will help improve relations and generate more cooperation," he stated in an interview. "[Arabs] will be more inclined to regard Israel as their country which, in turn, will increase their loyalty to the state." This issue will certainly dominate the political and social scene in Israel in the 1990s. Darousha formed his own Arab party in 1988.

The Labor Party, of which many of the founders of Israel were members, was able to form government coalitions that dominated Israeli politics until 1977. In that year, Labor was unable to sustain a majority alignment, and the more conservative Likkud Party was able to command a coalition majority. Under Prime Minister Menachem Begin, the Likkud Party (with the support of the National Religious Party and others) took office on June 20, 1977. Such a reversal of roles was indicative of an increase in Jews from Eastern and Arab countries (the so-called Oriental Jews) voting against the Labor coalition and the perceived inability of the Labor coalition to deal with domestic issues (inflation, labor strikes, social tensions, etc.). The death of beloved Labor leader and former prime minister Golda Meir in December 1978 brought to an end the era of the political "Founding Fathers" (and mothers!) of Israel.

By 1984 neither Labor nor Likkud could form an imposing majority. They banded together in a national unity coalition with a party-balanced cabinet. The respective major party prime ministers took turns at leadership during the four-year term (first was Shimon Peres of Labor and then Yitzhak Shamir of Likkud). In May of 1987 this national unity coalition showed signs of a Labor-Likkud division over a Peres proposal for an international conference on Middle East peace. This division appeared likely (in the words of Labor leaders) to "destabilize and paralyze" the functioning of the government of Israel. Nevertheless, Labor could not muster the 61 votes necessary to dissolve the government, and compromise was necessary once again. The *Jerusalem Post* editorialized in an article on May 14, 1987: "The national unity government has come to the end of its road. There is no turning back without either of the two major parties, or both of them, hopelessly compromising their utterly conflicting positions on the crucial issue of peace with the Arabs." And yet, the unity government was forced to carry on, an indication of both democracy and the close nature of the voting patterns of modern-day Israel.

RELIGION AND THE STATE

Such diversity encourages the wooing of minority parties to form coalitions, and increasingly the political spotlight has shifted to the religious parties. For instance, the National Religious Party (NRP) held five votes (five MKs) in the national unity government, which it cast for Likkud. If Labor had been able to woo those votes in the spring of 1987, it would have had a majority coalition and would have been able to call for new elections.

The NRP was formed in 1956 by the merger of two religious Zionist parties, and it views the political and security accomplishments in Eretz Yisrael as "the beginning of realization of the will of divine providence and of the processes directed toward complete salvation of the Jewish people in the land of its forefathers. . . . " It is joined by *Agudat Israel* ("Association of Israel"), a non-Zionist, ultra-Orthodox religious party (two votes in the 1987 unity government), in its efforts to support a religious-oriented society with religious-based laws. Founded in the early twentieth century *before* the Jewish state of Israel became a reality, Agudat Israel opposed any attempt to revive a Jewish political entity in Eretz Yisrael by human agency, including the political Zionist movement. Although Agudat Israel recognizes only God's personal (and future) reestablishment of a Jewish state under the Messiah, in 1948 it became an established political party within the state of Israel to fight for the observance of halakhah (religious law) in Israeli public life.

Because Israel is a Jewish state, most Israeli Jews believe Judaism is entirely relevant to public order and to Israel's political system. Judaism is not separated from the state, and Jewish religious tradition provides Israel's political symbols for official state ceremonies. The separation of religion and state is not on the same order as advocated in the United States Constitution. Whereas church and state are separated in the United States, Judaism and Israel are not separated in the same fashion. The close relationship stems from the inability to separate the Jewish state from Jewish nationality, rather than from legal favoritism of individual

Jews over non-Jews. However, Judaism of necessity has a preferred status in a "Jewish" state.

This certainly does not mean that most Israelis favor the imposition of halakhah by the Orthodox religious establishment. On the contrary, Israeli definitions of Jews, Judaism, and Jewish law are hotly debated. Religious identity and Jewish identity are almost universally accepted by the Israeli Jews, and a high percentage advocate some Jewish tradition in public life. And yet, for most Israeli Jews, Jewish identity transcends a religious identity. Most Israelis conceive of the Jewish people as a nation; and thus, the large majority of Israelis feel a special responsibility toward Jews outside of Israel. Persecuted Jews throughout the world are welcomed in Israel, despite numbers or drain on social institutions. Being Jewish is the natural state of affairs in Israel.

Nonetheless, the greatest debates in Israel today are over the questions, "Who is a Jew?" and, "How does Torah relate to civil laws?" When the ultra-Orthodox Israeli Jews demand that all transportation be terminated on the Sabbath, the majority of more broad-minded Jews fight against such strictures in the courts. When ultra-Orthodox Israeli Jews demand that only an Orthodox convert to Judaism be accepted as a "Jew"—nullifying both Conservative and Reform conversions—the vast majority of more broad-minded Israeli Jews advocate the acceptability of any Jewish convert.

Two recent examples will illustrate both the friction and the Jewish state's adaptability. Through political maneuvering the religious parties of Israel were able to pass the "Matzah Law" at the end of 1986. This religious legislation prescribed fines during the Passover holiday for vendors who displayed bread, rolls, cakes, noodles, biscuits, and the like, which contained *chametz* and were therefore not kosher for Passover. Instructions were distributed by Israel's Interior Ministry to municipal inspectors. The law did not apply to non-Jewish vendors in mixed communities or non-Jewish communities (as in Arab East Jerusalem). The law also did not apply to those who produced, transported, or ate such chametz.

The "Matzah Law" actually became unenforcible (as so much religious legislation does), with many Jewish-owned restaurants, pizzerias, and bakeries ignoring the law. Civil rights organizations advised retailers that they could circumvent the law by selling their chametz in closed bags. The majority of the Israeli population, although sensitive to some religious dietary strictures, would not tolerate the imposition of strict halakhah on their Jewish state!

The second example is that of Reform convert Shoshana Miller, whom the Interior Ministry (controlled by the ultra-Orthodox) refused to register as a Jew. The Israel State Attorney's office declined to defend the Interior Ministry's refusal to register non-Orthodox converts, and Interior Minister Yitzhak Peretz then proposed adding the word *convert* for all Jewish converts. Israel's High Court of Justice ruled that Miller must be registered as a Jew and that the word *convert* must not be added. In the court's opinion such a notation would create divisions in the Jewish people, which would be contrary to the purpose for which Israel was established. Peretz resigned as Interior Minister, and the religious parties vowed to continue their fight for an amendment to the Law of Return indicating who is a Jew according to their religious standards.

The Law of Return had been passed by the Knesset on July 5, 1950. It is one of the most basic laws of the state of Israel in that it declares that *every* Jew has a right to settle in the land, according to the age-old desire of the Jewish people to settle back in Eretz Yisrael.

On March 10, 1970, the Knesset adopted the "Who is a Jew" clause, which was the first attempt to define the word *Jew* in the Law of Return. It defines a Jew as "a person born of a Jewish mother or who has converted to Judaism and who is not a member of another religion." The amendment also gave the non-Jewish spouse, child, or grandchild of a Jew the rights of a Jew under the Law of Return. Ultra-Orthodox religious leaders at the time tried to add the words "according to halakhah" after the word "converted" in the definition. The Knesset soundly defeated the proposal to add those words, realizing that only Orthodox conversions would then be acceptable. The justice minister of that time, Y. S. Shapira, told the Knesset: "We are aware that there are Liberals, there are Conservatives, there are Reform Jews of all types, and they all perform conversions. We say that whoever comes with a conversion certificate from *any* Jewish community, as long as he is not of another religion, will be accepted as a Jew." The religious parties, however, have used their political power to attempt to pass such an amendment ever since.

In 1987, leaders of the United Jewish Appeal warned Likkud prime minister Shamir that the proposed amendment to the Law of Return by the religious parties—one that would render conversions to Judaism by non-Orthodox rabbis unacceptable—could weaken Judaism and Jewish causes. The Conservative and Reform movements are continually lodging their protests as well. The "Who is a Jew" issue appears to be a constant political issue in Israel (and throughout the Jewish world).

Because of the institutional monopoly in Israel of the Orthodox branch of Judaism, Conservative and Reform rabbis are not recognized as rabbis in Israel. They may conduct a wedding or conversion in Israel, but only an Orthodox rabbi can *register* a marriage or conversion. For Jews, there is no civil marriage in Israel, so the registration power of the Orthodox rabbi is quite significant. Although the non-Orthodox synagogue members in Israel number only a few thousand, they do receive some government support. This support is not as great as that received by a variety of Orthodox institutions and services through the Ministry of Religious Affairs and Ministry of Interior. For example, the Ministry of Education and Culture provides for a state religious school system parallel to the state nonreligious school system. In addition, chief rabbis (both national and local), the Chief Rabbinical Council, local religious councils, and an entire system of rabbinical courts are accorded government status and are funded by the state of Israel.

Amazingly, whereas non-Orthodox *Jewish* religious groups are discriminated against in Israel, non-Jewish religions are accorded full rights. Muslim and Christian religious courts are recognized by Israel and are given exclusive judicial authority in matters of their members' "personal status"—marriage and divorce. Muslim and Druze (a nominally Muslim group founded on gnostic principles conveyed by Ismail al-Darazi, who died in A.D. 1019) religious services and institutions are funded by the state of Israel. Christian groups declined government financial assistance when it was offered years ago. Furthermore, Israel places a priority on the protection of the holy sites of the various religious communities that inhabit its boundaries.

This extends even to the Temple Mount. When Israel captured East Jerusalem from Jordan in the 1967 Six-Day War, the decision was made not to alter the status of the rights of the various religious groups. Jerusalem police have standing orders not to let Jews pray on the Temple Mount because of the offense it gives to Muslims. In 1986 the confrontation between Israeli Jews who wanted to pray there and the Muslim community escalated with the establishment of the "Supreme Rabbinical Council on the Temple Mount." Headed by former chief rabbi Shlomo Goren, this council in August 1986 called on the government to "erase the disgraceful prohibition against [Jewish] praying" on the Temple Mount and even asked to build a synagogue there. The current Grand Mufti of Jerusalem, Sheik Sa'ad a-Din al-Alami, countered: "No Jew will pray on the Temple Mount . . . The Muslims are prepared to die for this." Religious Affairs Minister for the State of Israel, Yosef Burg, assured the

Muslims: "There is no need to add the dimension of religious struggle to the existing national struggle. I have always followed the ruling of Rabbi Avraham Kook who forbade prayers on the Mount."

Because the People of the Book are living in the Land of the Book, a purely secular religion cannot dominate the Israeli mentality. The more secular the state religion becomes in Israel, the more difficulty politicians and the government have in adapting Jewish symbols, institutions, consciousness, and culture. Israel today is far removed from the secular Zionist goal of creating a "new Jew." Rather, Israeli society is being integrated around Jewish tradition and uniting a nation of Jewish people. National motifs are thoroughly linked to historical religious motifs; religious symbols are thoroughly integrated into the national civil religion. The yearly cycle and life cycle of the Jewish people have an additional national cycle in Israel—Judaism is the primary source of Israeli political symbols. Israel's birth is celebrated in the Independence Day of the nation, a link directly related to the Exodus and Passover, and springing from the ashes of the Holocaust. Israel is viewed as lonely and isolated in this present world, surrounded by enemies who wish to destroy her, just as the Jews under Joshua or Ezra in the biblical period. Yet, the feeling is prevalent that Israel will survive, achieving peace and bringing blessing to the whole world, just as the prophets predicted. Most Israeli Jews believe that they are witnessing today a portion of this progress, scientific achievement, and blessing toward all humankind in their Jewish state. For the overwhelming majority of Israelis the "dream" is not "dying."

CREATIVITY

For Israeli Jews, Israel's greatest achievement is the existence of her democracy and democratic institutions, even in the midst of external and internal siege. Nearly its entire forty-year existence, Israel has been in a state of war or semi-war. And yet, Israeli Jews view their nation's active parliament, law and order, privileges of protest, independent judicial system, and free press as a beacon light in a dictator-ridden and fear-oriented Middle East. Israelis pride themselves on the fact that while the nations surrounding them honor terrorists and murderers, Israel brings charges against those Jews who revert (for even an instant) from the Torah principles of law and order; justice and compassion; honesty and fairness; human rights and love of neighbor.

From this democratic base, creativity has flourished. Kibbutzim and development towns have turned the desert into productive gardens and the wilderness into homes and businesses. Israeli pride goes out with the international exports of fruits and vegetables, and scientific agricultural techniques are bold and innovative. Israelis have been able to control the "salt stress" of brackish water by computer-controlled fertilizer and tubing techniques to nourish the roots of hybrid plants in the Negev desert. More than 250 thriving agricultural settlements dot the Negev, producing high-quality melons, tomatoes, peppers, dates, asparagus, avocados, zucchini, and eggplant in the desert sand. Even orchards of thousands of midget peach trees and fields of midget wheat produce more than those of regular size. Both Israeli farmers and scientists take pride in this feat.

A fine education system has been provided for the inhabitants of Israel from the primary through the university levels, and graduates are sent throughout the world to help and train others. History and tradition have been valued and honored in Israel in the past, and this respect is evident in Israel today. Israel by its very being represents a dialogue with the past in order to prepare for the future. Archaeology has prospered under Jewish domain, and archaeological sites have been protected where once they were neglected. Archives and collections of documents and artifacts have blossomed into new libraries and museums. Recently, the largest assemblage of artifacts to be found in the 120-year history of excavations in Jerusalem was unearthed. Some of the artifacts were four hundred years older than the Dead Sea Scrolls.

The head archaeologist of this excavation, Professor Gabriel Barkay, believes that his discovery proves conclusively that Jews continued to inhabit Israel after the destruction of the First Temple in 586 B.C. If proved, this would mean that the Chaldean destruction under Nebuchadnezzar was not total. Tiny ancient Hebrew scrolls encased in small cylinders were also found. Etched in silver was Numbers 6:24-26:

> The Lord bless you
> and keep you;
> the Lord make his face shine upon you
> and be gracious to you;
> the Lord turn his face toward you
> and give you peace.

Professor Barkay was particularly moved by this find because this traditional priestly benediction dates to 650 B.C. (the earliest original biblical passage found to date). "It is the text found in every Jewish prayer book," Barkay stated to the press, "and here I was on a scientific dig, and I found the same verses our people have been uttering in the same city for 2600 years."

Some of the finest medical facilities in the world are to be found in Israel, and the national health system is based on the community's obligation to care for all its members. Special efforts are made to see that the elderly and the poor are cared for. Israel's security situation has blossomed into an extensive and speedy emergency system. Casualty teams are noted for their efficiency, bravery, and preparedness. Israeli doctors and scientists take pride in publishing in scholarly journals throughout the world, and Israelis are noted for being on the cutting edge of many medical and scientific breakthroughs. Israeli specialists have been invited to help developing nations with their health problems, since Israel has experienced and conquered many of the diseases and conditions in its varied population that are common to the newly emerging states of Asia and Africa. Israel also trains doctors and nurses from other countries in special programs, including post-graduate seminars. With its tradition in Torah, Israel has been very active in the new discipline of medical ethics, discussing euthanasia, resuscitation, clinical death, organic transplants, and medical experimentation. In 1980 the Knesset restricted abortions to medically indicated cases only.

Israel is blessed with some of the finest musicians in the world. Orchestras, string quartets, and ensembles (as well as vocalists and bands, ranging from opera to pop artists) entertain an enthusiastic populace. The Israel Philharmonic Orchestra has gained an international reputation, and the number of Israeli finalists in competitions throughout the world has markedly increased. Similar strides have been made in dance, art, and theater. In the field of architecture, there has been a vigorous effort to preserve the ancient character of the land in some places, while creating a thoroughly modern aura in others. The vogue in Israel today is to have the public participate in the area of this "physical planning." Beautiful malls and shopping centers, multilevel with several below ground, often in ancient styles of stone, are being built throughout Israel. With aesthetically pleasing atmospheres that are climate-controlled, Israel's malls are the envy of the Middle East. Cities are also being revitalized. In 1987, for example, the older streets and buildings of Tel Aviv underwent restoration and refurbishing: parks were added; walkways and street lights improved; flowers planted; and even footpaths constructed.

Israel is also a sports-minded society, with deep interest in soccer, basketball, and tennis. Professional teams and individual stars are watched with great anticipation, and Israeli athletes compete in the international forum as well. Security has been significantly increased in international events, ever since Arab terrorists killed eleven Israeli athletes and coaches during the attack on the Olympic village at the 1972 Olympic Games in Munich. Israeli athletes are also competing on the international scene with success in areas such as hurdling, weightlifting, wrestling, sailing, shooting, and swimming. In 1986 American Little League-style baseball was organized in Herzlia. Arab children from neighboring villages, Jewish children from area kibbutzim, and Russian Jewish children from an area Absorption Center play together on teams.

Israelis take pride in their rescue of Jews throughout the world and their provision of a haven for the refugee. And Israel never forgets. When the Soviet Union made advances in 1987 to reestablish diplomatic relations with Israel, the topic of Soviet Jewry was on the top of Israel's agenda (much to the irritation of the Russians). More than two million Jews reside in the Soviet Union, making them the third largest Jewish community in the world (next to the United States and Israel itself). Although literate, generally well-educated, and active in Russian intellectual life, Soviet Jewry is restricted in religious practice and even persecuted.

The Soviet government has opposed emigration of Russian Jews and has tormented those who have applied to depart. Israel, in the meantime, has publicized the plight of Russian Jews, supported Soviet Jewish activists, and relentlessly petitioned for the release of those who want to immigrate to its shores. When Russia appeared to soften her opposition to Jewish emigration and began to increase Jewish exit visas to one thousand a month early in 1987, Israel immediately prepared for a mass influx. Soon the Russians were slowing emigration once again.

Ethiopian Jews found the same problem as Israel worked diligently to help them escape and prepared for them a home. By the summer of 1987, the situation of Ethiopian Jewry was deteriorating daily, and Israel's Absorption Minister, Ya'acov Tsur, was negotiating frantically through emissaries from other countries with communist Ethiopia for the more than ten thousand remaining Jews.

Such refugees find a home in Israel even in difficult economic times. The 1970s presented a grim economic picture in Israel. Taxes to fund the war effort and defense initiatives were high; inflation was out of control at more than 100 percent. Still, more than 180,000 Russian immigrants had come to Israel in little more than a decade. The views of these newcomers says something about Israeli democracy as well as the strenuous life in Israel. Many are amazed at the variety of foods and the crowds of individuals of differing personalities and opinions. They find the people of Israel friendly and communicative. Ironically, in spite of the threats of violence toward Israel from enemies within and without, Israeli Jews appear "relaxed" to Russian immigrants in comparison to Russian citizens.

And yet, the Russian Jewish immigrant will often say to friends, "I never expected it to be so difficult in Israel." Most come with no money and no experience with a Western-style financial system. Checking accounts and credit cards baffle them, causing more than a little problem. In spite of government help with temporary housing and permanent mortgages, expenses are high and salaries are modest. Everyone in the family that is old enough works. A sense of helplessness engulfs the new immigrant in reaction to a totally new culture, and nostalgia creeps up from time to time, even in those who have been in Israel for years. Nevertheless, Russian immigrants have a much higher percentage (nearly 95 percent) of remaining in Israel than the immigrant from the United States. Today, the economy of Israel is improving, and the spark of hope generated in native-born Israelis is shared by Jewish immigrants as well.

Many immigrants thrill at the exploits of Israel to help persecuted Jewry. News of the Entebbe raid of 1976, for example, had repercussions around the world (including Russia). Terrorists claiming to be from the Popular Front for the Liberation of Palestine hijacked an Air France jet on Sunday, June 27, 1976, finally landing in Uganda at the Entebbe airport. There they held the crew and 102 hostages, mostly Israeli Jews. On July 4, an Israeli commando unit made a daring rescue attempt by covertly flying 2,500 miles and releasing most of the hostages. Besides many terrorists, three civilians and the young Israeli commander of the strike force lost their lives in what many experts termed one of the most daring and successful rescue missions in military history. Most of the world thrilled at the news of Israeli success. President Gerald Ford became the first American president to congratulate Israel on a military action. United Nations secretary-general Kurt Waldheim, however, condemned the rescue operation as a "violation of Ugandan sovereignty," and the Organization of African Unity later denounced the action as well. Nevertheless, Jews around the world were elated, and Israeli Jews were ecstatic with national pride. It fed an indescribable dignity, self-confidence, and national trust that dwells deep in the Israeli Jew today.

FRUSTRATIONS

Notwithstanding, there are frustrations for the Israeli Jew. By the mid-1970s, the Israeli pound had been devalued twice in one year, and Israelis were paying the highest average tax rate in the world (approximately 65 percent). At the same time, some important tax deductions were being eliminated and government subsidies on fourteen staple products were reduced. The prices of some items, such as bread, milk, and cheese, nearly doubled overnight. Many Israelis are still recovering from this shock wave.

Furthermore, living dangerously is a way of life in Israel, and tensions often run high. By 1970, nearly half of all Israelis were native-born, and they had known very little but war and threats of war their entire lives. In addition, hundreds of thousands of Holocaust survivors and tortured and abused immigrants from Arab countries remember vividly their ordeals. One must realize that currently in Israel, Jews live in greater danger of their lives than people in almost any other place on the face of the earth. A full scale effort to grasp any opportunity to exterminate the Jews of Israel and totally conquer the area is on the drawing boards of scores of organizations and nations. Arab radicalism has escalated rather than moderated.

Yasser Arafat's Al-Fatah faction of the Palestine Liberation Organization attempted a guerilla suicide mission on Israel's northern border on the eve of the Palestine National Council's meeting in April 1987. Two Israeli soldiers were killed, and Arafat regained remarkable prestige with other groups in the Council (a "parliament in exile" according to the terrorists). He emerged once again as "first among equals" in the PLO, ready to escalate terrorism while claiming to be "moderate." His age-old lines appeared to have been effective in the world as he claimed once again: "We will maintain our armed struggle against Israel, not because we seek war, but because we want peace." Few realize, however, how deeply entrenched is hatred of the Jew in Arafat's upbringing. His relatives include the notorious collaborator with Adolf Hitler, Hajj Amin al-Husseini, the radical former Grand Mufti of Jerusalem.

By the conclusion of the eighteenth session of the Palestine National Council meeting near Algiers, Arafat had united the two largest factions that had opposed his "diplomatic efforts" and declared that "now all stand together, united until the final liberation of Palestine." He also insisted that "a just and comprehensive peace on the basis of the Palestinian right to self-determination" would include "an independent state with Jerusalem as its capital."

For many Israeli Jews, there is extreme frustration because the rest of the world does not recognize that Israel's plight goes beyond a "mere return" of Gaza and the West Bank—Israel itself is in serious danger. Israeli Jews believe that the state of Israel is treated differently in the court of world opinion than any other nation. Some Israeli Jews have decided that if the world will not help, but continually condemns, they will "go it alone"—with tradition, Torah, and God at their side. It is difficult to characterize such feelings among Israeli Jews, because even the right-wing nationalist religious Gush Emunim settlers are divided over issues of retaliation raids and vigilante activity in response to the Arab maiming and killing of Jewish women and children among the settlers. Such undemocratic reaction as vigilantism is clearly opposed by the general Israeli Jewish public—an opposition that more moderate conservative settlers realize would create an irreparable split in Israeli society. On the more liberal side of the spectrum, the *Shalom Akhshav* (Peace Now) organization launched in 1977 and composed of thousands of middle class and intellectuals is calling for an end to all war and the return of the West Bank and Gaza conquered in the Six-Day War. Thousands of Israeli Jews join their demonstrations.

Most Israeli Jews would gladly trade some land for genuine peace, but the prospects are bleak. They believe that there are no guarantees and that their return of land and their peace treaties of the past have been only regarded by Arabs as a prelude to future war. Even the return of the Sinai to the Egyptians for recognition by Anwar Sadat and a peace treaty resulted in Sadat's death and unbelievable pressures on his successor, Hosni Mubarak, to scrap the treaty. Egypt walks a thin line, trying to appear tough on Israel, to be friends with Arafat, while maintaining peace with Israel. Moderate Arabs are murdered; radicals and terrorists want the entire land. It is a frustrating situation. In a conference on the Mount of Olives the Palestine *Liberation* Organization was organized in 1964—*before* Israel had captured the Mount of Olives, East Jerusalem, Gaza, or the West Bank. Israeli Jews rightly ask, "What were they going to *liberate?*"

The situation, however, cannot be ignored. Before the Six-Day War there were approximately 220,000 Arabs in Israel. When East Jerusalem was captured during the Jordanian attack, 55,000 Muslim Arabs and 12,000 Christian Arabs were added to Israel proper. By the 1973 Yom

Kippur War, Arabs were 15 percent of the population; in 1986, they were 17 percent of the population; and by the year A.D. 2000 projections are that they will be 22 percent of the population (Israeli Jews growing to 4.1 million; Israeli Arabs growing to 1.2 million). One-half of these Arabs are youths under age fourteen and generally dedicated to Palestinian nationalism.

Added to this are the explosive situations in the Gaza and the West Bank, where an additional 650,000 and 520,000 Arabs, respectively, live. The Gaza has never adapted well under any occupation, and Israelis would certainly be glad to be rid of this sixty-square-mile strip of desert coast. Egypt controlled it until 1967, keeping it as one of the most despicable ghettos in the world and forbidding the construction of new mosques for fear of Islamic radicals (more than seventy new mosques have appeared since 1967 under Israeli control of the Gaza).

Today, Gaza has still not recovered from its past. It has 40 percent of all Palestinian Arabs in Israeli-controlled territories, and its population is doubling every generation. Most of these Palestinian Gazans are still concentrated in the eight refugee camps set up by the United Nations in 1948. Infant mortality, although lowered since 1967, is still four times the rate of that in Israel. Even though fifty thousand Gazans travel into Israel to work each day, living conditions are much worse in Gaza than on the West Bank. Israeli Jews have cried out to their government officials in the past few years to try to do more in Gaza to alleviate the poverty and inhospitable living conditions. The riots and violence that erupted in the latter weeks of 1987 and continued on into 1988 are indicative of the frustrations of a younger generation of Arabs with little hope for the future.

On the West Bank, refugee camps also exist and, like Gaza, are smoldering cauldrons for discontent, terrorism, and revolt. Cars of Israeli Jews are stoned; resulting fences and restrictions by Israeli troops are deeply resented. The six universities owned and operated by the Palestinian Arabs in the territories are filled with students who are not afraid to battle the Israeli army and to die for the cause of the PLO. These offspring of the refugee camps are steeped in PLO dogma and automatically plan an extra year or two to complete their degrees, because they know their actions will result in the periodic closing of their university. Some have totally shocked their more moderate parents, who had learned to live under Jordan's more stringent occupation. Yet, although it is possible for an Arab family on the West Bank to prosper, dreams of a separate Palestinian state loom large.

Such turmoil complicates the life of every young Israeli Jew who encounters the mandatory military service in the IDF (Israel Defense Forces). When they turn eighteen, Jewish teenagers in Israel (Israeli citizens and permanent residents) are required to serve in the IDF. In general, men serve two and one-half years, and women serve two years. New immigrants up to the age of twenty-nine are also liable for military service. After this conscript duty, every soldier is assigned to a reserve unit, where even forty-five to fifty-four year olds may spend two weeks a year in the Civil Defense organization. If the minister of defense determines that the state of Israel is in danger, a special duty of service may be ordered at any time. There are exceptions for conscript service for mothers or those who have religious reasons for not serving. Arabs are exempt from military service, but the Druze are well represented.

That Israeli Jewish eighteen-year-olds are thrust into the riots and turmoil, hatred and curfews of the West Bank and Gaza is a sobering experience. They must be ever on guard for assassins who roam the streets to kill any Jew and, they hope, some soldiers. On the border of Lebanon, ambushes with rockets, grenades, or mines are a constant danger. Little wonder that life for the Israeli Jew alternates between the depressing and the exhilarating, the tragic and the hopeful, war and siege. Little wonder that the Israeli conscripts take their oath at Masada, where Zealots and others held off the entire Roman army for three years, only to die free rather than to be paraded as slaves.

Streams of anti-Semitic literature are flooding the Middle East and Africa today, some financed by the Soviet Union, some financed by the Arab states. The infamous *Protocols of the Elders of Zion,* a forgery that has caused much Jewish suffering and death in the twentieth century, is once again popular, and, incredibly, Adolf Hitler's *Mein Kampf* is distributed by the tens of thousands in Arabic. It is not unusual to find *Mein Kampf* in an Arab home, even on the bedside reading table of an Arab teenager or college student. Thus, Adolf Hitler is once again becoming a hero in Arab circles, just as he was the hero of Haj Amin al Husseini, the Grand Mufti of Jerusalem before and during World War II. The Israeli Jew realizes that repeated verbal slanders are soon followed by violent physical deeds.

In spite of all this, the Jews of Israel are divided on the steps to be taken toward security and peace. Between the minority of hardliners on the right and on the left, a majority of Israeli Jews hold a kaleidoscope of moderate opinions. This majority is consumed with the daily burden of providing for a family and raising them to be responsible and caring human beings. In some ways Israel reminds one of the struggling years of the American democratic nation, pioneers with warts and blemishes as well as heroic feats, spectacular advances and, at times, extraordinary charity. America drew on the Judaic heritage for her benevolent concepts and neighborly values. For the Israeli Jews, however, this heritage is their special four-thousand-year tradition. And the mind-set, rugged individualism, and pride of the Israeli Jew can never be severed from the events and lessons of that four millennia of historical experience, including the sobering losses and hopeful gains of four decades of modern statehood.

Part 3

GROUPS AND RELATIONSHIPS

7

The Orthodox

Twenty-five minutes northeast of Jerusalem is Neveh Zion yeshiva, nestled in an Orthodox Jewish community and catering to American Jewish youth who have decided to give Orthodox Judaism "one last chance." Often sent by their distraught parents who have spent tens of thousands of dollars on their children's Orthodox Jewish education, these Jewish young men have many questions about the purpose and meaning of Judaism as they seek to capture (or recapture) the excitement of their Jewish faith. At Neveh Zion, the atmosphere is relaxed and nonrestrictive, and the rabbis and teachers are available at all hours to counsel students and to talk about Judaism and one's relationship to God. Students are invited into the teachers' homes and reinforced by the general community. For most, the traditions they learned from childhood gain new meaning and significance. They learn the reason behind their daily actions.

The struggle of these Orthodox young people underscores the problems the Orthodox community has faced throughout the world and especially in the United States. Until quite recently, many scholars had predicted the death of American Orthodox Judaism, just as they had predicted the demise of conservative Christianity. In both cases, the reasoning was that traditional religion could not (and would not) be able to withstand the lure of the modern world and the difficulty of religious commitment in a secular and mobile society. In both cases, the reasoning was erroneous. And yet, American society has had an effect on the Orthodox who have immigrated to her shores and has definitely created change in this Jewish group.

Orthodox Judaism considers itself the authentic bearer of the religious Jewish tradition. The *term* orthodoxy within Judaism first appeared at the end of the 1700s in response to the reform impulse and the attempt of some Jews to adapt Judaism to Western culture. The word *orthodox* means "right belief," and yet most of the early disputes were over "right practice." The Orthodox movement stresses the importance of halakhah, the legal part of Torah and the Talmudic tradition. *Halakhah* is derived from the Hebrew verb "to go" or "to follow" and in the singular refers to "law" in the general sense or, alternately, to a specific rule or regulation. Its plural, *halakhot,* refers to collections of laws. The authoritative law code recognized by Orthodox Judaism throughout the world is the *Shulkhan Arukh* formulated by Joseph ben Ephraim Caro (1488-1575).

Born in Spain, Joseph Caro lived at the time of Martin Luther. His family was affected by both the Spanish and Portuguese Inquisitions and migrated to the Ottoman Empire. It was in Adrianople that Joseph Caro began writing the *Beit Yosef,* his magnum opus, in 1522. He later completed it in Safed in 1542, where he headed a large yeshiva. As most Sephardim, Caro did not want to create new cultural values but was consumed with collecting and preserving the entire Jewish spiritual and religious heritage of previous generations. With intense love, diligence, and respect, he purposed to systematize the large number of Jewish law codes and religious rulings that had generated a confusing array of local customs. In essence, his attempt was to make order out of what seemed to be approaching legal chaos. His *Beit Yosef* attempted to investigate every single halakhah, to discuss each stage of its development, to relate ~very possible divergent view, and, finally, to arrive at a decisive ruling.

In order that his vast work might be accessible to the Jewish masses, Caro prepared the *Shulkhan Arukh* (Hebrew, "the prepared table"), an abridgment of *Beit Yosef* in clear, simple statements without the detailed academic discussion. It is divided in the same sections as the *Beit Yosef,* that is, (1) daily commandments, Sabbaths, and the festivals, (2) dietary laws, purity, mourning, and assorted topics, (3) marriage, divorce, and related topics, and (4) civil and criminal law. With notes and comments by Ashkenazic Moses ben Israel Isserles (1525?-1572), a Polish rabbi with whom Caro corresponded and who adapted Caro's work to the life of German-Polish Jewry, the *Shulkhan Arukh* became in the 1600s the authoritative code of Jewish law accepted by world Jewry, Sephardim and Ashkenazim alike.

In the next two centuries scores of commentaries appeared on the *Shulkhan Arukh* itself. One of the most famous is *Life of Man (Hayyei Adam)* by Abraham ben Jehiel Michael Danzig (1748-1820), a lay theologian from Vilna. In *Life of Man,* Danzig arranges and discusses the intricacies of the first section on daily conduct of the *Shulkan Arukh* in a clear writing style that both young people and laypersons could understand. *Life of Man* was so popular when it was first published in 1810 that nearly one hundred editions followed, and lay groups were formed for the regular study of it.

For instance, in 1897 a Hebrew/English edition appeared in New York City under the title *The Law of Israel.* Carefully compiled and arranged by Rabbi Bernard Abramowitz of Congregation Mishkan Israel Anshei Suvalk in New York, this edition not only gives an understanding of Danzig's work, but also gives one a perception of American Orthodoxy at the turn of the century. Abramowitz prefaced the work with an essay, "The Confirmation of the Law," including the subtitle explanation "Being a stirring appeal to the coming Jewish generation to demonstrate in every action of their daily life, that these laws of the SHULCHAN ARUCH for the preservation of which myriads of their ancestors suffered martyrdom, are imbued with eternal life." At the top of the title page is an arch with the words: "If I forget thee, O Jerusalem, let my right hand forget her cunning, If I do not remember thee, let my tongue cleave to the roof of my mouth, If I prefer not Jerusalem above my chief joy."

In "The Confirmation of the Law," Rabbi Abramowitz explains at the outset the fundamental principles of Judaism. He wrote:

> The foundations upon which the imperishable structure of Judaism has been reared are the thirteen fundamental principles of truth which form the groundwork upon which the Laws of Israel are firmly established; With more than mortal wisdom, with superhuman strength, with Divine intelligence did our ancestors dig in the quarry of Infinite Science and have hewn out these thirteen basal stones which they have solidified into the foundation of the UNITY,—that foundation upon which all the hearts of Israel are united, that everlasting foundation upon which the house of Israel was erected to stand for all eternity! The following are the principles which form the very consciousness of every Israelite—the faith inherent to his being—to believe:
>
> 1. In the existence of a Creator;
> 2. In His Unity;
> 3. That He is incorporeal;

4. That He is Eternal;
5. That to Him alone is it right to pray;
6. That all the words of the Prophets are true;
7. That the prophecy of Moses our teacher is true and that there has never yet arisen a prophet like unto Moses;
8. That Moses received the Torah on Sinai;
9. That God will not alter nor change His law;
10. That the Creator knows the deeds of the children of men and their thoughts;
11. That there is reward for the righteous and punishment for the wicked;
12. That the Messiah will come at the end of days;
13. That God will quicken the dead in His abundance of loving-kindness.

"The will of God," insists Rabbi Abramowitz, "is the Light of the *Torah* whereby He has caused Israel, His people, to become meritorious. It is the perpetual lamp that He·has commanded them to light in the temple of Judaism."

With the evident importance of Torah in Orthodox Judaism, it is little wonder that when the Union of Orthodox Jewish Congregations of America had its first meeting in 1898, the following statement headed its platform: "We believe in the Divine revelation of the Bible." It devoted itself to "advance the interests of positive Biblical, Rabbinical, Traditional and Historical Judaism." Because of this, it is not uncommon to hear Orthodox Jews refer to themselves as "Torah-true."

Today, the Union of Orthodox Jewish Congregations of America (UOJCA) is the largest organization of Orthodox synagogues in the United States. Through its organization for rabbis, the Rabbinical Council of America (founded in 1923), the UOJCA supervises the *kashrut* (Jewish dietary laws that assure food is *kosher*, "religiously proper" in both slaughtering and preparation). They are responsible for the "U" symbol that appears on some kosher products (signifying Orthodox Union). The "K" one finds on other products certifies that the food has been processed as kosher under rabbinic supervision. Since Orthodox Jews do not mix milk with meat, a "P" for *parveh* signifies that a product cannot be classified as milk or meat, and is safe to mix with either. Observant Jews maintain the Jewish dietary laws faithfully, and American Orthodoxy is painstakingly involved in monitoring the process.

Presently, more than 11 percent of the Jewish families in the United States describe themselves as "Orthodox." Although most Christians think of Orthodox Judaism as a monolithic movement, it is actually as diverse as Reform or Conservative Judaism. In fact, some would stress that it is more complex because an Orthodox synagogue may belong to one of three councils (UOJCA, the National Council of Young Israel, or the Yeshiva University Synagogue Council). And, Orthodox rabbis may be members of one of six rabbinical organizations.[1]

If Orthodox Judaism is united in any way, it is united in its rejection of modern biblical criticism. Even the professors at Orthodox Judaism's largest educational institution, Yeshiva University in New York (more than 7,000 students), unapologetically assert that the Hebrew text of the Torah is the text given to Moses by God and that the literal interpretation of the Bible is the foundation of the Jewish faith. The revealed Word of God is the essence of traditional Judaism.

Because of this, ceremonial law is obligatory. All of Torah is "binding" on the Orthodox Jew. Waking in the morning, he is to think of God before arising, thanking God for the return of consciousness and another day of life. "I give thanks before Thee," the Orthodox Jew prays, "King living and eternal, that Thou hast mercifully restored my soul to me; great is Thy faithfulness." When he rises, each movement is accompanied by a blessing to God. His undergarment is adorned with fringes as the Scripture requires. As he prepares for formal worship, he dons a large, outer prayer-shawl *(tallit)*, worn only during formal prayer and worship or during the study of the Torah. Then the two small leather boxes of the *tefillin* and the straps are wrapped around his head and arm for prayer. "Thou shalt bind them for a sign upon thine hand, and they shall be for frontlets between thine eyes," the Torah says.

Each act is accompanied by a blessing. "I will betroth thee unto Me forever; yea, I will betroth thee unto Me in righteousness, and in justice, And in loving kindness, and in compassion. And I will betroth thee unto Me in faithfulness; And thou shalt know the Lord." Only after the morning ritual may the Orthodox Jew eat his breakfast. In the afternoon and at dusk, he again engages in individual, formal worship of God. On retiring, he reaffirms his faith, commits himself to God's care, and falls asleep with the consciousness of God in his thoughts. The daily regimen for the Orthodox Jew thus ends as it began—with Torah on his lips and God in his thoughts.

1. Or privately ordained and not part of any such organization. Many Orthodox rabbis in America have never studied at an accredited college or university.

The Orthodox Jew is expected to conduct his business, professional life, and dealings with others according to Torah as well. The *Shulkhan Arukh* has a whole section on business practices, and Maimonides included the following outline as his "Laws of Ethics":

1. To follow in God's paths
2. To cling to His works (of benevolence)
3. To love our neighbors
4. To love strangers
5. Not to hate our brothers
6. To admonish (those who err)
7. Not to put one to shame
8. Not to oppress the weak
9. Not to backbite
10. Not to be revengeful
11. Not to cherish hatred

Cheating, stealing, and lying are forbidden, and charity is to be a way of life. One's word must be one's bond. Ethical rules are to be as binding as ceremonial rituals. Although Orthodox Jews are human beings with shortcomings and differing personalities like the rest of us, ethics are a central part of traditional Judaism.

In the past, women had almost no role in the Orthodox synagogue worship service. They were crucial in the home, the festivals, child-rearing, and food preparation, and they had their personal obligations (such as their monthly visit to the *mikveh,* "a collection" [of water] after their menstrual period for spiritual cleanliness). And yet, during worship they were separated from the men by a partition or curtain so that they would not distract the men. In many modern Orthodox synagogues, the celebration of Simchat Torah has served to bend these rigid lines of demarcation. Men carry the Torah scrolls through the women's section and allow them to kiss the Torah. In a few Orthodox synagogues, women are provided with a Torah in their section to dance with the Torah as the men do. English-speaking Orthodox synagogues are spreading, and a few have mixed seating. These developments are questioned as to being properly "orthodox," but modern society is having its influence on Orthodox Judaism as well.

It is an error to assume that Orthodox Jews in general isolate themselves from society. There are Orthodox university professors, doctors, and lawyers. The Association of Orthodox Jewish Scientists has more than fifteen hundred members, including biochemists, bacteriologists, and psychologists. Israel's Association of Religious Scientists uses its talents to find technical ways of avoiding the violation of the Sabbath in a society filled with modern conveniences.

Orthodox Jews are careful to observe the Sabbath and the festivals in every detail. They will not work, ride, write, or turn on the light switch during the Sabbath. Radio and television are not turned on either. Musical instruments and choirs are not permitted in Orthodox worship services. Men cover their heads at all times with the skull cap (Hebrew *kippah;* Yiddish *yarmulke)* or a hat as a sign of respect for God. Married women cover their hair with a kerchief or wig as a sign of modesty. Most people may view such Orthodox Jewish practices as restrictive and archaic, but Orthodox Jews believe they are embracing the total past and tradition of the Jewish people. They firmly accept that they are special participants in God's holy order, "free" to worship God in His Way of Torah, "free" from the "slavery" of office, telephone, television, and secular amusements. To the Orthodox Jew, one always has a master, and one has the option to choose God as one's Master.

Orthodox Jews believe in a personal Messiah. This individual will be a charismatically endowed descendant of David who will reign in Jerusalem, will rebuild the Temple, and will reinstitute the sacrificial system. Although some Orthodox rabbis at first opposed political Zionism because of its secular base, and others today oppose the state of Israel because the Messiah did not establish it, most Orthodox rabbis, leaders, and laypeople view the state of Israel as "the beginning of the redemption," God's guiding of human beings to prepare for the Messiah. Orthodox rabbis even speculate about the meaning of contemporary events in Israel and in the world in light of their messianic hope. In fact, Jews through *mitzvot* can actually help bring the Messiah—in Orthodox Judaism observance and a sanctified life advances the redemption of the world.

Most Orthodox rabbis have historically opposed dialogue with Christian clergy. They believed that such discussion and the inevitable debate was fruitless and foolish. They also feared that Christians proposed such dialogue as a prelude to covert missionizing and coercive missionary campaigns. Many still feel this way. Nevertheless, some Orthodox leaders have suggested that it may be proper for Jews and non-Jews to work together in areas of social concern and national morality.

One Orthodox rabbi who has entered the field of Jewish-Christian relations, and is one of the leading bridge-builders between the Jewish and Christian communities today, is Rabbi Yechiel Eckstein. A former national codirector of Interreligious Affairs for the Anti-Defamation League of B'nai Brith, Rabbi Eckstein has founded the Holyland Fellowship of Christians and Jews in Chicago, an organization that both Christians and Jews can contact for further understanding and dialogue. In his book, *What Christians Should Know About Jews and Judaism* (Word Books, 1984), Rabbi Eckstein explains concerning Christian-Jewish dialogue:

> The term "dialogue" represents more than just talk or conversation; it reaches beyond mere niceties. Dialogue is one of the most profound and compelling activities two people or groups can possibly engage in. In its ideal sense, dialogue involves an "I-thou" relationship (to use Martin Buber's terminology) wherein the quest for truth and authenticity is paramount and is built upon a solid foundation of openness and respect. Genuine dialogue demands that the parties treat one another *as they are,* and not attempt to use each other *as its* or impose their own categories of belief onto the other. While they may try to convince each other of their respective positions, their efforts must never involve manipulation, coercion, or deception. And while dialogue does not, necessarily, involve the acceptance of the other's viewpoints, it does imply openness to searching together for common understanding. (pp. 300-301)

Rabbi Eckstein finds that "the story of Christian-Jewish encounter is, unfortunately, a mostly sad and tragic one," but he firmly believes that "dialogue between Christians and Jews can be especially engaging and enriching." In Rabbi Yechiel Eckstein, the demanding life of Orthodox Judaism, the commitment and sacrifice to God and Torah, is coupled to the ever-rigorous task of bringing Jews and Christians together in a spirit of understanding, appreciation, and cooperation.

8

The Reform

At the founding of the Union of Orthodox Jewish Congregations of America in 1898, the Orthodox rabbis present made clear that they were "anti-Reform" and that Reform views were totally unacceptable. By the last quarter of the nineteenth century the Reform movement was strong and well-organized, whereas the Orthodox (in spite of new immigrants) felt divided, threatened, and weak. Whereas Orthodox Judaism coveted unity around traditional Judaism, the strength of the Reform movement was that it engendered and tolerated diversity.

Reform Judaism was the first of the contemporary reinterpretations of Judaism to emerge in response to the modern technological world and newly won freedoms. Early reformers were German laymen who had no intention of breaking with Jewish tradition. They sought only to adapt and modify the traditional synagogue service to modern culture, such as shortening the liturgy by avoiding repetition and using German as well as Hebrew, introducing the sermon, adding mixed choral singing, and so forth. A new generation of university-educated rabbis, familiar with modern biblical criticism, added theological impetus to the lay Reform movement. Quite independently, Jewish laymen in the United States incorporated such changes in their Orthodox synagogues. German Reform rabbis immigrating to America solidified the Reform movement in the United States. In a pioneer atmosphere with no traditional or organizational restraints, Reform Judaism in America went far beyond the more traditional Reform movement in Europe.

The first Reform congregation in America was in Charleston, South Carolina, a cultural and commercial hub on the eastern seaboard. In the

1820s Charleston had the second largest Jewish community in the United States, and it was a group of forty-seven worshipers at its old Beth Elohim synagogue who in 1824 requested a shorter service with a sermon in English. After their request was denied early in 1825, the petitioners established their own congregation, the Reformed Society of Israelites. This new Reform congregation instituted English prayers, a weekly sermon in English, and a commentary on the weekly Torah portion. Ironically, within a decade the leaders of Beth Elohim had changed their minds, and the old congregation became a Reform synagogue. They hired a German-trained Polish rabbi, Gustav Poznanski (1809-1879), who was asked to deliver sermons in English. They also voted in the use of the organ, elimination of some of the Hebrew prayers thought not to be central to the service, and did away with the second day of the festivals. Rabbi Poznanski is quoted as saying, "This synagogue is our *temple,* this city our *Jerusalem,* this happy land our *Palestine.*" As we have seen in chapter 5, Reform societies and synagogues spread rapidly across the United States.

Isaac Mayer Wise (1819-1900), a native of Steingrub, Bohemia, and the son of a poverty-stricken teacher, became an important leader in the Reform movement after immigrating to the United States in 1846. The free religious atmosphere in America dramatically affected Wise, and as rabbi of Congregation Beth El in Albany, New York, he introduced reforms such as mixed seating, a choir of men and women, elimination of Hebrew prayers that included reference to the Messiah, and confirmation for Jewish young people. In 1850 the congregation split, and Wise and his supporters organized Albany's first Reform synagogue. In 1853 Rabbi Isaac Mayer Wise was hired at Cincinnati's B'nai Jeshurun, where he spent the rest of his life as leader of Reform Judaism. For nearly half a century, Wise edited and published the *American Israelite,* and one can gain a keen understanding of this Reform rabbi from that periodical. His goal in the beginning was to unite *all* American synagogues into one organization.

In 1873 Wise established the Union of American Hebrew Congregations (UAHC), its primary purpose to support a seminary to train all American rabbis. The UAHC is regarded as the first nationwide cooperative organization of Jewish congregations. At first it included both traditional and "progressive" congregations. Today its headquarters is in New York City, and it is an association of approximately eight hundred congregations in the United States and Canada.

To Wise's delight, Hebrew Union College (HUC) was founded in 1875 in Cincinnati, the first extant institution of Jewish higher learning in America. Currently, Hebrew Union College-Jewish Institute of Religion (after the merger with Rabbi Stephen S. Wise's Institute in 1950, see below) has centers in Cincinnati, New York, Los Angeles, and Jerusalem. In addition to its rabbinical school, it has a school of biblical archaeology, a school of education, a school of sacred music (for training cantors), a school of Jewish communal service, and a school of graduate studies. Besides providing rabbis for Reform Jewish congregations, its graduates fill the need in many Conservative congregations as well as Jewish agencies. Hebrew Union College-Jewish Institute of Religion (HUC-JIR) is so highly respected in academic circles that its Ph.D. program has more Christians than Jews as candidates. A number of conservative Christian professors of Old Testament in Christian seminaries have received their Ph.D.'s there.

Rabbi Isaac Mayer Wise's plan that the Union of American Hebrew Congregations would be an umbrella organization for all of American Judaism kept the organization from radical changes during the first decade of its existence. The Union grew from an initial twenty-eight congregations that included some traditional synagogues to almost two hundred synagogues by 1880. The Reform movement had its greatest success among German Jewish immigrants, especially in the South and West. Alas, at a banquet celebrating the first four rabbinical graduates of Hebrew Union College to be ordained, nonkosher food was served. Offended, traditional Jewish leaders walked out, forever splitting the Union.

Reform Judaism moved immediately to a more radical position. In its 1885 meeting in Pittsburgh, the Union of American Hebrew Congregations adopted an eight-point program that would guide Reform Judaism for the next half century. After this Pittsburgh Platform was adopted, all hope for reunion with the traditionalists was dashed. The Pittsburgh Platform of 1885 read:

1. Judaism teaches the highest idea of God of any religion because it preaches ethical monotheism.
2. The Bible is the record of Israel's consecration to God.
3. Modern scientific and philosophical ideas are not opposed to Judaism since the teachings of the Bible merely reflect the primitive ideas of the time.

4. Only the moral laws of Judaism are binding. The ritual laws such as kashrut, priestly purity, and dress codes are of pagan origin and are no longer necessary to our spiritual upliftment.

5. We are no longer a nation, but a "religious community," and we no longer expect to return to Palestine or a Jewish state or offer sacrifices in a Temple.

6. Judaism must work with Christianity and Islam to bring truth and righteousness to mankind.

7. The notions of Heaven and Hell and bodily resurrection of the dead are no longer meaningful.

8. Jews must participate in the task of solving the problems of society through a program of social justice.

In chapter 5 we discussed Reform Judaism's initial opposition to Zionism, as well as the gradual change within the movement because of the rise of pogroms and Adolf Hitler.

Reform Judaism of the latter nineteenth and early twentieth centuries became quite radical. It declared that Hebrew was no longer necessary because it was not the native language of the American "holy land," and that the Talmud and the codes of Jewish law (such as the *Shulkhan Arukh)* were no longer binding on Jews. It dropped the requirement of a *ketubah,* or marriage contract, and also dropped the *get,* or Jewish divorce. Reform Jews eliminated the wearing of *tallit* and *tefillin,* wore no head coverings and, in many cases, instituted Sunday services. Late Friday evening services replaced or supplemented the traditional Saturday morning service, and in the 1890s Reform rabbis ruled that circumcision was no longer required when a male converted to Judaism. Reform Judaism moved further and further from Jewish tradition. In some cases, Reform synagogues became almost indistinguishable from Protestant churches.

Some Reform rabbis could scarcely believe the outlook of the revolutionary reformers. For example, Reform Rabbi Stephen S. Wise was so displeased with the teaching of Hebrew Union College in Cincinnati and the radical direction of Reform Judaism, a movement he believed was becoming increasingly out of touch with the Eastern European Jewish masses, that he set up the Jewish Institute of Religion in New York City. Only after HUC and Reform Judaism began to change would the Jewish Institute of Religion merge with HUC.

In 1889 the third arm of the Reform movement (in addition to UAHC and HUC) was created—the Central Conference of American Rabbis (CCAR). This national association of Reform rabbis today has a membership of approximately 1,500. Regarding itself as the successor to the Reform rabbinical councils in nineteenth-century Germany, the CCAR was a pioneer in areas of American social action, religious education, and Christian-Jewish relations. As its members followed the lead of Zionist Reform rabbis, such as Stephen S. Wise, the CCAR progressively supported a Jewish state in Eretz Yisrael and adopted a less radical platform. When Reform rabbis gathered in Columbus, Ohio, in 1937 to consider its Commission to Redraft the Principles of Judaism's "Guiding Principles of Reform Judaism," a much more traditional constituency was present than had been at the Pittsburgh meeting in 1885. Although quite a battle took place between factions, the resulting Columbus Platform of 1937 was a watershed for the change in direction for Reform Judaism. In stark contrast to the 1885 statement, the Columbus Platform stressed the uniqueness of Judaism and the importance of Torah. Both the written and oral Torah was said to remain the "dynamic source of life" for the Jewish people.

Distinctly Zionist language was carefully worded into a support for the Jewish homeland, and a demand for social justice to "all, irrespective of race, sect, or class" was a firm affirmation of the CCAR's bold social stands. The Columbus Platform also underscored the centrality of the Sabbath and the Jewish festivals to Jewish faith in the home and the synagogue. Even the importance of the Hebrew language was stressed. Changes in the Reform movement were gradual, but a post-World War II period of growth witnessed a move back toward a more traditional practice. Nevertheless, Reform Judaism today remains a distinctive entity from either Conservative or Orthodox Judaism in its principles, practices, and worship.

Like its nineteenth-century precursor, modern Reform Judaism still believes that halakhah is created by human beings, not God. Because Judaism is a changing, evolving, and growing religious tradition, human beings have the option to change or modify Jewish practices. It strives to maintain a balance between such adaptation to modern culture and the perpetuation of the historic Jewish tradition. Reform Judaism continues to teach that revelation is progressive, that is, God reveals new rules to the Jewish community. Some Reform philosophers insist that God reveals *only* His presence, not laws, commandments, and so forth. Reform Judaism accepts modern biblical criticism and evolutionary theory and believes in a coming messianic age, rather than in a personal Messiah. Ideas about God and the future vary greatly within the movement, and

Reform Judaism is careful not to dictate the theology or practice of its adherents. It strongly upholds the autonomy of the local congregation. In fact, Reform Judaism is so flexible that some Reform rabbis have been calling for an official guide or code to regularize Reform Jewish practices.

In the area of observance, Reform Judaism prefers that people rest on the Sabbath but does not command such observance. *Kashrut,* or the dietary laws, are not usually observed in Reform homes, but it is not uncommon to find Reform rabbis' homes judiciously observing kashrut (even with separate dishes). Most Reform Jews today have their sons circumcised (although not necessarily in a religious ceremony), and the Bar Mitzvah has been reinstituted (as well as a Bat Mitzvah for girls). The confirmation ceremony for teenagers sixteen or seventeen years of age that nineteenth-century Reform Judaism had originally substituted for Bar and Bat Mitzvah is still held as well. This prolongs the period of Jewish education, and "classes" of Jewish young people are usually "confirmed" in a ceremony during the holiday of Shavuot. These young people recite various selections from the Bible and publicly declare their devotion to Judaism. They receive special certificates, the hearty support of their congregation, and often additional gifts: prayer books, Bibles, and other things.

Reform Jews often refer to their synagogues as "temples," sometimes to show that they no longer pray for the rebuilding of the Temple in Jerusalem. And yet, the movement is very supportive of the state of Israel and the importance of a Jewish nation (although the battles with the Israeli Orthodox movement discussed in chapter 6 still rage). Head coverings are not usually worn in Reform services, and *tallit* and *tefillin* are almost never used. Men and women sit together in services, and HUC-JIR ordained its first female rabbi in 1972. Since then, an increasing number of young women have chosen to enter the rabbinate, and Reform Judaism's continued emphasis on social justice has led it to affirm strongly equal rights for women in the synagogue, work place, and society at large. Female presidents of congregations are not uncommon, and women enter into every dimension of Reform Jewish worship.

Instrumental music and choirs are often part of the Reform service, and the sermon is considered the highlight of the Reform Sabbath ceremony. Most Reform congregations now have a combination of English and Hebrew in the service, including Hebrew songs and recitations. The Friday evening service is usually the most important service of the week, and many Reform congregations do not have regular Shabbat morning worship. These are increasingly reading the Torah on Friday night. Most Reform congregations have Sunday schools and even weekly Hebrew schools. There is total affirmation in Reform Judaism of both the yearly cycle and life cycle. The Jewish festivals are celebrated, although the second days of festivals such as Sukkot, Passover, and Shavuot are not observed (in keeping with ancient biblical practice and as done in Israel today). Unlike Orthodox and Conservative Jews, Reform Jews celebrate Simchat Torah on *Shemini Atzeret* as is done in Israel.

In contrast to the traditional Hebrew prayer books, which read right to left, the Reform *Union Prayer Book* (first published in 1892, and revised in 1922 and 1940) and its new *Gates of Prayer* (1975) read left to right. However, changes in Reform Judaism and diversity in congregations are certainly evident in that *Gates of Prayer* is available in a Hebrew format, opening right to left. It even includes the benedictions for putting on the *tallit* and *tefillin*.

Reform rabbis have been extremely active in Jewish-Christian relations, most becoming active members of their local ministerial associations. Rabbi Joshua O. Haberman of the Washington Hebrew Congregation in Washington, D.C. (founded in 1852 and one of the largest Reform congregations in the United States) has played an important part in furthering understanding between Jews and Christians on the national scene as well as in local dialogue. In his six-page booklet "If Jesus Visited a Modern Synagogue," Rabbi Haberman wrote:

> The moment Jesus walked into any modern synagogue he would feel a sense of "at homeness" because of the Hebrew prayers which are spoken there and are inscribed on the walls usually above the ark of the synagogue. He would recognize immediately the sentence known as the "shema" which, translated into English, says "Hear, O Israel, the Lord our God, the Lord is one." This sentence from Deuteronomy 6:4 is recited at every service. It is likewise inscribed inside the "Mezuzah," the little tube which is affixed at the door of every Jewish home as a reminder of God's presence and the mystery of His unity. Jesus, I think, would be pleased with the extraordinary prominence of the shema statement in the modern Jewish faith. . . .
>
> Looking around the modern synagogue, Jesus would likewise be very familiar with at least two sacred symbols: the perpetual lamp hanging over the ark and the seven-branched candelabrum called the "Menorah." The perpetual lamp, based upon the passage in Exodus 27:20, is still meaningful to us as a symbol of the eternal Presence of God, and

the seven-branched candelabrum, which is described in Exodus 25:37, is generally understood to represent the six days of creation to which the Sabbath was added as the seventh day, a day of rest, in recognition of God's creatorship.

Of all the prayers Jesus would hear in the synagogue, the one most likely to move him deeply would be the popular "Kaddish" which opens in words of striking similarity to the Lord's Prayer: "Hallowed be the name of God throughout the world which he created according to His will. May His kingdom come speedily."

Today, Reform practice has drawn closer to Conservative Judaism than at any other time in its history. Notwithstanding, it continues to assert that a Jew should be free to exercise his or her individual judgment in choosing the basis of commitment and knowledge. Flexibility of belief and diversity of views remains the group standard of Reform Judaism. As the introduction to *Gates of Prayer: The New Union Prayerbook* (New York: Central Conference of American Rabbis, 1975) states so well: "We are a diversified people. Within our Reform community are proponents of many viewpoints. There is disagreement among us on many issues. ... We do not assume that all controversy is harmful."

9
The Conservative

Like Reform Judaism, Conservative Judaism has roots firmly planted in the soil of Western Europe. Zacharias Frankel (1801-1875), a scholar and rabbi born in Prague, was called in 1836 by the government of Saxony to be chief rabbi of Dresden. The first Bohemian rabbi to have both a talmudic and a secular education (in Budapest), Frankel founded the "positivist-historical" school of Jewish thought, advocating moderate change within the boundaries of halakhah. He was one of the first rabbis to preach in German, and he insisted that only moderate reforms that were not in conflict with the spirit of historical Judaism should be permitted in traditional ritual. When the reformist Frankfort Rabbinical Conference of 1845 sought to do away with Hebrew in the synagogue liturgy, Frankel broke with that reform movement.

Frankel's policy of moderation was attacked by both Reform Judaism on the left and Orthodox Judaism on the right, so he decided to found his own *Jüdisch-Theologisches Seminar* (the Jewish Theological Seminary) at Breslau in 1854, an institution he directed until his death. At this European Jewish Theological Seminary, Frankel laid the basis for Conservative Judaism, a movement that would become popular in the New World rather than in Europe. This institution also set the standard for modern rabbinical curriculum and training.

Conservative Judaism holds many of the basic precepts of its nineteenth-century forebearer, Zacharias Frankel. The Conservatives believe that modern culture necessitates some adaptation and change. They believe that the entire history of Judaism was a succession of changes, and that change is valid in light of biblical and rabbinic precedents. To the

Conservatives, the Jewish peoplehood is a living organism that historically responded with creativity to new challenges. And yet, such change is to be made with only the greatest reluctance, because Conservative Judaism maintains the validity of the traditional forms and precepts of Judaism. There is an essential commitment of Conservative Judaism to the observance of kashrut, the Sabbath, the yearly and life cycles, reestablishment of the Jewish state in Eretz Yisrael, and devotion to the Hebrew language.

These attitudes are clearly evident in the American pioneer of Conservative Judaism in the United States, Rabbi Isaac Leeser (1806-1868). Leeser grew up in Prussia, receiving both a talmudic and secular German education. He emigrated to Richmond, Virginia, in 1824, and attracted wide notice when he defended Judaism in an essay responding to a defamatory attack in a New York newspaper. In 1829 the Sephardic Philadelphia congregation, Mikveh Israel, appointed him to be its *chazzan* ("minister"),[1] and Rabbi Leeser was the first to introduce a sermon in English into an American synagogue service. He remained at Mikveh Israel for the next twenty-six years, introducing a few readings in English into the service and yet devoting himself to the retention of the traditional Hebrew liturgy. His views are quite evident in the monthly periodical he founded in 1843, *The Occident,* which (among other things) helped raise support for Jewish colonies in Palestine.

In the field of Jewish education, Isaac Leeser remains a legend. He published the first Hebrew primer for children in America in 1838 and founded the first Hebrew high school in 1849. He was instrumental in the Jewish Sunday school movement and wrote numerous texts for young people. He even translated into English the Sephardic prayer book (1848) and provided the first American translation of the Hebrew Bible (1845). Rabbi Leeser founded Maimonides College of Philadelphia in 1867, the first American Jewish rabbinical school. Although his college failed in six years (due largely to Leeser's death in 1868), it produced the first rabbis trained in the United States.

Rabbi Isaac Leeser tried to adapt traditional Judaism to the American culture. He did not like being called a Reform Jew, yet he tried to cooperate with Isaac Mayer Wise in realizing the dream of a consensus among Jews in America. It was the moderate rabbis that surrounded Leeser who tried to work with the leaders of the emerging Reform Judaism, moderates such as Rabbi Benjamin Szold (1829-1902) of Balti-

---

1. Today, the word *chazzan* refers to a cantor in the synagogue.

more's Congregation Oheb Shalom, Rabbi Alexander Kohut (1842-1894) of New York's Congregation Ahabath Chesed, and Leeser's successor at Mikveh Israel in Philadelphia, Rabbi Sabato Morais (1823-1897). Rabbi Szold had studied under Frankel in Breslau, and Rabbi Kohut was ordained in 1867 at the Jewish Theological Seminary of Breslau (after earning a doctorate in oriental languages at the University of Leipzig in 1865). It was Szold and Morais who were to walk out of the first graduation exercises of Hebrew Union College in 1883 when nonkosher food was served, and the Pittsburgh Platform of 1885 would sever the relationship of all three rabbis with Reform Judaism.

Under the direction of these moderate Conservatives and others (such as the rabbi of Shearith Israel in New York, H. Pereira Mendes, a champion of "modern enlightened Orthodoxy"), Jewish Theological Seminary of America (JTS) was founded in 1887 in New York City as an alternative to Reform Judaism's Hebrew Union College. At the opening exercises, Rabbi Kohut used the term "Conservative Judaism" to describe their movement. It was one of the earliest recorded usages of the name that would come to characterize a major Jewish tradition. The JTS Articles of Incorporation declared that the seminary was dedicated to "the preservation in America of the knowledge and practice of historical Judaism as ordained in the law of Moses expounded by the prophets and sages in Israel in Biblical and Talmudic writings."

Today, the Jewish Theological Seminary of America is the educational and spiritual center of the Conservative movement, with one of the largest Jewish libraries in the world, a prestigious rare book and manuscript collection, the principal patron of the Jewish Museum of New York, extensions in Los Angeles (the University of Judaism) and Jerusalem (the American Student Center), a Teachers' Institute and Sacred Music school, and a College of Jewish Studies for extension course work. The JTS and its faculty have historically been more traditional than many Conservative congregations, and currently remain so.

This vibrant educational institution may not have come to fruition had not dedicated Reform and Conservative laymen rescued JTS from lack of funds at the turn of the twentieth century. These individuals believed that the masses of East European immigrants needed an alternative to the radical Reform movement. Indeed, Conservative Judaism soon bridged the gap between Orthodox Judaism and Reform Judaism for the children of Jewish immigrants who wanted to modernize somewhat without giving up their attachment to tradition. By the 1950s, every study of religious preference among Jews showed that approximately half of all Jews in the United States considered themselves Conservative Jews.

Much of the groundwork for this broad base was laid by Rabbi Solomon Schechter (1847-1915), a professor at Cambridge University and the University of London, who was convinced to emigrate to the United States and become president of Jewish Theological Seminary in 1902. He is considered the chief architect of Conservative Judaism in the twentieth century and was to Conservative Judaism what Isaac Mayer Wise was to Reform Judaism. Schechter himself was regarded as one of the finest biblical scholars of England, and he reorganized the seminary with a staff of highly trained scholars. He firmly believed that the purpose of JTS must be to connect Jewish people with their past, and he steadfastly maintained that the future of Judaism was in the United States. "The rabbi should be the greatest of his brethren," Dr. Schechter told his students, insisting that "the observance of the Sabbath, the keeping of the dietary laws, devotion to Hebrew literature, and hope for Zion are as absolutely necessary for maintaining Judaism in America as elsewhere." He was fond of repeating: "It is not the mere revealed Bible that is of first importance to the Jew, but the Bible as it repeats itself in history, in other words, as it is interpreted by Tradition."

Under the leadership of Solomon Schechter, the United Synagogue of America was founded in 1913. This association of Conservative synagogues in the United States and Canada has grown from the original 22 to approximately 850. The founders of the United Synagogue of America committed themselves to eight goals:

1. The advancement of the cause of Judaism in America and the maintenance of Jewish tradition in its historic continuity
2. To assert and establish loyalty to the Torah and its historic exposition
3. To further the observance of the Sabbath and the dietary laws
4. To preserve in the service the reference to Israel's past and the hopes for Israel's restoration
5. To maintain the traditional character of the liturgy with Hebrew as the language of prayer
6. To foster Jewish religious life in the home, as expressed in traditional observances
7. To encourage the establishment of Jewish religious schools
8. To embrace all elements essentially loyal to traditional Judaism

These goals were Solomon Schechter's goals, and Conservative Judaism has attempted to maintain them in the twentieth century.

Whereas congregations that permitted the use of musical instruments and permitted men and women to sit together during the service were allowed to join the United Synagogue of America at its inception, any congregation that used the Reform *Union Prayer Book* or that worshiped without head coverings was not permitted to join. In 1952 the United Synagogue attempted to raise standards of conduct for its member congregations by adopting a "Guide to Standards for Congregational Life." In 1959 a similar "Statement of Standards for Synagogue Practice" became binding on all affiliated synagogues.

Nevertheless, the United Synagogue does not have as much authority in the Conservative movement as its counterpart, the Union of American Hebrew Congregations, has in Reform Judaism. It is actually the Rabbinical Assembly of Conservative Judaism that debates and articulates the position of the movement on most issues, and the Jewish Theological Seminary that exercises great influence on standards. Existing as an alumni association for JTS in 1901, this body of rabbis was called the Rabbinical Assembly of America by 1920 and was finally incorporated in 1929 under that name. In 1962 this organization was renamed the Rabbinical Assembly, the International Association of Conservative Rabbis. Simply referred to as the Rabbinical Assembly (RA), it is the Conservative counterpart to the Reform movement's Central Conference of American Rabbis.

In the past few decades, decisions such as allowing women the right to receive *aliyot* (to be called forward to recite the blessing over the Torah) and to be counted in the *minyan* (quorum of ten required for communal prayer) have been made by the RA, subject to the policy of the individual Conservative congregations. In recent years, the subject of women's ordination has initiated a great deal of debate. In 1979 at the convention of the RA, the Conservative rabbis voted to leave the decision of women's ordination with the faculty of the JTS, even though a commission they set up recommended that qualified women be admitted to the JTS rabbinical school.

After much debate in the early 1980s, women were finally permitted ordination in the Conservative movement. The JTS faculty was so divided over the issue that the outcome was in doubt until the last moment. Proponents of women's ordination had often pointed out that technically there was no prohibition in halakhah against women performing rabbinic functions and that it was in proper order with Conservative Judaism's historical commitment to "change." Opponents argued that women's ordination was a departure from Jewish tradition and that such a vote would alienate traditional Conservative Jews, pitting the right wing against the moderate and left wing within the movement. Some more traditional Conservative congregations have threatened to leave the movement over the issue.

Presently, Conservative Judaism continues to preserve its stance that halakhah is an essential element in Judaism. Officially, the Conservative movement expects its members to lead their lives according to the principles outlined in the Torah. In contrast to Reform Judaism, Conservative Judaism insists that Jewish law is binding. A Conservative Jew is expected to observe the Sabbath and kashrut. In practice, however, many Conservative Jews are not strict in their observance. This is in spite of the fact that the RA has contributed rulings and changes over the years that have made observance easier in a modern culture.

For example, Conservative Jews are permitted to use electricity on the Sabbath (the RA ruling that it is not the same as fire), are allowed to drive a car to services (most do), are permitted to eat a dairy meal in a nonkosher restaurant, and to use foods containing gelatin (from nonkosher animal tissues) when it has been so chemically altered that it is no longer in its original form. The RA has even ruled that the observance of the second day of festivals be optional, since Israel uses the biblical calendar. Only a few Conservative synagogues, however, have opted for a one day observance. In contrast to Orthodox Judaism, therefore, Conservative Judaism believes that Jewish law and ideology were not set once and for all at Sinai, but rather have evolved and changed. To be historically authentic, Judaism must be allowed to adapt and modify.

In a Conservative synagogue, men and women usually sit together in the worship service, and men wear head coverings. English prayers are used during the service, but there is a predominance of Hebrew. Prayer books have been modernized—the Hebrew and English are both included in the Conservative texts. The rabbi preaches a sermon in English at the Friday evening service, and this service is generally the one with the greatest attendance (although Sabbath morning service is also held). A Sunday school is part of the weekly activity, and the Conservative movement holds tenaciously to the events of the life cycle as well as the yearly cycle. Male children are circumcised in a religious service; female children are named in the synagogue service. In addition to Bar and Bat Mitzvah, a confirmation class is usually held for teenagers. Jewish education is stressed, and a Conservative rabbi is not permitted to marry a Jew to a non-Jew if the non-Jewish partner does not convert. Conservative males are expected to pray daily with *tallit* and *tefillin*, and a Conservative woman is expected to run a kosher home and light the Sabbath candles. Conservative women usually do not go to the mikveh (the exception to this is during the conversion process). The trend in the Conservative movement is to give women equal status with men, and Conservative Judaism is extremely concerned about social justice. The Conservative movement expects its members to live moral and ethical lives of the highest quality. The movement has also been a firm supporter of the state of Israel; but it has been contending with the Orthodox Israeli for the right to equal recognition and the right to found synagogues, camps, and schools in the Jewish state.

Conservative Jews have been very active in Jewish-Christian relationships. Because most Conservatives believe in a messianic age rather than a personal messiah, they acknowledge that Christians and Jews must join together to better understand each other, combat prejudice, and build a better society. One of the most active Conservatives in this endeavor is JTS graduate Rabbi Marc H. Tanenbaum, for many years national director for interreligious affairs for the American Jewish Committee (AJC) and currently director of international relations of the AJC. Rabbi Tanenbaum has often asserted that "since Hitler and the founding of the United Nations, more persons have been killed by massacre than by traditional wars that have kept the world on edge."

Seeing a definite progression from verbal aggression to violence, from rumor to riot, and from gossip to genocide, Rabbi Tanenbaum has frequently called for Christian-Jewish cooperation. In a number of speeches he has underscored the following points:

1. Christians and Jews must help engender a national and international attitude of scorn and contempt for those who use violence or who advocate the use of violence. We must work to deromanticize all appeals to use violence and terrorism as means of liberation or of institutional oppression, since from a moral standpoint, no ends can justify such antihuman means.

2. Christians and Jews must work to curtail the resort to inflammatory propaganda, especially from international forums that have psychological impact on an international scale.

3. Christians and Jews must work toward educational development and communication among peoples to reduce the abrasive effects of "differences." Differences, as we have learned in the pluralistic experience of America, can be a source of enrichment rather than a threat.

4. Christians and Jews should engage in a massive effort . . . to restore the biblical value of the infinite worth and preciousness of each human life.

10

Other Groups

As the Jewish people have continued to interact with their tradition and with the world about them, as they have sought relevance, interpretation, meaning, and spirit, other groups have become a part of the Jewish milieu. Although these groups differ significantly from one another, a brief sketch of background and place within the Jewish peoplehood will help round out the Christian's knowledge of this diverse, creative, and vibrant people.

RECONSTRUCTIONIST JEWS

Out of Conservative Judaism came a rabbi and scholar who developed a distinctly American-born movement. The rabbi was Mordecai M. Kaplan (1881-1983). The movement was Reconstructionism. It has been described as the left wing of the Conservative movement and is so distinct and so intrinsically linked with the powerful dynamism of its founder that its influence is felt beyond its small constituency.

Mordecai Kaplan was born in Lithuania and emigrated to the United States with his family in 1890. He was raised in the Orthodox tradition, and his father (a rabbi) became an assistant to Rabbi Jacob Joseph, the chief rabbi of New York. Mordecai's American experience had a profound effect on his life, for he immediately was faced with the difficulty of living as an Orthodox Jew in the modern non-Jewish world. Graduated and ordained at the Jewish Theological Seminary in 1902 (with other work at City College of New York and Columbia University), Rabbi Kaplan became an associate rabbi of the prominent Orthodox synagogue in New York City, Kehillath Jeshurun.

Conservative Judaism's Dr. Solomon Schechter discerned the promise of this young man, and in 1909 appointed Kaplan dean of the new Teachers Institute of the Jewish Theological Seminary. An excellent orator, Kaplan began teaching homiletics within a few months in J.T.S.'s rabbinical school and soon became professor of Midrash and philosophies of religion. He thus affected hundreds of Hebrew teachers and three generations of rabbis in his five decades as a professor at J.T.S.

An active Zionist, Rabbi Kaplan was one of the founders of the Orthodox Young Israel movement (1912), and he organized the first synagogue-center, the Jewish Center, in Manhattan (1915). Completely observant as an Orthodox Jew, Mordecai Kaplan's philosophy and theology was becoming increasingly un-Orthodox. In 1922 he formed his own synagogue, the Society for the Advancement of Judaism, a laboratory for Kaplan to address the challenges posed by modern culture to traditional Judaism. Gathering students, rabbis, and laypersons who shared his views on "reconstructing" Judaism and Jewish values, the Society gave birth to the Reconstructionist movement. *The Reconstructionist* magazine was begun in 1935, and the Jewish Reconstructionist Foundation originated in 1940. One of his students noted that Rabbi Kaplan was not only a great scholar and teacher in his prime, but also was "a titanic force, reshaping the landscape around him."

And reshape it he did. Kaplan's more traditional colleagues at Jewish Theological Seminary almost forced his resignation in the 1920s, and his followers formed a separate party within the Conservative movement, winning some Reform rabbis as well as some secularists. The explosion created by his 1934 book, *Judaism as a Civilization: Toward a Reconstruction of American Jewish Life,* caused a furor that took decades to subside. In this book, his first, Kaplan proposed that the *Jewish people* rather than God be viewed as the center of Jewish life. He suggested a "reconstruction" of historical Judaism without supernatural revelation and reference to God's "choosing" the Jews. To Kaplan, everything must be done to preserve the Jewish people, even though it might mean discarding old ideas. Kaplan was confident that modern Jews could create the new, if they would no longer insist "that God is a mighty Sovereign, or that the universe is the work of his hands." Launching a scathing attack on all three branches of Judaism, Mordecai Kaplan sought to reach the remaining Jews of America who were not members of the other groups. His dream was to bring together all Jews in "organic communities" or *kehillot.*

In 1941 Kaplan edited (with others) a Reconstructionist service for the Passover Seder, *The New Haggadah*, and in 1945 published a Reconstructionist *Sabbath Prayer Book*. Even his friends at Jewish Theological Seminary criticized him for this, and a few Orthodox rabbis burned the new prayer book. Calling Kaplan a "nonbeliever" and a "heretic," they held an Orthodox excommunication service. Kaplan insisted that he was not a "secularist," because secularism did not appreciate the basic role of religion in Jewish culture as he did.

Increasingly isolated from many in the Jewish community, Rabbi Mordecai M. Kaplan emigrated to Israel in the 1960s. He had often stated that Judaism must be centered in Israel, and he believed that reconstruction of Jewish life had already begun in Israel (whereas it was only "in the talking stage" in the United States). He returned to the United States in his later years. He was more than one hundred years old when he died.

Although the Reconstructionist movement for many years insisted that it was not a new denomination, in 1959 Kaplan's son-in-law, Rabbi Ira Eisenstein, formed the Fellowship of Reconstructionist Congregations (later changed to the Federation of Reconstructionist Congregations and Fellowships, and now called Federation of Reconstructionist Congregations and Havurot). In 1968, the Reconstructionist Rabbinical College was established in Philadelphia and ordained its first class in 1973. In 1974 the Reconstructionist Rabbinical Association was founded. By 1970, however, only ten congregations were affiliated with the Federation, representing 2300 Jewish families. Today, less than one hundred men and women belong to the Reconstructionist Rabbinical Association, and approximately fifty congregations are affiliated with the movement.

In *Questions Jews Ask: Reconstructionist Answers* (New York: Reconstructionist Press, 1956), Rabbi Kaplan answered the question, "What is right and what is wrong with Orthodox, Reform, Conservative, and Secularist Judaism respectively?"

He answered that Orthodox Judaism was right in "its insistence on Judaism as a way of living and not merely a way of speaking, its emphasis on expressing our religious faith not merely in vague and abstract ideals but in specific norms of behavior." Nevertheless, he believed Orthodox Judaism to be wrong in "its intolerance, its claim to having a monopoly of religious truth, its assumption that all non-Orthodox Jews are sinners."

To Kaplan, Reform Judaism was right in "its acceptance of evolution, its recognition of the historic processes by which Judaism changes in response to changing conditions, and yet retains its identity, by virtue of the sense of historic continuity." But Reform Judaism was wrong in "its imperfect realization of the intimate relation of Jewish religion with Jewish peoplehood and the secular aspects of Jewish culture." Although Reform Judaism had reversed itself on Eretz Yisrael, pockets of Reform Judaism (such as the anti-Zionist American Council for Judaism) remained anti-Israel.

Conservative Judaism, Kaplan emphasized, was right in "its stress on *k'lal yisrael,* the unity and integrity of the Jewish People, its greater stress on practice than on dogma as evidence of religious loyalty, and the recognition that the same standards of behavior may be justified by different rationales." Conservative Judaism was wrong (according to Kaplan) in "its failure to come to grips with the challenge to tradition. It has tended to make a virtue of inconsistency, thus justifying, in no small measure, the charge of its opponents that it is ruled by expediency rather than by principle."

Kaplan would only consider Secular Judaism under the rubric of those Secular Jews who were positive toward Jewish survival. "What is right," he explained of them, "is their recognition of the values of Jewish peoplehood and of Eretz Yisrael as the creative center of Jewish cultural life." Nevertheless, Rabbi Mordecai M. Kaplan had considerable differences with Secular Judaism. He declared (*Questions Jews Ask,* p. 440):

> What is wrong with Secular Judaism is the failure of its adherents to understand the basic role of religion in Jewish culture. Identifying religion only with those manifestations of it which have stood in the way of cultural development and human progress, they tend to deprecate its value for Jewish life today. But human nature demands faith in the possibilities of human development, and to inculcate that faith is the essential function of religion. Jewish Secularists, by their aloofness, both fail to participate in the necessary reconstruction of Jewish religion, and deprive their own cultural efforts of the stimulation and direction which religion at its best affords.

One can easily see that both friends and foes, as well as scholars of Jewish movements, have to contend with the twentieth-century thought of Rabbi Mordecai M. Kaplan.

In summary, the Twelve Principles of Reconstructionism give one insight into both the man and his message.

1. Judaism, or that which has united the successive generations of Jews into one People, is not only a religion; it is a dynamic religious civilization.

2. Judaism has passed through three distinct stages in its evolution, and is now on the threshold of a fourth stage. It was primarily *national* in character during the First Commonwealth era, *ecclesiastical* during the Second Commonwealth era, and *rabbinical* from then until the end of the eighteenth century. It is now developing into a *democratic* civilization.

3. The emergence of the next stage calls for the reconstitution of the Jewish people and its enhancement, the revitalization of Jewish religion, and the replenishment of Jewish culture.

4. The reconstitution of the Jewish People is predicated upon the following:
    (a) The reclamation of the Land of Israel as the home of the historic Jewish civilization;
    (b) The renewal of the covenant binding all Jews throughout the world into one united People, with the Jewish community in Israel as the core;
    (c) The formation of organic Jewish communities in all countries of the Jewish Diaspora.

5. An organic community is one in which all activities and institutions conducted by Jews for Jews are interactive, and in which the fostering of Jewish peoplehood, religion, and culture is given primacy.

6. The revitalization of Jewish religion can be best achieved through the study of it in the spirit of free inquiry and through the separation of its organized institutions from all political authority.

7. The revitalization of the Jewish religion requires that the belief in God be interpreted in terms of universally human, and specifically Jewish, experience.

8. By reason of the prevailing diversity in world outlook, there has to be room in Jewish religion for different versions of it.

9. The continuity of a religion through different stages, and its identity amid diversity of belief and practice, are sustained by its *sancta:* these are the heroes, events, texts, places, and seasons that the religion signalizes as furthering the fulfillment of human destiny.

10. The traditional conception of Torah should be expanded to include:
    (a) ethical culture, the fostering of love and justice in all human relations;
    (b) ritual culture, the fostering of the religious *sancta* with all of their symbolic significance;
    (c) esthetic culture, the fostering of the arts as a means of expressing the emotional values of Jewish life.
11. Every people, Jewish and non-Jewish, is nowadays confronted with the problem of living in two civilizations. It has to blend its *historic* civilization with the modern national civilization of the country in which it lives.
12. Loyalty to Judaism should be measured by active participation in Jewish life, in keeping with the foregoing principles.

In its 1980 convention, the Reconstructionist Rabbinical Association placed the authority to determine halakhah within the respective congregation rather than in a rabbinical authority. Local congregational customs were to evolve "democratically."

Secularist Jews

In halakhah, a child born of a Jewish mother is considered a Jew. If the child is born into a family in which one parent is a Jew and the other is a Gentile, the Talmud states that the status of the child follows the status of the mother. "Thy son by an Israelite woman is called thy son, but thy son by a heathen woman is not called thy son" *(Kiddushin 68b)*. Traditional practice required that the child of a non-Jewish mother undergo ritual conversion. In modern times, this definition has been questioned, and the debate over "Who is a Jew?" has been tempestuous. Reform Judaism, for example, recognizes that the status of the child as a Jew may derive from either the mother or the father. The debate in Israel has been discussed in chapter 6.

But what if a child is Jewish (even by talmudic standards) and is secularist in both belief and practice? Such was the case of Baruch Spinoza (1632-1677), a Dutch philosopher. Born in Amsterdam to Sephardi parents, Spinoza began to question whether Adam was the first man, debated against Moses' writing the Pentateuch, and argued that natural law took precedence over Torah.

In later writings he would replace religious tradition completely with rationalism and scientific reasoning. For Spinoza there was no possibility of prophecy or miracles; the Bible was neither mysterious nor divine. God is Nature, Nature is God, with no purpose or goals for humankind. By that time Spinoza had been excommunicated by leaders of his Jewish community who had tried to dissuade him from his "evil ways." The rabbinical pronouncement declared on July 27, 1656, that all the evidence "having been examined in the presence of the rabbis, the council decided, with the advice of the rabbis, that the said [Baruch de] Spinoza should be excommunicated and cut off from the Nation of Israel." He was twenty-four years of age.

Today, few Jews consider themselves secularist, "nonbelievers," or "non-Jewish Jews." In the 1960s it was not uncommon for Jewish young people in college to claim to be "agnostics," but there has been considerable return to Jewish practice and belief since that turbulent decade. Only a small percentage of Jews would describe themselves as atheists (deniers of God) or would even question the existence of God. For example, more than 80 percent of American Jews define themselves in religious terms or as part of a religious movement. This would also be true of Christendom as a whole, but the ethnic identification of the Jewish people adds another dimension of determining "Jewishness" with which contemporary Jewish movements must contend. Certainly the courts in Israel have had to grapple with the issue in modern times. Judaism as a "way of life," the importance of mitzvot, and the sanctifying nature of participation in Jewish causes and organizations further complicate the issue for the present-day Jewish community. In Judaism, the concept of activism is basic. Furthermore, the diversity of belief and practice within established Jewish movements has been evident throughout our study.

In a conference on secularism and pluralism sponsored by the Spinoza Institute in Israel in 1987, scholars debated the possibility of a secular Judaism. Some Jewish scholars believed that Judaism that called itself "secular" was in trouble, often replaced with decadence and anarchy. Others explained that secularism originally penetrated Judaism as a foreign influence and was intrinsically linked with assimilation. Nonetheless, fears were expressed by some that Orthodoxy led to a "barbaric," exclusive form of Judaism, contrary to a pluralistic Jewish state.

Under a portrait of Baruch Spinoza, Professor Yirmiyahu Yovei gave the closing remarks to the participants and audience. He made evident to all involved that the secularist Jew had no intention of going away:

Secularism is a value system competitive to religion. It's neither nihilistic nor transcendental. It is superior to religion and harder to live by, because it insists on individual responsibility. Spinoza tried to be secular and to stay a Jew. He wasn't allowed to do it. But times have changed. I and we can do it. We must struggle to keep the possibility alive for ourselves and others.

HASIDIC JEWS

Hasidim ("pious ones, pietists") is a term used in rabbinic literature to designate those more rigorously observant of religious and moral commandments. In popular usage in the medieval European Jewish communities, it meant a good, just, and upright person. In the 1700s in Lithuania and Poland, the name came to denote an enthusiastic Jewish movement. Today, Hasidic Jews are the charismatic pietists of Judaism.

Drawing heavily from a heritage of Jewish mysticism, the founder of Hasidism, Israel ben Eliezer (c. 1700-1760), gave the poor and persecuted Jews of Eastern Europe new hope of God's love and the ability of any man or woman to experience that love. In the 1730s, Israel ben Eliezer began working miracles and healing the sick. His fame spread, and many followers were drawn by his charismatic personality and deep wisdom. He became known as *Baal Shem Tov* ("Master of the Good Name"). Although he was not the first to hold this title (the words literally mean "Possessor of the Name" and referred in the medieval period to those who possessed secret knowledge and worked miracles), the name and its initials *(Besht)* have been associated with him ever since.

The Baal Shem Tov never put his teachings and parables into writing, but his disciples spread them orally during his ministry. After his death, his teachings were written down by his followers, and tales concerning him were spread all over Europe. His successor, Rabbi Dov Baer of Mezhirech (1710-1772), collected tales from sources he considered reliable into the manuscript *Shivhei ha-Besht (In Praise of the Baal Shem Tov).* "In each case I wrote down the name of the person from whom I heard the tale," Rabbi Dov Baer wrote, "and praise God, who endowed me with memory, I neither added nor omitted a single detail. All is true and irrefutable. I have not changed a single detail."

Well respected as a talmudic scholar, it was Rabbi Dov Baer who organized the movement and sent emissaries to promote the new teaching in other Jewish communities. He instituted the *tzaddik,* or saintly leader, over a variety of Hasidic communities. Thus, Hasidic dynasties were formed as the succession was passed from *tzaddik* (or *rebbe*) to oldest son and, in turn, grandson. When the tzaddik did not have a son, the succession was passed to his son-in-law. In this way the Hasidic movement not only proliferated, but also developed varying customs, traditions, and beliefs.

By the 1830s the major spread of Hasidism had declined in Europe, and it had become a way of life for the majority of Jews in the Ukraine, Galicia, and central Poland. Sizable groups of Hasidic Jews were also to be found in Lithuania and Hungary. The mass emigration of European Jews to the United States in the latter nineteenth and early twentieth centuries spread the Hasidic movement to the West, and the largest centers of Hasidism are currently found in the United States and in Israel. Some Hasidic Jews had traveled to Eretz Yisrael in the mid-1700s and established communities there. The Baal Shem Tov had often talked of traveling to Eretz Yisrael himself.

Today, Hasidic Jews dress like their forebears of two centuries ago. They think like them, eat like them, pray like them, and are governed in the same community manner as they were. They refuse to compromise with modern culture, shunning television and movies, adhering strictly to halakhah. Originally opposed in eighteenth-century Europe by the traditional Jewish community because of the Hasidic ecstasy, visions, miracles, wild dancing during prayer and worship, and seeming emphasis on emotionalism instead of Torah study, Hasidic Jews have been accepted (sometimes guardedly) by Orthodox Judaism as part of the Orthodox movement. The historic opposition to the Hasidic Jews is somewhat analogous to the opposition pentecostal or charismatic Christians have encountered in conservative Protestant circles.

Although varying widely, from the tolerant Lubavitch movement that sends out missionaries to draw nontraditional Jews back to Judaism to the rigid and sectarian Satmar community that is violently opposed to the state of Israel, the heart of Hasidic teaching is the principle of *devekut* ("adhesion" or "union") with God. Through faith, the soul of the Hasidic Jew is to form union with God, not only in times of worship and prayer, but also in daily acts, social contacts, and even business affairs. Clinging to God in this way, a physical act becomes a religious action. In prayer, an ecstatic state may be obtained where the soul of the Hasid is directly linked with the divine. Self is abandoned; communion with the divine is obtained. Also through the study of the Torah, a Hasidic Jew believes that he may link the letters of the Torah to their root, thereby becoming joined to the heavenly source and receiving mystical revelations. Humility, enthusiasm, joy, and community service are all virtues taught and practiced by the Hasidic Jew. Today's tzaddik or rebbe is turned to for advice on a wide variety of topics and is often responsible for mediating between his community and God.

It is recorded in *Shivhei ha-Besht* that once Tsevi, the son of Baal Shem Tov, traveled with him to visit a local rabbi. Tsevi saw many pieces of silverware in the rabbi's home. On the way back to their own home, Baal Shem Tov perceptively said to his son, "You are doubtless envious because your father does not possess any silverware." "Yes," the boy replied. Baal Shem Tov responded: "If your father had money for silverware, it would be better used to provide for poor people and the rest to give for charity."

Across the East River from Manhattan in the Williamsburg section of Brooklyn, tens of thousands of Hasidic Jews live, maintaining hospitals, nursing services, private bus services, interest-free loan agencies, employment agencies, butcher shops and bakeries, publishing enterprises, burial societies, synagogues, and the largest private Jewish school system in the world. One might say that the Baal Shem Tov traded his silverware for this spiritual offspring.

11

Loving the Neighbor

Throughout this book we have dealt with relationships—relationships between Christians and Jews, between Jews and Jews, between Jews and the world in which they lived. As we have sought to understand Jews and Judaism, the principles of interaction and relationship have faced us at every turn, both the good and the bad. With this background, it is important that we confront our personal situation.

In recent years dialogues and convocations have brought the leadership of Christian and Jewish communities together in an effort to build relationships and understanding. I have participated in many such meetings.

And yet I believe firmly that the major accomplishments are those made at the local level by lay Christians and Jews. These men and women have taken the time to get to know one another, building day-to-day friendships that are fruitful and enduring.

Perhaps you are a person who wants to get to know Jewish people, who desires friendship and interaction. Perhaps you are asking, "Where do I start?"

Start with yourself by examining your own maturity level and capacity to love. Make sure your sense of well-being and worth are from the Lord, not based on what *you* know and what *you* can do. In this way you will be in a position to give. Then, ask God to guide you in your efforts and contacts.

FEEL THE PAIN

One must view with horror the pain with which the Jewish people have been inflicted in the past by those who called themselves "Christians." The finest preacher of the fourth century, Chrysostom, filled his sermons with anti-Jewish rhetoric. The cross-carrying Crusaders burned Jews in a Jerusalem synagogue while singing "Christ, We Adore Thee!" Hebrew Christians were forced to persecute their own Jewish people to prove their loyalty to the Christian faith.

Martin Luther is a classic example of a person who was enthusiastic about Christian-Jewish relationships, but became disappointed and angry when the Jewish community did not respond to his ideas and meet his expectations. He then called for the burning of synagogues and Jewish schools, the destruction of Jewish homes, the burning of prayer books and talmudic writings, and forbade rabbis to teach. Even Adolf Hitler used the name of Jesus and claimed biblical support in exterminating more than six million Jewish men, women, and children. Famed missionary statesman Oswald J. Smith insisted that Hitler had the support of "true Christians."

The Jewish community appreciates one who has grappled with the injustice of this history and has felt pain and regret over what has been done. I have seen Holocaust survivors who were deeply moved upon seeing tears in the eyes of some of the Christian students in my classes in which the survivors were relating their experiences. They knew these young men and women cared. Unless you have embarked on this distressing journey back through time or are willing to do so, you will lack sensitivity and understanding and are not ready to explore the realm of friendship with Jewish people.

COMPASSION AND UNCONDITIONAL LOVE

The norm governing relationships between human beings in Judaism and in the teaching of the Jewish Jesus is *compassion* and *love*. In chapter 1, we saw that the Jewish concept of Torah included a daily pattern to glorify God *and* to love one's neighbor as oneself. Jesus' parable of the Good Samaritan is based on this divine command. In this instance Jesus used Leviticus 19 which implores the man or woman of God to "not pervert justice," but to "judge your neighbor fairly" (v. 15); to "not do anything that endangers your neighbor's life" (v. 16); to "not hate your brother in your heart" (v. 17); but to "love your neighbor as yourself" (v. 18). God endorses these statements with the reminder, "I am the Lord."

A viable interaction is that which is built on love and concern. Both love and concern can grow, blossoming into friendship. But friendship takes place only where there is mutual respect and a spirit of humility. Humility is the realization that all your gifts and abilities are given to you by God and are nothing for which we can take any credit. Without these God-given endowments, we would have nothing to bring to any relationship. Humility of spirit, like compassion and unconditional love, never comes easily to anyone. Nevertheless, it is the attitude best exemplified for the Christian in Jesus. It is love without strings attached; love that looks for ways to meet needs; love that feels the pain of injustice and makes reconciliation its task. It is the love of listening and learning, rather than the spirit of conquering. As a Hasidic Jew once stated: "To know the needs of men and to bear the burden of their sorrow—that is the true love of man."

RESPECT AND HONESTY

In the realm of Christian-Jewish relationships, there is an immediate task of reconciliation. Some emotional and spiritual healing must take place, because close relationships have been hindered by preconceptions, caricatures, and stereotypes.

It is no secret that when Jewish people meet a dedicated Christian they *expect* to be put under considerable pressure to convert. Furthermore, they anticipate deception and a cunning, calculating presentation. Jewish people receive the same knot in their stomachs that most Christians do when a pair of Jehovah's Witnesses rap on the door with their briefcases bulging with tracts, books, and magazines.

A professor once asked me, "Have you ever won a Jew to the Lord? I've always wanted to win a Jew!" His whole body shook with anticipation. Quite frankly, most Jews have the impression that the major Christian objective is to add a Jewish person to one's trophy case of converts. Indeed, as we have seen, such Jewish fears have a historic foundation, because the Jew's only escape from persecution in medieval "Christian" society was to convert to Christianity. In fact, the Nazi regime was the first time in history that the act of conversion could not save the Jew. Sad to say, Christians often have committed themselves to a conquest instead of to a person; to their pride and fleshly instincts instead of to the Lord.

Can a good relationship be built on a bad history?

I believe the answer is yes, if there are no conscious hidden agendas and one maintains an attitude of respect for the other person. Jews and Christians have much in common and can learn much from one another. A sound view of the sanctity of life—of a human being that God loves and cherishes; of the uniqueness of every human soul—will help the Christian and the Jew interact and grow in the knowledge of each other's faith. Certainly, a legacy of mistrust and suspicion must be overcome, but through personal contact the old slogans and fears come tumbling down. Each person (Christian and Jew) is in some respects entering another culture for the first time. Through friendship they move beyond the caricatures of each other's community into a realm of understanding and respect, compassion and love. Many times I have seen fledgling encounters become rewarding experiences. Understanding and reconciling with one's Jewish neighbor can only enhance a Christian's life.

In a way, Jews and Christians are strangers. And yet, both of their traditions speak specifically to dealing with a "stranger." Leviticus 19:33 states: "When an alien [stranger] lives with you in your land, do not mistreat him. The alien living with you must be treated as one of your native-born. Love him as yourself, for you were aliens in Egypt. I am the Lord your God."

In comparison, Hebrews 13:1-2 reminds Christians: "Keep on loving each other as brothers. Do not forget to entertain strangers, for by so doing some people have entertained angels without knowing it."

To the question, "And who is my neighbor?" (Luke 10:29) Jesus replied with the story of the Good Samaritan, a religious and racial outcast who, though despised, proved to be a neighbor. Mercy, justice, and compassion are stressed by Jesus in this passage, not only to one's own, but also to those despised by our friends, acquaintances, peer group, and culture. Jesus also practiced what He preached when He entered the culturally forbidden religious and racial ghetto of Samaria (John 4).

VULNERABILITY

Such attitudes leave the Christian open to vulnerability, a vulnerability with which Jesus was familiar. He risked being challenged and stereotyped by part of His community for the personal contacts He made and the reconciliation He attempted.

In Christian-Jewish relationships both parties are at risk. There is the risk of rejection. There is the risk of misunderstanding. There is the risk of being exposed as ignorant of the other's tradition. Ironically, an encounter in mutual respect, humility, and sensitivity overcomes the discomfort of vulnerable situations and allows the relationship to prosper. As Christian and Jew learn about each other's life and traditions, hopes and aspirations, career and culture, barriers indeed melt, and friendship begins to develop. Both individuals begin to "understand" a bit more. In addition, you have become aware of the fact that you have given a very rare and intimate gift—*yourself.*

The Christian learns that the Jewish people want him or her to *be* a Christian; in fact, they are appreciative of the Christian who lives in the way of the Jewish Jesus, rather than in the way of historical pseudo-Christian society. By getting to know each other on a one-to-one basis, caricatures a Jewish person may hold about you or your faith are usually dispelled rather quickly. I realize that we live in an age instilling "basic communication skills." But words are not nearly as important as the personal encounter in changing perceptions. Sincerity is always recognized and appreciated.

It is important to learn that the Jewish people will ask you soon enough what *you* believe, if you have first won their trust and have by your conduct earned the right to represent your views. Too many Christians are so busy emphasizing their own beliefs that they do not take the time to try to understand why others feel the way they do. Vance Havner used to say, "Some Christians are like matches—they only strike on their own book!"

Because of the historical anti-Semitism of the Christian church and the legacy of mistrust engendered, I believe it is the Christian who must go the extra mile to foster the relationship—to listen rather than expound. This takes a very special kind of Christian person and is a process that most do not have the patience or courage on which to embark. Many succumb to the pressure from some circles either to "reel them in *any* way possible" or "shake the dust off your shoes and move on." Ironically, the "cults" are noted for the same "divine deception" and misplaced fervor.

In contrast, dismantling of erroneous views and the construction of a meaningful relationship takes considerable time and considerable effort. It is built on small insights and an ever-growing trust. Through the process, Jew and Christian will find themselves growing stronger in their tradition, faith, and knowledge of God, while they gain new respect for each other.

FRIENDS ARE PEOPLE

Friends are "people," and your Jewish friends will differ widely in personality, practice, and background just as does any other group of individuals. It is hoped that your study of contemporary Judaism in the earlier chapters of this book has alerted you to this fact and given you a deep appreciation for the diversity among Jews, both in belief and custom. The more diverse your acquaintances among the Jewish community, the richer your experience and the greater your opportunity for personal growth.

We have discussed much about *love* in the Christian-Jewish relationship. We have viewed a history of Christian-Jewish encounter sadly lacking in love. Frankly, however, there can be no expression of love without interaction. We may feel a deep affection for the Jewish community, an intense desire to give loving service to Jewish people, but these are feelings based on admiration. On the other hand, engendering one's desires from emotion or intellect, we may base a relationship on all of the *practical* benefits one might obtain from such an encounter. Love and friendship go beyond such dimensions. A viable relationship, a love relationship, is based on communication of personhood, a sincere, demonstrated caring for the flesh-and-blood Jewish acquaintance who has his or her own dreams, desires, worries, expectations, convictions, and moods.

I suggest that you get to know more about the Jewish community in your area. The local synagogue provides the perfect atmosphere for such an encounter. I have known individuals who have traveled fifty miles or more in states that have a small Jewish population in order to visit a synagogue. Rabbis are more than delighted to have a church group visit a service and to give an educational tour afterward. Many groups today arrange such an excursion.

But more Christians should consider going to the synagogue on their own and meeting Jewish people personally at the Friday evening service. The Jewish people are kind and hospitable. They will endeavor to help the Christian who sits next to them through those portions of the service with which he or she may not be familiar. You will find that the rabbi will take special note of your presence and call out the page numbers of the prayer book to help you along. The more frequently you attend, the more friends you will make, *if* the attitudes that have been outlined are exemplified in your person. Although knowledge of Judaism and Jewish people will enhance any person's own Christian understanding, if one is lacking in the attitudes of love so indicative of the Jewish Jesus, it is best to leave the friendship and interaction to some other Christian. Otherwise, the dreary history of Christian-Jewish encounter will have another ghastly episode.

The challenge is laid at our door, because Christian-Jewish relations today desperately need quality interaction, an interaction that encompasses compassion, unconditional love, respect, honesty, vulnerability, and knowledge. The Bible teaches that each human being is created in the image of God and as such is not to be treated as a project or an object. Human life is sacred and not to be toyed with—human beings are of infinite worth in God's sight. God's four-thousand-year love affair with the Jewish people is undeniable; the contribution of Judaism and the Jewish people to Christianity unparalleled.

Some reading this book have been given the responsibility of embarking on the voyage of healing Christian-Jewish relations. In light of history, the Jewish people should *not* be expected to meet Christians halfway. Building bridges of understanding, razing walls of bitterness, is not only praiseworthy but actually is to walk with God.

> He has showed you, O man, what is good.
> And what does the Lord require of you?
> To act justly and to love mercy
> and to walk humbly with your God.
>
> (Micah 6:8)

Glossary

Amidah: Lit., "standing," i.e., prayer recited while standing, also called *tefillah*, meaning "prayer." With the *Shema*, one of the two pillars of Jewish prayer and worship. It is the main prayer recited at all services. It is of ancient origin and includes praise, petition, and thanksgiving.

Ark: The receptacle or cabinet containing the Torah scrolls.

Ashkenazim: Pl. of *Ashkenazi*. A biblical term (Genesis 10:3; Jeremiah 51:27) that the Jews of medieval northwestern Europe used for their territory. The term became extended to Eastern Europe and today refers to the full heritage of the entire area, in contrast with Sephardic heritage, rituals, and dialect.

Bar Kokhba: "Son of the Star." A charismatic soldier who led the Jewish rebellion of A.D. 132-35 and was declared a messianic figure by Rabbi Akiva. This Second Jewish Revolt was crushed by Emperor Hadrian's Roman forces.

Bar mitzvah: "Son of commandment" or "commanded son." A joyous milestone ceremony wherein a young Jewish boy formally assumes personal moral and religious responsibility and accountability. Usually conducted in the synagogue on the Sabbath following the thirteenth birthday.

Bat mitzvah: "Daughter of the commandment" or "commanded daughter." Ceremony for girls parallel to *bar mitzvah,* and a recent development in Judaism. Girls become *bat mitzvah* at the age of twelve in traditional congregations; in Reform, often at age thirteen.

B'rit milab: The "covenant of circumcision" ceremony performed on the male infant's eighth day of life, confirming the special covenant relationship with God. A joyous occasion symbolizing partnership with God.

Chametz: Trans. "yeast," cf. Exodus 12:15, 19. The leavening product caused by fermentation that results from water touching grain. A symbol of corruption and impurity. The home is thoroughly cleansed of *chametz* in preparation for Passover.

Diaspora: "Dispersion." All Jewish people residing outside *Eretz Yisrael*, including historic Jewish settlements.

Eretz Yisrael: "Land of Israel." The Promised Land, or Holy Land, which is indissolubly linked with the people of Israel and their God.

Gemarab: "Completion." Commentaries on the Mishnah by scholars from Babylonia and *Eretz Yisrael* known as the *Amoraim* ("interpreters"). Together, the Mishnah and the Gemarah form the Talmud.

Haftorah: "Conclusion." The portion from the prophetical books of the Bible recited after the designated Torah reading on Sabbaths and holidays.

Haggadab: Also spelled *Aggadah*; from *baggeyd*, "to tell." In the popular sense, the text used for the festive Passover seder. It contains the account of the Exodus and explains the symbols inherent in that story, including songs and prayers. *Aggadah* is in a broader sense used for the nonlegal contents of the Talmud and Midrash.

Halakbab: "The way one goes." The collected legal rulings of the scribes who clarified and amplified written Torah so that its precepts could be lived out fully. *Halakbab* is more than rules of conduct. It can be described as the "Jewish way of life." In contrast to *Aggadah* (see above), this refers to the legal contents of Talmud and Midrash.

Hallab: Also spelled *challab*. Special Sabbath bread symbolic of the showbread in the Temple. The two covered loaves on the Sabbath table are symbolic of the double portion of manna given in the wilderness.

Ha-Motzi: The blessing over the bread ("Blessed art Thou, O Lord, King of the Universe, who brings forth bread from the earth").

Kaddish: Beautiful Aramaic prayer recited by mourners in memory of the dead. It does not mention death, but rather praises the Creator. It is a regular part of the daily and Sabbath service, recited at the close of principal segments of the service as a liturgical doxology.

Kashrut: "Religously fit or proper." Term referring to the Jewish dietary laws regulating slaughter, processing, and preparation.

Ketubah: The marriage contract stating the obligations of the bride and groom and read aloud as part of the ceremony. In the past it was an important legal document that specified the obligations of the husband to his wife. Today, it stresses the moral responsibilities of the couple.

Kiddush: Lit.,"sanctification." A ceremony setting apart as holy the incoming Sabbath and festivals, consisting of a prayer recited over a cup of wine.

Kippah: Pl. *kippot.* The traditional head-covering, or skullcap, worn to acknowledge reverence for God. One explanation is that the wearing of the *kippah* traces its root to ancient times when the uncovered head symbolized freedom and human strength. The Yiddish word is *yarmulke* (see below).

Kittel: A white robe worn by traditional men on Yom Kippur, symbolizing purity and forgiveness. Also worn by a bridegroom.

Knesset: "Assembly." The state of Israel's lively, democratic parliament, composed of many political parties.

Kosher: Also spelled *kasher;* lit., "proper, fit." Term applied to ritually proper foods and dietary customs.

Matzah: Unleavened bread specially prepared under rabbinic supervision from the harvesting of the grain to the baking. To be kosher for Passover it must be baked under supervision within eighteen minutes after the flour is mixed with water. This guarantees that it is free from *chametz* (see above).

Menorah: Ancient symbol of Judaism named for the seven-branched oil lamp used in the Tabernacle and the Temple. Also, the eight-branched candelabrum that commemorates the golden lampstand in the inner sanctuary of the Temple that was kept lit by oil, which miraculously lasted for eight days and nights during the Maccabean rededication of the Second Temple. Menorahs are lit in remembrance of that event during Hanukkah, the Festival of Lights.

Mezuzah: A small container, usually wooden or metal, fastened to the upper right-hand doorpost. It holds a rolled parchment inscribed with the *Shema*.

Midrash: Method of interpreting Scripture to elucidate legal points (*halakhah*) or to bring out lessons by stories or sermons (*aggadah*). Also refers to collections of sermonic interpretations.

Mikveh: Jewish ritual cleansing bath, precursor to baptism. In traditional practice, it is always part of the Jewish conversion ritual.

Minyan: Lit., "number" or "count." Term referring to the ten men (age thirteen or older) required by tradition to hold religious ceremonies and communal prayer. A Jewish quorum.

Mishnah: "Repetition." A compilation by Judah ha-Nasi (c. A.D. 200) of the halakhic teachings. The *Mishnah*, which is divided into tractates, is the earliest codification of the Jewish Oral Torah and is the foundation of the Talmud.

Mitzvot: Pl. of *mitzvah*, "commandment." Refers to the obligations and good deeds incumbent upon the Jewish people by biblical or rabbinic law. *Mitzvot* will further faith, not substitute for it.

Omer: "Sheaf" (of grain). The first sheaf cut during the barley harvest, offered in the Temple on the second day of Passover. From Leviticus 23:9-16, the injunction to count off fifty days from Passover to Shavuot is known as the "counting of the omer."

Oneg Shabbat: Lit., "joy" or "delight of the Sabbath." A joyful time of fellowship and refreshment, which follows the Sabbath services.

Rebbe: Affectionate term of respect for a rabbi or spiritual leader, especially used of the *tzaddik* (see below) of a Hasidic community.

Sanhedrin: The assembly of ordained scholars that functioned as a supreme court and a legislature before the destruction of the Temple in A.D. 70. It was the highest legislative body and court of appeal for Jewish people during the Second Temple period, being nearly autonomous even under Roman rule.

Seder: "Order." Home celebration on the first night of Passover, conducted by family members. The celebration is repeated on the second night by Orthodox, Conservative, and some Reform Jews. The *Haggadah* (see above) is recited, containing the Exodus story, prayers, songs, reflections on the meaning of freedom and slavery. Special foods are served at a festive meal.

Sephardim: Pl. of *Sephardi*, note Obadiah 20. A term used for the descendants of Jews who lived in Spain and Portugal before the expulsion of 1492. Contrasted with the Ashkenazim (see above).

Shabbat: The seventh day, which God ordained as a sanctified day (including the cessation of creative work). The day, which begins at sundown Friday and goes until Saturday night, is not only sacred but also is beloved as a bride.

Shema: Lit., "Hear!" From the first word of Deuteronomy 6:4, "Hear, O Israel: The Lord our God, the Lord is one." This is the great Jewish confession of faith. It is a major feature of the morning and evening prayer service, proclaiming the unity of God (cf. Numbers 15:37-41; Deuteronomy 6:4-9; 11:13-21). It is one of the two pillars (with the *Amidah*) of Jewish prayer and worship.

Shulkhan Arukh: "The prepared table." The authoritative law code recognized by Orthodox Judaism throughout the world. It was formulated by Joseph ben Ephraim Caro (1488-1575).

Siddur: The Jewish prayer book used in both home and synagogue, containing fixed liturgy that originated from the spontaneous prayers of previous generations. In Judaism, prayer is never to be rote but rather is the offering of one's soul to God.

Tachrichim: White burial shroud made of cotton or linen.

Tallit: The beautiful, traditional, four-cornered prayer shawl with fringes worn by adult males during formal prayer and worship and for the study of the Torah.

Tefillin: Or phylacteries. Parchments inscribed with Torah passages and encased in two black leather boxes. The boxes have long straps used for attaching the tefillin to the left arm and head. They are worn during weekday morning prayers by traditional Jews.

Torah: "Teaching." Torah can refer to the Pentateuch (the five books of Moses) but also to the entire body of Jewish teaching and godly knowledge. Torah is a gracious, revelatory gift from God and should not be translated merely as "Law."

Tzaddik: The saintly leader of a Hasidic community; Rebbe.

Yarmulke: Abbreviation of Yare Me-Elohim ("Stand in awe of God"). The skullcap worn to show humility before God. See *Kippah*.

Yeshiva: Lit., "sitting." An academy or place of study where Jewish sages and their pupils learn Torah and Talmud. In modern Hebrew, *yeshiva* is also used to mean "meeting" or "session."

Zionism: From "Zion," an early synonym for Jerusalem, later tied to a hope for return to the Promised Land. The movement to rebuild the Jewish state in the land of Israel. Although having historical precedents, the political Zionist movement arose in the 1890s due to Theodor Herzl's call to reestablish a Jewish state in *Eretz Yisrael*.

Suggested Reading

Many of the following books contain extensive reading lists and bibliographies. Differing in content and perspective, yet delightful to read, each book will lead the Christian student of Judaism and the Jewish people into further study and understanding.

Eban, Abba. *Heritage: Civilization and the Jews.* New York: Summit, 1984.
> Now in a beautifully illustrated softcover edition, this is the companion volume to the Peabody Award-winning Public Broadcasting television series of the same name. A well-known Israeli statesman, diplomat, scholar, and writer, Eban describes the history and culture of the Jewish people, covering many aspects of Jewish contribution to the arts and humanities of the civilized world (from the Mesopotamian desert to the modern state of Israel).

Eckstein, Yechiel. *What Christians Should Know About Jews and Judaism.* Waco, Tex: Word, 1984.
> This book is written by an Orthodox rabbi who is deeply involved in Christian-Jewish relations today. Founder and president of the Holyland Fellowship of Christians and Jews in Chicago and an entertainer and recording artist of Israeli-Hasidic music, Rabbi Eckstein describes the faith, customs, and empowering emotions of Judaism from a traditional perspective. Chapters 9-13 relate his views concerning the Jewish-Christian encounter. As a former national co-director of the Interreligious Affairs division of the Anti-Defamation

League of B'nai B'rith, Rabbi Eckstein brings a wealth of experience as well as knowledge.

Encyclopedia Judaica. 16 vols. Jerusalem: Keter, 1972.
This encyclopedia may be found in many libraries, public and academic. This reference set is one of the finest sources for illustration and explanation of Jewish life, thought, and history, and contains numerous yearbooks. Volume 1 is a massive index for easy reference to the content of the remaining volumes. Because of its penchant for accuracy and the listing of additional sources, the *Encyclopedia Judaica* is highly recommended to the student of Judaica.

Flannery, Edward H. *The Anguish of the Jews: Twenty-Three Centuries of Antisemitism.* Revised and updated. New York: Paulist, 1985.
This is a new paper edition of a classic history of anti-Semitism written by a Roman Catholic priest who is deeply involved in Christian-Jewish relations. First published in 1964, this groundbreaking book did much to expose historical anti-Semitism from the ancient world through the church and into modern society. This latest edition includes new material covering the last two decades, considers developments in the Middle East, and explores the impact that Judaic studies have had on Christian thought.

Gates of Prayer: The New Union Prayerbook. New York: Central Conference of American Rabbis, 1975.
This Reform prayer book has a variety of liturgies and services, both traditional and modern. The Hebrew appears in the text and is translated as well, making it easy for the uninitiated Christian to follow. It also includes songs and hymns as well as transliterations of recurring passages. Nearly eight hundred pages long, it contains an abundance of services and prayers for weekdays, Sabbaths, and festivals in synagogue or home.

Greenberg, Blu. *How to Run a Traditional Jewish Household.* New York: Simon & Schuster, 1983.
Written by the wife of an Orthodox rabbi, this is a delightful book that sweeps one along through the joys and trials of being a traditional Jewish homemaker. The mother of five children gives helpful insights and hints (even recipes!) in addition to a thorough understanding of Jewish festivals and customs. Blu Greenberg symbolizes the modern traditional Jewish woman in that she is a popular au-

thor and lecturer; has advanced degrees in clinical psychology, religious education, and Jewish history; and has taught on the college level. Her first book, *On Women and Judaism* (1981), met with high praise.

Greenstein, Howard R. *Judaism: An Eternal Covenant*. Philadelphia: Fortress, 1983.

Written by a Reform rabbi, this 160-page book is designed to explain God, Torah, and Israel as the three basic components of Judaism and directly relate them to contemporary interpretations in Reform, Conservative, Reconstructionist, and Orthodox Judaism. Rabbi Greenstein is a successful rabbi in the Reform movement and is the author of *Turning Pont: Zionism and Reform Judaism* (1981).

Holtz, Barry W., ed. *Back to the Sources: Reading the Classic Jewish Texts*. New York: Summit, 1984.

A very readable guide to the great books of the Jewish tradition. Essays are written by leading Jewish scholars and cover Bible, Talmud, Midrash, medieval Bible commentaries, medieval Jewish philosophy, Kabbalistic texts, teaching of the Hasidic masters, and Jewish prayers and the prayer book.

Johnson, Paul. *A History of the Jews*. New York: Harper & Row, 1987.

A highly readable four-thousand-year survey of Jewish history and the interaction of that history with Western culture. The six-hundred-page book is divided into seven parts: Israelites, Judaism, Cathedocracy, Ghetto, Emancipation, Holocaust, and Zion. It has a glossary, source notes, and index. Johnson's *Modern Times: The World from the Twenties to the Eighties* (1985) was noted for its freshness and insight. This latest book brings some of those same qualities to the study of Jewish history.

Rausch, David A. *A Legacy of Hatred: Why Christians Must Not Forget the Holocaust*. Chicago: Moody, 1984.

This book uses the history of anti-Semitism and the Holocaust to lead the Christian to better understand the Jewish people and the racist groups that threaten them in the modern era. As a case study, the Holocaust not only provides an important insight into the modern Jewish community, but teaches valuable lessons about the cancer of racial and religious prejudice.

Rudin, A. James, and Marvin R. Wilson, eds. *A Time to Speak: The Evangelical-Jewish Encounter.* Grand Rapids: Eerdmans; Austin, Tex: Center for Judaic-Christian Studies, 1987.

Based on the proceedings and papers from the third national conference between evangelicals and Jews held at Gordon College in Wenham, Massachusetts, from February 28 through March 1, 1984, this book is produced in an easy reading format with study questions at the end of each chapter. Essays include such topics as "The Place of Law and Good Works in Evangelical Christianity" and "The Place of Faith and Grace in Judaism," with proper responses by members of each community. Self-definition, the place of each community in American culture, attitudes toward the state of Israel, perceptions of the other, and "shared nightmares" are some of the other important areas covered in this fine work. Dwight A. Pryor, president of the Center for Judaic-Christian Studies, P.O. Box 202707, Austin, TX 78720 offers a strong selection of tapes, booklets, and books to those who wish to pursue these areas and others. Write for his free publication brochure.

Sarna, Jonathan D., ed. *The American Jewish Experience.* New York: Holmes & Meier, 1986.

A helpful and readable guide to American Jewish history containing essays by experts in each area. The book is divided into five parts (twenty chapters): (1) The American Jewish Community Takes Shape (three chapters); (2) The "German Period" in American Jewish History (four chapters); (3) The Era of East European Immigration (five chapters); (4) Coming to Terms with America (four chapters); and (5) The Holocaust and Beyond (four chapters). Dr. Sarna is associate professor of American Jewish history at Hebrew Union College-Jewish Institute of Religion in Cincinnati and Academic director of its Center for the Study of the American Jewish Experience. Certainly knowledgeable in this field, he has provided an excellent introduction, suggestions for further reading, and appendix. His second chapter, "The Impact of the American Revolution on American Jews," is very helpful.

Singer, David, ed. *American Jewish Year Book, 1987.* New York and Philadelphia: The American Jewish Committee and the Jewish Publication Society, 1987.

A yearly publication of facts and statistics on the Jewish people. In addition to current population statistics broken down into countries, states, territories, and so forth, it includes pertinent essays on the events and trends in American and global Jewish life. It also includes a listing of national Jewish organizations and calendars of the Jewish year. This is an extremely helpful and fascinating study tool.

Tanenbaum, Marc H., Marvin R. Wilson, and A. James Rudin, eds. *Evangelicals and Jews in Conversation on Scripture, Theology, and History.* Grand Rapids: Baker, 1978; and *Evangelicals and Jews in an Age of Pluralism.* Grand Rapids, Baker, 1984.

The papers and presentations from the first and second national conferences between evangelicals and Jews. In their quest for understanding and honesty, the scholars from each respective community discuss a broad range of theological and social issues and concerns.

General Index

Moody Press, a ministry of the Moody Bible Institute, is designed for education, evangelization, and edification. If we may assist you in knowing more about Christ and the Christian life, please write us without obligation: Moody Press, c/o MLM, Chicago, Illinois 60610